MERCHANTS OF LABOUR

MERCHANTS OF LABOUR

Editor
Christiane KUPTSCH *

Contributors

Beate ANDREES
Cesar A. AVERIA Jr.
Ibrahim AWAD
Bernd BALKENHOL
Nilim BARUAH
John CONNELL
Mary CUNNEEN
Luc DEMARET
Mohammed DITO
Bruce GOLDSTEIN
Eric GRAVEL
Ellen HANSEN
Christian HESS

Christiane KUPTSCH
Philip MARTIN
Alan MATHESON
Anna di MATTIA
Susan MAYBUD
NG Cher Pong
Rajendra G. PARATIAN
Dan REES
L.K. RUHUNAGE
Verena SCHMIDT
Tasneem SIDDIQUI
Barbara STILWELL
Christiane WISKOW

* I wish to express my sincere gratitude to both Anna di Mattia and Kristen O'Connor for their most valuable assistance with the English language editing of this volume and thank Anna di Mattia for her support, dedication and hard work in organizing the 'Merchants of Labour Policy Dialogue' where the idea for this book was born.

International Institute for Labour Studies   Geneva
International Labour Office   Geneva

Published by the International Institute for Labour Studies

The *International Institute for Labour Studies* (IILS) was established in 1960 as an autonomous facility of the International Labour Organization (ILO) to further policy research, public debate and the sharing of knowledge on emerging labour and social issues of concern to the ILO and its constituents — labour, business and government.

Copyright © International Labour Organization (International Institute for Labour Studies) 2006.

Short excerpts from this publication may be reproduced without authorization, on condition that the source is indicated. For rights of reproduction or translation, application should be made to the Director, International Institute for Labour Studies, P.O. Box 6, CH-1211 Geneva 22, Switzerland.

ISBN (Print) 92-9014-780-6
ISBN (Web PDF) 92-9014-782-2

First published 2006

Cover photocredit: http://gemaelde-archiv.gemaelde-webshop.de/gemaelde/std/paolo-uccello-predellatafel-zum-hostienwunde-09945.jpg

The responsibility for opinions expressed in signed articles, studies and other contributions of this volume rests solely with their authors, and their publication does not constitute an endorsement by the International Institute for Labour Studies of the opinions expressed.

Copies can be ordered from: ILO Publications, International Labour Office, CH-1211 Geneva 22, Switzerland. For on-line orders, see www.ilo.org/publns

Photocomposed in Switzerland   BRI
Printed in France   NOU

Contents

List of contributors

Beate ANDREES
   Anti-Trafficking Specialist, Special Action Programme to Combat Forced
   Labour, InFocus Programme on Promoting the Declaration, ILO

Cesar A. AVERIA, Jr.
   President, EDI Staffbuilders International Inc., Philippines

Ibrahim AWAD
   Director, International Migration Programme, ILO; formerly Director,
   ILO Subregional Office for North Africa – Cairo, Egypt

Bernd BALKENHOL
   Head, Social Finance Programme, ILO

Nilim BARUAH
   Head, Labour Migration Service, International Organization
   for Migration (IOM)

John CONNELL
   Professor of Geography, School of Geosciences, University of Sydney, Australia

Mary CUNNEEN
   Director, Anti-Slavery International, United Kingdom

Luc DEMARET
   Focal Point for Migration, Bureau for Workers' Activities, ILO

Mohammed DITO
   Policy Development Manager, Bahrain Economic Development Board;
   formerly Head, Employment Services Bureau, Ministry of Labour and Social
   Affairs, Bahrain

Bruce GOLDSTEIN
   Co-Executive Director, Farmworker Justice Fund, Inc., United States

Eric GRAVEL
   Team on Employment and Social Policies and Tripartite Consultations,
   International Labour Standards Department, ILO

Ellen HANSEN
> Senior Employment Services Specialist, InFocus Programme
> on Skills, Knowledge and Employability, ILO

Christian HESS
> Senior Adviser, Bureau for Employers' Activities, ILO

Christiane KUPTSCH
> Senior Research Officer, International Institute for Labour Studies, ILO

Philip L. MARTIN
> Professor of Agricultural and Resource Economics, University of California-
> Davis, United States

Alan MATHESON
> Australian Council of Trade Unions

Anna di MATTIA
> Research Officer, International Institute for Labour Studies, ILO

Susan MAYBUD
> Health Services Specialist, Sectoral Activities Department, ILO

NG Cher Pong
> Divisional Director, Foreign Manpower Management Division,
> Ministry of Manpower, Singapore

Rajendra G. PARATIAN
> Senior Labour Market Policy Specialist, ILO Sub-Regional Office
> for Southern Africa – Harare, Zimbabwe

Dan REES
> Director, Ethical Trading Initiative, United Kingdom

L.K. RUHUNAGE
> Employment and Welfare Counsellor,
> Sri Lanka Consulate, Dubai, United Arab Emirates

Verena SCHMIDT
> ILO Coordinator of the Global Union Research Network (GURN),
> Bureau for Workers' Activities, ILO

Tasneem SIDDIQUI
> Professor of Political Science and Chair of the Refugee and Migratory Move-
> ments Research Unit (RMMRU), University of Dhaka, Bangladesh

Barbara STILWELL
> Coordinator, Department of Human Resources for Health, World Health
> Organization (WHO)

Christiane WISKOW
> Director and Research Consultant, Salumondi, Health Personnel
> and International Public Health, Geneva, Switzerland

Foreword

The present volume contains the papers that were presented at 'Merchants of Labour: Policy Dialogue on the Agents of International Labour Migration' held on 28 and 29 April 2005.

'Merchants of labour' are public and private agents who move workers over national borders. Their practices as well as the implications for migrants are among the most under researched topics in migration research. This is due to lack of reliable data and wide variation in policy regime in different regions of the world, ranging from laissez-faire vis-à-vis private recruiters to a state monopoly on labour exchange activities. There is, however, recognition that recruitment can play a key role in creating vulnerabilities in the final employment stage.

Despite knowledge gaps, one sentiment is also widely shared: overall, the significance of private recruitment agencies in deploying migrant workers has risen considerably in the last decades, often to the detriment of bilateral agreements and public employment services. Thus, when the ILO tripartite constituents of governments, employers and workers during the 2004 International Labour Conference requested that a non-binding multilateral framework "proposing guidelines and principles for policies based on best practices and international standards" be developed, they saw best practices in the area of "licensing and supervision of recruitment and contracting agencies" among the important points that the framework should cover.[1] Similarly, the World Commission on the

---

[1] For details please refer to "Resolution concerning a fair deal for migrant workers in the global economy", ILC92-PR22-269-En.doc: http://www.ilo.org/public/english/protection/migrant/download/ilcmig_res-eng.pdf

Social Dimension of Globalization argued that the emergence of new private institutional mechanisms reinforced the need for a multilateral framework and called on those concerned to work towards a regime of discipline to be imposed on intermediaries.[2]

The International Institute for Labour Studies decided to fill some of the knowledge gaps alluded to above and reveal best practices by organizing an experts meeting that brought together the ILO's constituents, agents directly involved in the recruitment of migrant workers from the private and public sectors, representatives from NGOs, academia, international organizations and colleagues from the International Labour Office. The 'Merchants of Labour Policy Dialogue' assessed the current situation in selected regions and focused on future options. Participating experts discussed the different interests and challenges and presented examples of good/best practice in recruitment and agency regulation – economically efficient and ensuring that human rights standards are upheld.

The meeting covered a wide range of issues related to migrant recruitment, which is echoed in this book, including reflections on 'merchants of labour' from a historical perspective; a comparison between private recruitment agencies and money transfer operators that channel migrant remittances; and a discussion of special challenges in particular economic sectors. The book puts 'merchants of labour' in the wider context of changing employment relationships in globalized labour markets. The country and regional case studies offering good practice examples should provide food for thought and might inspire emulation.

I hope that this book will encourage more research and debate so that practical solutions can be found to end malpractices such as contrived job offers, contract substitution, and physical and psychological abuse of migrant workers.

Gerry Rodgers

Director, International Institute for Labour Studies, ILO

---

[2] World Commission on the Social Dimension of Globalization, A Fair Globalization: Creating opportunities for all, ILO, Geneva, 2004. See pp. 95-98.

Introductory overview

Christiane Kuptsch[1]

The role of private recruiters in the emerging global migration infrastructure is evolving, but the ultimate shape of the industry is not clear. First, global sources and destinations of migrants are diversifying, as more countries send workers abroad and recruit or tolerate the entry of migrants. Within sending countries, migrants are being drawn increasingly from the top and bottom rungs of the job ladder. Second, the role of fee-charging private recruiters may diminish as migration flows mature, because migrants returning for a second or third overseas assignment may be able to avoid the services of a recruiter or use social networks to arrange employment, which suggests that optimal government regulation of recruiters may have to change with the maturity of the labour flow. Third, international organizations and governments can shape the emerging recruitment industry, much like they shaped the evolving remittances industry.

Until development makes emigration unnecessary, essentially three strategies are available to regulate recruiters and to protect migrants:

- registration to make recruiters identify themselves to government agencies, which facilitates the enforcement of laws protecting migrants;
- issuing licences subject to recruitment agents passing a test that demonstrates their knowledge of protective labour laws; and
- bonding, e.g. requiring recruiters to post a financial guarantee so that if migrants who paid the recruiters for their services suffer losses, there are funds to compensate the migrants.

---

[1] Senior Research Officer, International Institute for Labour Studies, ILO.

Complementary strategies to protect migrants include having a public employment agency that provides overseas recruitment services in addition to private recruiters, so that migrants have an alternative to the private agents and the government has a more concrete understanding of how the recruitment industry works. Furthermore, self-regulation among recruiters can be encouraged and recruiters made jointly liable with foreign employers to honour migrant contracts.

'Merchants' of various types: yesterday and today

In part I of this volume entitled "'Merchants' of various types: yesterday and today", *Philip L. Martin* makes these and other suggestions in his issue paper and also discusses two potential best practice examples concerning the recruitment of migrant workers: policies developed by the Philippines as a sending country,[2] and the bilateral agreement concluded between Canada and Mexico on seasonal agricultural workers. Martin views as the best protection for migrants the power to say no - when workers have the opportunity for decent work at home. He also points out that if there are migrants who want to go abroad, and jobs available for them, most countries find it better to allow and regulate private recruiters than to outlaw or ban them, because the latter move tends to drive recruiters underground rather than eliminate them.

Bernd Balkenhol examines similarities and differences between private recruitment agencies and money transfer operators (MTOs), another type of 'merchants', to gain insights into the scope for making the recruitment of migrant workers as 'business like' as remittances handled by MTOs. The fundamental difference lies in the nature of the service traded. Balkenhol underscores the limits to the negotiability of labour; recruitment bureaux thus face constrains in optimizing their performance. In a discussion on institutional efficiency, he points out that MTOs are profit maximisers that measure success in terms of maximum return on inputs whereas recruitment agencies cannot measure success by their return in financial terms alone, but must also analyse the quality and stability of social outcomes as a result of the placement of migrants. Costs for the client and the service provider are compared and contrasted; and the issue of market perfection is examined, observing inter alia that

---

[2] See also the contribution of Cesar A. Averia, in Part II.

information asymmetry is detrimental to the migrant worker in both the recruitment and the remittances markets. Policy entry points are also discussed.

A historical perspective on 'merchants of labour' is provided by *Bruce Goldstein*, who discusses labour subcontracting that became known as "the sweating system" during the late 1880s and early 1900s. He describes the history of the system and attempts at legislation to ameliorate the problem of labour exploitation in the United States during the 19th and 20th centuries. Goldstein parallels past efforts at reform in the garment industry and current efforts in agriculture, concluding that in the 21st century, the United States seems to be fighting the same labour practices that were used during the 1880s to weaken workers' bargaining power and suppress improvements in wages and working conditions. Reformers have learned from the past that they have to look at the employment relationship and focus on the larger entities that contracted with labour recruiters, those who have the economic power to change the system, namely the companies that retain the subcontractors.[3]

The empirical framework: Country and regional experiences

Part II of the present volume is devoted to case studies. Authors from different parts of the world share country and regional experiences to reveal good practice in the area of migrant recruitment. Private recruiters are most widespread in the Asian region, and Asian countries have been in the forefront of devising policies and mechanisms to protect migrant workers in the recruitment process; empirical evidence from this region is therefore dominant.

Nilim Baruah examines developments in major migrant sending countries in Asia, some of which are presented in more detail by other authors in the subsequent contributions. Baruah reports about complaints by migrant workers and the policy and operational responses they have triggered in different nations and with regional and international bodies. In Baruah's analysis the most prevalent protection and regulation tools used in Asian labour sending states are the following: licensing requirements for recruitment agents and limits on the fees that such agents

---

[3] A similar view is taken by Alan Matheson, see Part II.

can charge the migrants; setting standards for employment contracts, exit controls, welfare services for migrants, posting of labour attachés abroad, and cooperation with countries of destination. He remarks that the experience of Asian labour sending states is a rich source of ideas for any country wishing to embark on a pro-active overseas employment programme.

Cesar A. Averia offers a list of best practices from his perspective as President and CEO of a private recruitment agency based in the Philippines. This includes niche marketing, setting up strategic partnerships as well as branch operations in mature markets, and not charging placement fees to potential migrants. He also reviews the important economic and socio-cultural effects that labour migration has for the Philippines, e.g. via remittances, and notes that tripartite cooperation — among the migrants, the private recruitment companies and the government agency that supervises the deployment of migrant workers in foreign countries — is a must for any successful overseas employment programme.

In his Sri Lanka country report, *L.K. Ruhunage* traces the development of institutional monitoring and controlling of migrant recruitment, from the establishment of a Sri Lanka Bureau of Foreign Employment to the involvement of Sri Lanka overseas missions in the recruitment process. All recruitment agencies in Sri Lanka have to be licensed. Among other things, agents have to place cash bonds with the Sri Lanka Bureau of Foreign Employment; the Bureau can conduct enquiries, demand compensation for workers and cancel licences; there is a final exit clearance and an airport surveillance desk; overseas missions register all foreign agencies and companies that wish to recruit Sri Lankan workers. Yet despite elaborate government control mechanisms, problems and conflicts in the placement process remain, some of which can be attributed to the existence of sub-agents and middlemen who operate widely unmonitored and without liability. Regarding Sri Lanka, Ruhunage also demonstrates the dominance of private recruitment agencies in the deployment of overseas workers. Merely about 25 percent of all Sri Lankan migrant workers find foreign jobs through relatives and friends; this concerns mainly unskilled jobs and people from rural areas. Very few persons, essentially professionals, are capable of making direct contacts with foreign employers.

Tasneem Siddiqui focuses on Bangladesh, one of the major labour-sending countries in the global labour market, and the challenges that this country faces in ensuring effective governance of the migration sector as a whole, and of the recruitment industry in particular. Siddiqui observes and examines the growth of different legal instruments and institutions for governance of labour migration in Bangladesh. She emphasises the need for a pro-active migration policy and actions involving the public and private sectors as well as civil society to ensure the protection of migrants and provides concrete suggestions for policy improvement. In her view, effective governance of migration will lead to greater economic and social benefits to the state, communities and the migrants.

In analysing what might be 'good practice' for Australia, *Alan Matheson* points out that migration systems, labour market systems and industrial systems are all dynamic and evolving and that it is imperative to understand and regulate the triangular relationship between worker, employer and 'merchant of labour' (i.e. labour hire, private employment agency, contractor, subcontractor, or hire company). Matheson gives an overview of the agencies and individuals involved in the identification, recruitment and employment of workers from overseas in Australia. He also shares the Australian Council of Trade Unions' (ACTU) checklist for determining whether the use of skilled migrant workers might be appropriate. In concluding, he lists principles of good practice.

Ng Cher Pong outlines how Singapore, a country with a large percentage of migrant workers, which has historically maintained a very open labour market, has taken a multi-pronged approach to managing foreign labour. Responsibility is placed on the employer, the migrant worker and the employment agency alike to ensure worker safety and that employers afford proper treatment to migrants. Singapore's Employment Agencies Act stipulates that the Ministry of Manpower shall license all recruitment and placement agents providing services to employers; licenses are screened regularly. In addition, Singapore has established a mandatory accreditation scheme for employment agencies placing foreign domestic workers, with particularly stringent provisions to protect vulnerable domestic helpers – a potential best practice. Because of the cross-border nature of the recruiters' work, Ng urges the coordination of the regulatory and enforcement efforts of different governments because they will be fully effective only if both host and source countries are equally committed to introducing and enforcing rules to govern the behaviour of employment agents.

Mohammed Dito raises the question of lessons that can be learned from Bahrain's recent labour market reform. Bahrain, as the other Gulf Cooperation Council states, suffered from labour market inefficiencies created through a system whereby foreigners work in private sector jobs

5

for low wages, are tied to their employers or 'sponsors' and do not enjoy the same rights as local workers. Bahrain developed a dependency on foreign workers and at the same time neglected the training of local workers. These and other problems have now been tackled in a labour market reform package. Among others, Dito sees the following lessons that can be learned from the process that led to this reform: Bad conditions for foreign workers are a breeding ground for worsening conditions for locals; vacancies should be filled based on a fair competition between local and migrant workers where 'cost competitiveness' is not a function of lack of rights. Bureaucratic foreign worker management systems carry the risk of resulting in corrupt practices whereas effective migration management relies on proper information systems, good governance and the active participation of the social partners.

In taking Egypt as a case study for 'merchants of labour' in the Middle East and North Africa, *Ibrahim Awad* first gives an overview of the migration system that Egypt is embedded in and highlights differences in labour flows to the Gulf States and the Mediterranean, with largely regular streams to the Arab countries and essentially undocumented migration to Europe. He makes observations concerning the functional importance of 'merchants of labour' – which is negligible where clandestine migration takes places – and discusses the regulation and the realities of access to overseas employment in Egypt. Awad outlines the respective roles of public and private institutions in recruitment, in presenting inter alia the cases of two reputed private agencies. His empirical research shows that the effectiveness and professionalism of private recruitment agencies is correlated with the labour market segments and occupations they deal with. He therefore suggests to first increase the role of agencies involved in the placement of highly skilled workers, along with stepped up supervision, if one wishes to modernize labour markets.

Rajendra G. Paratian examines South Africa's move towards a modernized migration policy and highlights the importance that a regional approach to migration might play in bringing about equitable solutions, e.g. as outlined in the Southern African Development Community (SADC) Draft Protocol for the Free Movement of Persons within Southern Africa. He points out that in the South African context the pertinent question might not be how to better regulate existing temporary foreign worker schemes and recruitment under these schemes but whether temporary employment schemes might be an instrument for regularizing and legitimizing the status of foreign workers who are at present without any significant protection.

Recruitment and ILO standards

In Part III of this volume, ILO officials address the issue of ILO standards on employment services and their relevance for regulating migrant recruitment and preventing migrant abuse.

Eric Gravel traces the history of ILO standards concerning employment services, outlines their main provisions, and reports on comments made by the Committee of Experts on the Application of Conventions and Recommendations, an independent body composed of high level jurists. Early ILO standards in this area considered that the public service would ensure the needs of workers and the business community as far as recruitment was concerned. For example, Unemployment Convention (No. 2), adopted as early as 1919, provided for the creation of a system of free public employment agencies; and Convention No. 96 on Employment Agencies (1949) called for the abolition or at least the regulation of fee-charging agencies and the simultaneous establishment of a public employment service. A climate of economic liberalism and international competition then led to the recognition that private employment agencies could contribute positively to the functioning of the labour market. The fact that public employment services, with their resources being downsized in several countries, were unable to provide all job seekers with services, contributed to the debate. In 1997, new international labour standards on private employment agencies were adopted, namely Convention No. 181 and Recommendation No. 188.

Christian Hess offers the employers' perspective on Convention No. 181. He emphasizes that this standard was adopted with the support of the employers and in their view represents major progress over Convention 96 on Employment Agencies (1949) because it recognizes the importance of flexibility in labour markets and the role of private agencies. Hess also suggests possible actions that the ILO, in cooperation and coordination with its constituents, could take to promote Convention 181, including steps for collecting, developing and updating material on the implementation of Convention 181 in a tool-box approach and assisting in the organization of awareness-raising campaigns.

Luc Demaret presents the trade unions' perspective. He points out that ILO Convention 181 offers both protection to migrant workers and an opportunity for employers to reduce unfair competition and disassociate themselves from malpractices and images of abuse. In critically examining a 2004 European Union draft directive on services (known as the 'Bolkestein Directive') and developments under so-called 'mode 4' of the General Agreement on Trade in Services (GATS), Demaret raises the question whether Convention 181 will prevail over liberalization strives in services and points to the role of the ILO and that of trade unions in this respect.

In reviewing implementation issues pertaining to ILO Convention No. 181, *Ellen Hansen* notes how this standard balances firms' needs for flexibility to expand or reduce their workforce with workers' needs for employment stability, a safe work environment, decent conditions of work, and a safety net when they are unable to work. Based on the ILO's experience with commenting on draft legislation concerning private employment agencies, Hansen offers insights into good practice in regulation. For example, effective national legislation includes a clear definition of the term 'private employment agency' and determines basic prerequisites for the legitimate operation of an agency. Most importantly, the laws and regulations established should be within the capacity of the government to enforce thoroughly.

Beate Andrees emphasizes that recruitment can play a key role in creating vulnerabilities in the final employment stage. Drawing on recent ILO research carried out in Europe, she describes illegal and abusive recruitment leading to forced labour. Andrees' contribution highlights good practices in combating criminal activities in the recruitment of migrant workers. She sees an improved understanding of how the industry works as a first step in this process and stresses the importance of coordinated action between different law enforcement agencies in both origin and destination countries. Moreover, it is vital that law enforcement authorities can use a wide range of evidence to ensure convictions. Last but not least, Andrees argues for relying on a combination of ILO and UN Conventions that stipulate administrative as well as criminal sanctions against abusive recruitment agents.

Innovative policy and possible protection strategies

Part IV of this volume is a collection of papers that call for comprehensive approaches in developing protection strategies for migrant workers and that look through the lens of specific sectors at migrant recruitment, licensing and supervision of agents and other types of regulation with the purpose of protecting migrants. For example, innovative policy and possible strategies in agriculture and health care are studied.

Mary Cunneen examines forced labour in the context of migration and particularly as it occurs in the informal economy of different parts of the world. She gives practical examples from the work at Anti-Slavery International, looking at the experiences of migrant workers themselves. She reports on bonded labour in South Asia; migrant nurses in the United Kingdom's National Health Service; and migrant domestic workers in the Middle East. Cunneen urges that in developing protection strategies, it is necessary that policies fall within a comprehensive human rights framework, protecting both migrant rights and core labour standards. The provision of legal migration channels that can reduce vulnerabilities and the regulation of recruitment agencies are both important. However, these policy aspects should not be seen in isolation and it is essential to address exploitation and abusive labour practices at the same time.

Verena Schmidt analyses migrant recruitment in the wider context of temporary migration and focuses on recruitment agencies for migrants as one particular form of temporary work agencies. In offering theoretical reflections as well as evidence from trade union work in several world regions, she discusses five different kinds of protection strategies adopted by unions: campaigns to change the legal framework for temporary migrant workers; organizing temporary migrant workers; offering practical support to temporary migrant workers; information campaigns for temporary migrant workers; and specific measures to include and integrate migrant workers within trade unions. Which policy options towards migrants a trade union will choose depends on a variety of factors such as its internal organization, its power position in the economy or the migration history of the country concerned.

In examining the role of information campaigns for curtailing migrant abuse, *Anna di Mattia* discusses the different aspects of campaigns to be considered such as target groups, mode of dissemination, content, providers and evaluation. She gives specific examples of successful campaigns and case examples from other subject areas which may be adapted to information campaigns targeting labour migrants. She concludes that information campaigns can be a very helpful prevention tool to curb malpractice but that they should be used as an integrated element of broader labour recruitment campaigns since their effectiveness has not yet been conclusively demonstrated.

Dan Rees provides a concrete example of licensing and supervision. He reports on measures that have recently been taken in the United

Kingdom to tackle exploitation in the agricultural industry. Rees presents the main provisions of the Gangmasters (Licensing) Act 2004 as well as the Act's enforcement regime. The Act was adopted partly thanks to lobbying by the Temporary Labour Working Group — a consortium of retailers, growers, suppliers, labour providers and trade unions. This Group took the view that a twin-track strategy to protect workers needed to be adopted: legislation and voluntary action. Thus, in parallel to the Gangmasters Licensing Act, it also developed a code of conduct and audit procedures to assess compliance with this code. Rees emphasizes that worker-focused inspection should be one component of a licensing regime. In concluding, Rees offers some general lessons: A public interest case can be built to address responsible treatment of migrant workers but for this a broad based alliance is essential. Voluntary initiatives are most effective when employers are willing to change and not sufficient to protect the most vulnerable workers. Rees also notes that there may be limits associated with the focus on a single industry.

The last two papers of the present volume focus on another sector, namely health care. *Susan Maybud* and *Christiane Wiskow* reflect on the question whether health worker migration constitutes a brain drain, brain gain or brain waste. They underline that the international recruitment of health care workers has adverse effects on strained health systems of poor countries, which raises moral concerns. They describe the vulnerability of migrant health workers and discuss regulation as a measure for their protection, in particular regulation in the form of codes of practice regarding international recruitment. Finally, Maybud and Wiskow outline the social partners' particular responsibilities and roles in making the migration of health care professionals sustainable.

The issues of migrant vulnerability and that of possible forms of regulation are also taken up by *John Connell* and *Barbara Stilwell* who discuss the role of recruiters within the global health care chain. This chain of interlocking health worker movements has developed over roughly the last decade and goes from the poorest African and Asian states and the relatively small and poor island states of the Caribbean and the Pacific, to the developed world, culminating in the United States. Connell and Stilwell observe that the migration of skilled health workers has become more complex, with new actors such as China and Central and Eastern European countries on the global market. An important novelty is also that recruitment agencies do not merely satisfy demand but, through their advertisements and promotions, actively create a desire for further migration. There is increasing evidence that the intention to migrate occurs even before entry into the health system. In terms of policy directions for this particular sector, Connell and Stilwell view bilateral agreements, in a general context of managed migration, as possibly a more powerful tool than codes of practice.

Part I: 'Merchants' of various types: yesterday and today

Regulating private recruiters: The core issues

Philip Martin[1]

Introduction

Merchants of labor are private intermediaries who, for a fee, help workers to find jobs at home or abroad. Private intermediaries have long played important job matching roles in labor markets, using their competitive advantage of knowing about employers seeking workers and the languages and expectations of workers to establish the businesses of labor market matching. Private recruiters (headhunters) have become the norm in matching high-level executives and managers with corporations and nonprofits, and have become more common in matching professionals such as nurses with hospitals.

In most cases, recruiters act as brokers between workers and employers. However, some of the largest private employers in industrial countries are firms such as Adecco, Manpower, and Labor Ready that recruit and act as the employers of workers who are assigned to firms to complete assignments. These employment agencies have largely avoided recruiting workers in one country to place or assign to jobs in another, except in areas such as the European Union that guarantee freedom of movement; in the European Economic Area (EEA), employment services firms employ EEA nationals seeking placement anywhere in the EEA.

Economic theory views job-matching as an information problem, with workers seeking the best wage, benefit, and working condition package available given their skills and labor market conditions and employers seeking the best workers available at the least cost. Viewed in this way,

---

[1] Professor of Agricultural and Resource Economics, University of California-Davis, United States.

13

the most efficient job-matching institution is the one with maximum information: one that collects and shares information on employers seeking workers and workers seeking jobs.

The economies of scale implicit in job matching have led to public no-fee employment services (ES) in virtually all countries. However, the market share of ES agencies has declined in most countries, and most match fewer workers and jobs than they did several decades ago; many make less than 10 percent of worker-job matches in a country. Instead, significant employment services[2] or recruitment industries[3] have emerged in most countries, often matching more workers and employers than the public ES agencies. The ILO recognized the importance of private employment agencies in Convention 181, whose Article 2 allows states to "prohibit...private employment agencies from operating in respect of certain categories of workers or branches of economic activity" while Article 7.1 asserts that "Private employment agencies shall not charge directly or indirectly, in whole or in part, any fees or costs to workers," although Article 7.2 allows exceptions.

Recruiters and migrants

There has long been a private recruitment industry in areas inside countries. Its activities were most noticeable when employers and potential employees did not share the same language or culture, or when there was significant physical distance between jobs and workers. In immigrant countries such as Canada and the US, bilingual go-betweens were common to assemble crews of workers and often stayed with them on the

---

[2] There is no standard terminology. In the United States (US), employment services is the umbrella term for three distinct kinds of entities (1) *employment placement agencies* are job matchers that list employment vacancies and place permanent employees, (2) *temporary help services* or temporary staffing agencies provide employees to other organizations on a contract basis to supplement the workforce of the client, and (3) *professional employer organizations* assign workers to client locations and act as their employer—they may also provide other human resources functions to clients on a contract basis. In March 2002, employment services employment was 3.2 million, including 925,000 in office and administrative support occupations, 730,000 in laborer and similar occupations, and 600,000 in production-related occupations. Median hourly earnings of e.g. laborers were lower if they were employed by employment services, e.g. $7.90 versus $9.50 an hour. See Employment Services. http://www.bls.gov/oco/cg/cgs039.htm.

[3] Most private agencies in what the United Kingdom (UK) calls the recruitment industry are small: the top 15 companies control just over 25 percent of the job placement market, with Adecco having the largest market share. Marketing Week (January 13, 2005, p30) reported that the UK had 14,700 employment agencies in 2004 and generated revenues of £24.5 billion for making two million placements, 90 percent of which were temporary.

job, even though the railroad or farm where the crew worked was the employer of the migrants. Private recruiters or labor contractors remain significant in sectors in which there is a seasonal demand for workers and when workers and employers do not have a common language, as with Spanish-speaking farm workers in the US. Recruiters can also play important job-matching roles when language is not a barrier but distance is, as with the recruitment of workers inside Brazil or Thailand.

Private recruiters charge for job-matching services. If workers are ranked by their level of education or skill from low to high on the X-axis, and if the share of job-matching fees paid by workers is on the Y-axis, the line showing the cost of recruitment paid by the worker falls from left to right, as lower-skill migrants tend to pay a higher percentage of any job-matching fees (if the share of fees paid by employers are on the right-hand side Y-axis, the share-of-cost paid by the employer line rises from left to right). Migrants and employers can avoid recruitment fees via direct job matching, which can occur via social networks, as when current employees tell friends and families about job vacancies, and perhaps vouch for and train those who are hired. Employers can advertise for workers, screen and test those who apply, and thus pay for recruitment costs internally.

Private recruiters can get into the job-matching business with few start up costs; their major asset is their contacts with workers seeking jobs and employers seeking workers. The recruitment industry that is most like the public ES, providing job-matching services, tends to be two-tiered: at one end are multinational, national, and regional firms with a network of offices and offering a range of types of workers and screening options, and at the other are smaller firms that tend to operate in only one area, industry, or occupation, and sometimes for only one or a few employers.

Matching workers and employers over borders introduces complications. First, information gaps are likely to be greater, which can enable workers going abroad with one recruiter to pay a different fee and have a different contract abroad than migrants going to work in the same type of job who use a different recruiter. There may be less standardization in the absence of bilateral agreements, multinational firms, and government oversight of contracts. There is also an asymmetric information problem: worker recruiters may know the abilities of the workers they interview, but not have details about the job abroad. Meanwhile, employers or job recruiters abroad may know what the job entails, but not know the qualifications of workers in another country.

15

Whether recruiters deal directly with employers or work in pairs, with one in the sending country and another in the receiving country, there is an upper limit on what they can charge migrants for their services that is some fraction of the gap in wages between labor-sending and -receiving countries. Migrants may be willing to pay higher recruiting fees if there are prospects for settlement abroad, if it is difficult to migrate via social networks or illegally, and if there are far more workers seeking to go abroad than there are contracts available.

Sending country example: Philippines

Almost a million Filipinos a year, an average 2,700 a day, are "deployed" abroad. The Philippines is an island nation, so most Filipino migrants leave legally by air, enabling the government to erect a framework to regulate the activities of recruiters, including requiring them to provide contracts to the migrants they send abroad. The major protective agency is the Philippine Overseas Employment Administration (POEA), which regulates recruitment, checks the workers' contracts, and provides pre-departure orientation to migrants; it finances its activities with a P3,000 ((US $60) processing fee collected from migrants. [4]

Table 1. Filipino Migrants Deployed: 1985-2002

	2002	2000	1995	1990	1985
Total	891,908	841,628	653,574	446,095	372,784
Land-based	682,315	643,304	488,173	334,883	320,494
Sea-based	209,593	198,324	165,401	111,212	52,290
Saudi Arabia	193,157	184,645	168,604	169,886	185,837
Hong Kong	105,036	121,762	51,701	34,412	22,020
Japan	77,870	63,041	25,032	41,558	16,029
UAE	50,796	43,031	26,235	17,189	15,093
Taiwan	46,371	51,145	50,538	54	9
Kuwait	25,894	21,490	9,852	5,007	21,167
Singapore	27,648	22,873	10,736	4,698	10,047
Italy	20,034	26,386	5,829	3,229	1,413

Source: POEA, 2004

---

[4] The POEA issues a number of booklets that outline living and working conditions in various countries.

16

Fees paid to recruiters are generally the largest expense of migrants seeking overseas jobs. Many of the migrants who know that there are more applicants than jobs are willing to pay more than the one month's wages abroad limit on recruiter fees, or 4.2 percent of the wages expected to be earned under a 24-month contract. Despite POEA campaigns against illegal recruitment and overcharges, there are almost daily press reports of migrants paying fees for non-existent overseas jobs or paying for a contract but waiting 4, 6, or 10 months before going abroad to earn wages. [5]

Between 1992 and 2002, the POEA filed 650 cases alleging illegal recruitment, but only 66 of the cases that were recommended for prosecution resulted in a criminal conviction, a result attributed to the inefficiency of the Philippine court system and the reluctance of many migrant victims to file formal charges and testify. [6] Some victims refuse to testify because the recruiter is a relative, friend or resident of their town, and in other cases victims who initially allege that they had to wait too long to be deployed are in fact sent abroad, which stops the case.

Many violations of POEA regulations occur overseas, as when a migrant is required to sign a supplemental contract that requires the payment of additional fees. Migrants in such cases could complain to labor attaches at local consulates, but most do not, fearing that they could be dismissed by the employer and required to return to the debts they incurred to go abroad. To protect migrants in such situations, Philippine law makes Filipino recruiters jointly liable with foreign employers to fulfill the provisions of the contracts that each migrant leaving legally must have. This helps to protect migrants but prompts some recruiters to complain that their revenues and profits depend on deploying migrants to employers abroad whom they may not know well.

Most Filipino recruiters are small; the largest private recruitment agencies deploy 3,000 to 5,000 migrants a year. The government would like fewer and larger licensed recruiters, which would simplify enforcement, and has doubled the capital required to get a recruiting license from one to two million pesos (from US $20,000 to US $40,000) and has proposed requiring agencies to deploy at least 100 migrants a year to be re-licensed.

---

[5] Most police stations in the Philippines have an Overseas Foreign Worker (OFW) desk to receive complaints.

[6] In November 1998, a Malaysian, a Briton and an Australian were arrested after they recruited Filipinos for jobs in a fictitious country, the Dominion of Melchizedek, said to be in the South Pacific (in the Old Testament, Melchizedek was a model priest to whom Abraham and others paid tithes).

The Philippine system is often considered a model for sending countries that want to regulate recruitment and protect migrants abroad. However, there is an active debate about whether the regulation of recruitment raises the costs of Filipino migrants "too much." Most recruiters as well as the Union of Filipino Overseas Contract Workers (OCW-Unifil) want less government regulation, arguing that regulation increases their costs and enables recruiters from China, Indonesia and Vietnam to erode the market for Filipino migrants.

Bilateral best practice example: Canada-Mexico

The Commonwealth Caribbean (since 1966) and Mexican (since 1974) Agricultural Seasonal Workers Program allows foreign workers to be employed on Canadian farms up to eight months a year. About 60 per-cent of the almost 20,000 migrants are from Mexico, and 80 percent are employed on fruit, vegetable and tobacco farms in Ontario, where the average stay is four months. The migrants, who fill about 20 percent of Ontario's seasonal farm jobs, usually work 10- to 12-hours six days a week.

Table 2. Canadian Guest Worker Employment in Agriculture
Canadian Guest Workers Admitted for Agriculture, 1987-2002

	Mexicans	Caribbean*	Total	Mexican %
1987	1,547	4,655	6,202	25%
1988	2,721	5,682	8,403	32%
1989	4,468	7,674	12,142	37%
1990	5,149	7,302	12,451	41%
1991	5,111	6,914	12,025	43%
1992	4,732	6,198	10,930	43%
1993	4,710	5,691	10,401	45%
1994	4,848	6,054	10,902	44%
1995	4,884	6,376	11,260	43%
1996	5,194	6,379	11,573	45%
1997	5,670	6,705	12,375	46%
1998	6,480	6,901	13,381	48%
1999	7,528	7,532	15,060	50%
2000	9,222	7,471	16,693	55%
2001	10,446	8,055	18,501	56%
2002	10,778	7,826	18,604	58%

Source: Citizenship and Immigration Canada

*From Barbados, Jamaica, and Trinidad and Tobago http://www.cic.gc.ca/english/pub/facts2002-temp/index.html

The Mexico-Canada program is governed by an MOU between the Mexican Ministry of Labor and Human Resources Development Canada (HRDC).

The admissions process begins with farm employers applying to local Human Resources Centers (HRCs) for certification of their need for migrants at least eight weeks before they expect work to start. Farmers must offer the Mexicans at least 240 hours of work over six weeks, free approved housing and meals or cooking facilities, and the higher of the minimum wage (C$7.15 an hour in Ontario in 2004, projected to rise to C$8 by 2007), the prevailing wage, or the piece-rate wage paid to Canadians doing the same job.

HRDC approval to hire migrants is sent to an organization funded by farmer-paid fees, Foreign Agricultural Resource Management Services (FARMS), which transmits the job offer to the Mexican labor ministry. Migrants go to the Canadian consulate in Mexico to receive entry papers, and a FARMS affiliate arranges and pays for transportation to Canada and the employer's farm.[7] Workers are on probation for two weeks after their arrival, and farmers provide written evaluations of each worker at the end of the season that are placed in sealed envelopes and delivered by returning workers to Mexican authorities. Farmers may specify the names of workers they want, which they do over 70 percent of the time, so that the average worker interviewed in one study had seven years experience in Canada (Basok, 2002). Farmers face fines of up to C$5,000 and two years in prison for hiring unauthorized workers or lending migrants to other farmers, but such fines are rare.

Farmers say they turned to Mexican migrants after negative experiences with local workers, recounting stories of workers threatening to break equipment in order to get fired and return to the welfare rolls, or workers "breaking faith" by walking away during busy times after being "helped" by growers who kept them on the payroll when there was little work available. Reliance on migrants seems to be increasing. In one study, 40 percent of the jobs in 40 vegetable greenhouses were filled by migrants, up from 10 percent a decade ago (Basok, 2002).

---

[7] FARMS began to play this role in 1987, when the program was changed and the private sector played a greater role in program administration. Transportation is arranged by CAN-AG Travel Services. Employers deduct four percent of worker wages (up to C$575) to recoup transport costs; farmers also deduct payroll taxes and insurance costs from workers' pay.

Most of the Mexican migrants are married men who leave their families in rural Mexico, and many go into debt in order to get into the program.[8] Initially, only married men from the Mexico City area were recruited by Mexican authorities, but after 1989, women could go— about three percent of the 12,000 Mexican workers in 2003 were women, whom some employers prefer for fruit and vegetable harvesting and packing.[9] Approved workers receive passports from the Ministry of Foreign Affairs (special three-year passports for 165 pesos), temporary departure forms from the Ministry of the Interior, and get medical exams at Canadian-approved health centers in Mexico City. The share of workers from provinces surrounding Mexico City began to drop after workers could come from anywhere in Mexico, but in 2003 some 70 percent of the Mexican migrants were still from four Mexican states: Tlaxcala, Guanajuato, Mexico and Hidalgo. Unmarried men have been allowed to participate since 2003.

In Canada, the migrants usually live on the farms where they work. They report spending very little, enabling them to save 70 percent of their earnings—savings average C$1,000 a month.[10] Mexican consular officials can inspect worker housing and solicit grievances, but they cannot deal with the most common migrant complaints, which often involve deductions from their earnings. Employers deduct up to C$425 to recoup travel expenses, and there have been deductions since 1993 for Employment (Unemployment) Insurance and social security[11] (for workers earning more than C$3,300); migrants are not eligible for unemployment insurance payments.[12] Income taxes are deducted, but can be refunded to workers earning less than C$14,000—78 percent of Mexican workers applied for income tax refunds in one survey. Migrants are eligible for health insurance coverage upon arrival in Canada—the usual

---

[8] The Mexican government advertises the ability to work in Canada via its 139 State Employment Service offices, but workers must, on average, make six trips to Mexico City at their own expense to actually complete procedures. Since May 2002, the Mexican government has provided most first-time workers with 3,000 pesos (US $280) to travel to Mexico City, where they learn about the work they will do in Canada and their rights and obligations.

[9] To participate, Mexicans must have experience working in agriculture and have at least three and no more than 12 years of schooling, with men aged 22-45 and women 23-40. Men until 2003 had to be married with children who stayed in Mexico, and women must have dependent children who also stay in Mexico.

[10] The Caribbean migrants have 25 percent of their pay deducted in a forced savings program.

[11] Workers who are at least 60 can apply for pensions— 360 have so far.

[12] The United Food and Commercial Workers says that Mexican and Caribbean migrants paid a total C$8.2 million in Employment Insurance Act premiums in 2002—C$3.4 million by workers and $8.2 million by employers.

three-month wait for coverage under provincial health care programs is waived.

Some migrants went on strike on April 29, 2001 and were deported, which led the United Food and Commercial Workers Union to protest on behalf of the migrants. The UFCW operates Migrant Worker Centers and calls the migrant program "Canada's shameful dirty secret;" it has sued provincial authorities for excluding farm workers from the Occupational Health and Safety Act and for not protecting farm workers engaged in union activities.

Canadian Foreign Affairs Minister Pierre Pettigrew called the Canada-Mexico program a "great success" in a visit to Mexico City in August 2004, while Mexican Foreign Secretary Luis Ernesto Derbez said the program "shows our colleagues in Spain and the United States the success of a program established correctly." Prime Minister Jean Chretien, in Mexico in March 2003, said "This program where your farmers can come and work in Canada has worked extremely well and now we are exploring (ways) to extend that to other sectors. The bilateral seasonal agricultural workers program has been a model for balancing the flow of temporary foreign workers with the needs of Canadian employers."

The potential best practice aspects of the Canadian seasonal farm worker program include:

*   the active involvement of farm employers in program design and administration,
*   Mexican government involvement in recruiting migrants and monitoring their conditions in Canada and
*   the health insurance coverage.

Worker organizations do not play a role in program design or administration, and their complaints focus on legal restrictions that apply to all farm workers, such as the lack of rights for farm workers to form unions and bargain collectively. Researchers emphasize that most migrants arrive in debt, and thus have an incentive to be good employees and follow program rules so that they can return, repay debts, and accumulate savings in the second or third years of program participation. Note that the Mexican Labor Ministry and experienced migrants are an effective substitute for private recruiters in Mexico, and FARMS handles recruitment, travel, and deployment activities in Canada.

Remittances and migrants

Remittances are monies transferred from migrants abroad to their countries of origin. The remittance business collects funds in small amounts from millions of migrants abroad, many of whom do not have banking accounts, and sends the money to family and friends abroad, who may also lack a bank account. The global money transfer industry often measures remittances in transactions rather than the amount of money transferred, since the major revenue generating unit for the companies is a transaction in which US$200 or US$300 is sent over borders.

Like the recruitment business, the money transfer business consists of two types of firms. At one extreme are large firms that have thousands of branches in countries where migrants work and where they live. The largest is Western Union (www.westernunion.com/), a subsidiary of First Data Corp. (www.firstdatacorp.com). [13] First Data Corp's payment services division had revenues of US $2 billion and profits of US $581 million in 1999, a profit margin of 29 percent. Western Union advertises 80,000 agents and almost 200,000 outlets in 190 countries to collect and distribute payments, and says that its goal is "one location for every 25,000 to 35,000 population." Some competitors accuse Western Union of "locking up" agents by offering signing bonuses, but then requiring the agents to deal only with Western Union.

At the other extreme are small mom-and-pop agents, often trusted friends who act as couriers and take cash from one country to another (conductors on Russia-Moldova trains perform this role). The price, reliability, and timeliness of such remitters varies enormously, and surveys of migrants often find that bad experiences with small remitters encourage them to pay the premium normally collected by Western Union.

Remittances and remitters have become an important, profitable, and respectable part of the global migration infrastructure. Three interrelated trends seem important. First, the amount of remittances surged in the past decade, increasing the interest of governments in flows that are now twice the size of Official Development Assistance (ODA) to developing countries. Second, governments in some sending and receiv-

---

[13] FDC says it has four major divisions, including payment services, which includes "Western Union, Integrated Payment Systems ("IPS"), and Orlandi Valuta Companies and is the leading provider of nonbank domestic and international money transfer and payment services to consumers and commercial entities, including money transfer, official check and money order services."

ing countries have cooperated to educate migrants about how to send remittances at minimal cost, including in the case of Mexico and the US, the Mexican government issuing matricula consular IDs, which the US government declared were acceptable documentation to open US bank accounts (the US government also makes ITINs available to those who are not legally present and thus cannot get Social Security numbers).

Third, the cost of remitting funds fell with competition while the diversity of ways to remit funds increased. Banks generally charged lower fees than money transfer firms such as Western Union, and as US banks acquired Mexican banks, or forged banking relationships with banks that had Mexican branches, they began to advertise their low-cost remittance services. Mexican consulates helped to educate migrants by surveying the various money remitters and preparing charts that compared costs and services. New ways to remit money appeared, including depositing money in a US institution and having beneficiaries in Mexico withdraw the funds from a local ATM, or paying for housing and other supplies in the US and having them available or delivered in Mexico, which allowed the migrant to control how remittances were spent.

The evolving remittance business was heavily shaped by governments aiming to channel more funds via formal channels and thus undercut funding for terrorist, drug, and other organizations. The recruitment industry has received less attention from governments, especially in labor-receiving countries in which many of the migrants are unauthorized. However, the agreements signed by southern European nations such as Italy and Spain include provisions for sending country governments to accept the return of their nationals and cooperate to combat illegal migration and trafficking, but also give sending country governments a role in recruiting workers to fill sending country quotas.

Potential best practices

The ILO identified best practices to move migrants over borders in Convention 97 in 1949, viz., have public employment services in labor-sending and labor-receiving countries operate under the terms of bilateral agreements to ensure that the contracts of migrants are respected. The ILO in 1997 recognized the growing importance of private recruiters, and urged that countries sign bilateral agreements that include regulation of private recruiters as well as foster cooperation between private recruiters and public employment services.

Most international migration for employment does not occur under the auspices of bilateral agreements and public employment services. Instead, a diverse array of private recruiters moves workers over borders. Most are small, placing fewer than 1,000 migrants in foreign jobs each year but, with few barriers to entry and relatively low start-up costs, recruiting attracts those with knowledge of workers willing to migrate. Recruiters generally have more information than migrants, and recruiting can slide into smuggling and trafficking. The best way to protect migrants is economic growth that makes emigration unnecessary—if migrants are not desperate to leave, they are less likely to fall into the hands of recruiters who abuse them. Until then, educating migrants about their rights at home and abroad and using the media and victims to campaign against unauthorized recruitment and trafficking as well as punishing violators severely offer the best overall protections for migrants.

There are also three types of more specific policies that can help to prevent abuses of migrants by private recruiters: licensing, minimum size standards, and joint liability:

- Get recruiters to identify themselves by requiring them to have licenses, and make the issuance of recruitment licenses conditional on the recruiter passing tests that demonstrate knowledge of labor and immigration laws. Recruiters can also be required to provide written contracts to migrants that must be approved by labor-sending and -receiving government agencies, and to post bonds so that if migrants have legitimate complaints against them, there are funds available for compensation.

- Labor brokerage generally offers economies of scale, and the logic of having one place with information on employers seeking workers and workers seeking jobs is the justification for public employment services. Labor-sending countries can require recruiters to deploy at least a minimum number of migrants each year, and labor-receiving governments can also impose a minimum size requirement, which can make enforcement of the recruiting industry more efficient.

- Recruiters can be made jointly liable with the employers of migrants, so that migrants who may find it hard to ensure enforcement of their contracts abroad have recourse upon their return.

Joint liability may make recruiters more careful about the employers they deal with abroad.

As with remittances, governmental interest, education of migrants, and economies of scale can make the recruitment industry more competitive as well as a better protector of migrants.

References

Abella, Manolo. 2004. The Recruiter's Share in Labour Migration. in Massey Douglas and Edward Taylor. Eds International Migration. Prospects and Policies in a Global Market. Oxford University Press. Pp201-211.

Abella, Manolo, Philip Martin, and Elizabeth Midgley. 2004. Best Practices to Manage Migration. The Philippines. Mimeo.

Basok, Tanya. 2002. Tortillas and Tomatoes: Transmigrant Mexican Harvesters in Canada McGill-Queens University Press.

Canada. HRDC/CIC. 2003. Caribbean and Mexican Seasonal Agricultural Workers Program. http://www.on.hrdc-drhc.gc.ca/english/ps/agri/overview_e.shtml and http://www.cic.gc.ca/english/pub/facts2002-temp/index.html

ILO. 1997. Report of the Tripartite Meeting of Experts on Future ILO Activities in the Field of Migration. April 21-25. http://www. ilo.org/public/english/standards/relm/gb/docs/gb270/meim97-4.htm

Miller, Mark J. and Philip L. Martin. 1982. Administering foreign-worker programs: Lessons from Europe. Lexington, MA: Lexington Books, D.C. Heath and Company.

Ruhs, Martin. 2003. Temporary foreign worker programmes: Policies, adverse consequences, and the need to make them work. Perspectives on Labour Migration, no. 6. Geneva. International Labour Office.

Sobieszczyk, Teresa Rae. 2000. Pathways abroad: Gender and international labor migration institutions in Northern Thailand. PhD Dissertation. Cornell University.

Recruitment bureaux and money transfer agencies: Similarities and differences

Bernd Balkenhol[1]

Introduction

The symmetry in the movements of labour and money in the wake of migration invites a comparison of the key institutional actors. Migrant workers cross borders to make a better living and earn higher wages and salaries; part of their earnings travels back crossing international borders to provide a buffer to the consumption and incomes of the families and communities left behind. In these movements two types of institutions play a particular role, more or less in all corridors of migration: recruitment bureaux and money transfer operators (MTOs).

The comparison is appealing because MTOs thrive as monopolist providers but also in competition with each other and other types of financial service providers, like banks and microfinance institutions. Comparing the two types of operators might therefore yield insights into the scope for making the recruitment of migrant workers as "business" like as remittances handled by MTOs are already.

A fundamental difference

Despite the similarity of the corridor movements of labour and money, the fundamental difference lies in the nature of the service traded. There are absolute limits to the negotiability of labour, which sets it apart

---

[1] Head, Social Finance Programme, ILO.

from other services and products. Labour is not a commodity; this includes migrant labour.

Recruitment bureaux are thus constrained in optimising their performance in ways that MTOs are certainly not: money transfer agents can modify fees, commissions at short notice; they can fix an exchange rate at a level that is unrealistic but may be accepted by the remittance sender because of information gaps.

By contrast a recruitment bureau should abide by social and labour legislation: the fee charged must be in a reasonable proportion to the future earnings of the migrant worker; there are obligations to inform the migrant candidate concerning working conditions, wage protection, social security and rights to complain. Of course, this presupposes that the recruitment agency is licensed...

Institutional efficiency

MTOs are private profit maximisers. Their efficiency is in terms of maximum return on human, physical and financial inputs. This applies also to recruitment agencies if they are privately owned. However, public or mixed recruitment bureaux cannot be measured by their return in financial terms alone, but by the quality and stability of social outcomes as well: satisfaction of employer; satisfaction of migrant; precision of matching.

MTOs are basically single-product operators, while recruitment bureaux often come with a package of services, like information, advice, training.

MTOs are organized in international networks, whilst recruitment agencies are defined by national boundaries. Due to the range of operations, MTOs can also tap economies of scale, unavailable to recruitment agencies.

Transaction costs for both client and service provider are high in proportion to the amounts sent, but decreasing rapidly as soon as the market gets more transparent and competitive. Remittance transaction costs are low under near perfect competition. On the other hand, the client transaction costs can be high in dealing with recruitment agencies in which there are more cumbersome and protracted proceedings.

Opportunity costs for migrants are of two variants. They can be in terms of time lost in interacting directly with the service provider or they can also be in terms of non-delivery of the contract by the service provider. A mismatch in jobs that can be attributed to a recruitment agency's poor selection is dramatic for a migrant worker; this also includes cases of abuse and of ill treatment in so-called preparatory centres before migrant workers are sent off by recruitment agencies (Indonesia). However, the loss of a single transfer is absorbable. In the remittance field there is – usually – choice, there is always the informal market segment. That choice does usually not exist with recruitment agencies.

On the whole it would seem that the many of the drawbacks of recruitment agencies in terms of institutional performance could be addressed with appropriate changes in the governance, i.e. ownership of recruitment agencies, as well as licensing conditions that provide incentives for quick and efficient delivery.

Market perfection

On the demand side, high price elasticity is favourable in the case of remittances because of the existence of an underground informal alternative; because of the state monopoly that some recruitment agencies enjoy, this price elasticity of demand is low when it comes to recruitment.

Concerning the supply side, MTOs are perfectly demand responsive, so they can deliver as much and as frequently as migrant workers want to send money. The supply of jobs for which recruitment agencies select migrant workers is contingent on external factors outside of the control of the recruitment agencies. Market entry obstacles are high on both sides.

Competitiveness is always a market concern. In the US-Mexico corridor the monopoly profits that Western Union enjoyed before 2001 melted away within four to five years as a result of the entry of new MTOs and banks. By contrast, the recruitment market is first of all domestic, not cross-border, and distorted in some cases by the co-existence of public and private operators.

Information asymmetry in both markets is detrimental to the migrant worker.

29

Policy entry points

There is a place for public policy to shape the market for remittances in such a way that migrant workers can choose from a variety of safe, reliable and accessible MTOs and other agencies. The question – here as in other policy domains – is: how much direct government intervention is actually required? Governments may take a strong interest in remittances because they help to cut down on public investments in social and economic infrastructure in areas that receive a disproportionately large share of remittances, they may see remittances as a substitute for public investment.

Whatever the underlying motive or hidden agenda, the list of possible entry points includes at least the following:

- Governments could design the fiscal regimes in ways to encourage MTOs to go for large numbers of transfers, rather than large volumes; or award a preferential tax status to MTOs that interact with credit union networks and other financial intermediaries known to cater more to those who are not well off;

- Ownership of transfer agencies: In corridors where there is no competition in transfer agencies, governments could create their own agency, with a sunset date before it would completely pull out, and not more than a minority ownership from the beginning;

- Incentives for market entry: Alternatively and more in line with market principles, governments should carefully review the entrance requirements for newcomer MTOs, especially minimum capital requirements;

- Licensing, regulation and supervision;

- Information campaigns for migrant workers: Financial education of migrants who wish to send remittances should focus on the costs and risks of the small print in remittance orders; the public sector may not necessarily be best suited to do financial education. Worker and employer organisations would be more appropriate – directly or via subcontracted specialized firms.

'Merchants of labor' in three centuries: Lessons from history for reforming 21st century exploitation of migrant labor

Bruce Goldstein[1]

The International Institute for Labour Studies is justifiably concerned about conditions for international migrant workers and the practices of employment agencies and recruiters. Advocates for migrant workers in the United States have found valuable lessons by studying the experiences of labor advocates during the great wave of immigration from the 1880's through the beginning of the 20th century. Those lessons followed from attempts to improve workers' wages and working conditions by reforming the practices of labor intermediaries.

Reformers learned they needed to focus on the larger entities that contracted with labor recruiters, and not focus solely on the labor recruiters. The removal of one labor contractor will usually lead to his replacement by another who engages in similar conduct. The business with the real economic power is not the recruiter but rather the one that actually uses the labor to produce commodities for profit. Effective reform will occur only by focusing on the financial interests of the business that actually uses and benefits from the workers' labor. Such businesses must be considered an "employer."

Labor subcontracting, or "The sweating system"

During the late 1800s and early 1900s, labor contracting in the U.S., Great Britain and Australia was commonly referred to as the "sweat-

---

[1] Co-Executive Director, Farmworker Justice Fund, Inc., Washington D.C., USA.

ing system." The contractor, or middleman, was called the "sweater" because he "sweated his profit" out of the difference between what the bigger business paid him and what he paid the workers.

Garment manufacturing and other occupations where the sweating system was widespread were called "the sweated trades." Originally, a "sweating shop" was a place where the workers worked under the supervision of a "sweater" for the benefit of a larger business. Garment manufacturers and other companies reduced their costs of labor by hiring contractors to supervise workers in locations outside their factories. Once the sweatshops gained a reputation for poor wages, long hours, child labor, and unsanitary working conditions, the term "sweatshop" eventually became associated with any miserable place to work, even if there was no labor contractor. The origins of the "sweatshop," however, are in labor contracting.

Because subcontracting required little skill or capital, there was intense competition among the sweaters, who "use every device to get the work done as cheaply as they can." The contractors' principal method of lowering their costs to win bids from the manufacturers was to reduce the wages they paid. (Willoughby 1900: 4; Boris 1994: 53-54). To save money, the sweaters also used children as workers and subjected the workers to unsafe working conditions.

Strategies to end sweating system abuses: Aiming at the manufacturers

It became apparent to workers, reformers and legislatures that regulating sweaters (contractors) was important but was difficult and ultimately inadequate in the effort to stop exploitation. "The first attempts at legislation were all defective in one vital particular. The prohibitions were all directed against and the penalties imposed on the petty sweater or the family [performing homework]. Experience soon showed that unless an army of inspectors was employed, it was impossible to ferret out the thousands of small shops located in cellars, attics and back buildings of tenement houses. In most states, therefore, amendments were enacted placing the responsibility on the wholesale manufacturer and on the merchant. These were no longer allowed to shelter themselves behind the statement that they gave out the work to contractors and did not know where or under what conditions it was made up" (Willoughby 1900:10,15).

Reformers and legislatures used a variety of methods to attempt to place responsibility on the larger companies that utilized the contractors. For example, in New York in 1899 and several other states at the time, the manufacturer had to keep a record of the names and addresses of all contractors it used and had to stop using contractors whose conditions had been found by state inspectors to violate health and safety laws.

Reformers, such as the Consumers' League, created "white labels" which manufacturers were permitted to purchase and place in their garments if produced in accordance with the League's standards. Under these standards, the goods had to be produced in a factory, rather than a sweatshop, and without child labor. Through organizing and publicity, the reformers encouraged consumers to purchase only goods that included these labels to ensure fair treatment of workers. Manufacturers who relied on sweatshops were subject to boycotts.

State legislatures also began to broaden the answer to the question "who is the worker's employer?" The traditional English common law definition of employment relationships allowed companies to easily avoid status as a worker's "employer" by claiming that that they had not hired a worker and did not directly supervise the worker's daily activities on the job. New laws in the 1880's began defining employment relationships more broadly. These definitions, which eventually were used in labor laws in every state, would consider a company to be the employer of a worker if it "suffered or permitted" the work of that person. A company "suffers" someone to work if it tolerates or acquiesces in someone's performance of work. Thus, a business that benefits from a person's work and knew or should have known that the work was being performed will be considered an "employer" of the worker even if a labor contractor hired and supervised the worker.

An official with the National Child Labor Committee in 1905 said: "Legislation should definitely prohibit not only the employment of young children but their *permission* to work. The name of every person working on the premises, whether that person is officially employed or is simply "permitted or suffered to work," should appear on the roll of the firm or corporation. Otherwise factory inspection is a farce. In states failing to make this definite prohibition little children, sometimes pitifully young, have been found in the mills and factories working as helpers of older members of the family. They are not technically employed..." (Lovejoy 1905: 47, 51).

When Congress enacted the federal minimum wage, overtime pay, and child labor restrictions in the Fair Labor Standards Act of 1938 (FLSA), it adopted the "suffer or permit" standard. 29 U.S.C. § 203(g). The Supreme Court recognized the expansiveness of the definition when it held that a slaughterhouse was the "employer" of meat deboners, despite the presence in the slaughterhouse of a contractor who had been retained by the slaughterhouse to operate the deboning operation. More recent examples of the usefulness of this definition include a federal district court decision, which applied this concept to hold that a garment manufacturer was an employer of the workers supervised by a contractor. *Lopez v. Silverman*, 14 F. Supp. 2d 405 (S.D.N.Y. 1998). Congress also used this broad definition when it enacted the Migrant and Seasonal Agricultural Worker Protection Act of 1983 ("AWPA"), an employment law that, among other things, requires farm labor contractors to be licensed and requires farmers to only use licensed contractors. In AWPA cases, the workers frequently attempt to persuade the court that the larger company (the grower) and the labor contractor "jointly employ" the workers and are therefore jointly responsible for any violations of wage and other obligations. The larger company usually argues that it does not "employ" the farmworkers on its farm and that the sole employer is the labor contractor. In most, but not all cases, the federal courts of appeal have held that the farmer and the labor contractor are "joint employers" of the workers and are jointly liable for nonpayment of wages and other violations. See *Antenor v. D & S Farms*, 88 F.3d 925 (11th Cir. 1996).

Labor unions have long recognized the need to address the roles of manufacturers and contractors. Union organizing and collective bargaining picked up momentum in the garment industry around 1891. Unions, through large-scale strikes in the garment industry in various cities began to break apart the sweating system. They organized not only at the manufacturers but also in the sweatshops and began preventing manufacturers from using the subcontracting system to push down wages. (Willoughby 1900:18). For years, there would be ups and downs in the unions' efforts to enforce and "improve upon the conditions already wrested from the wholesale firms through their subservient tools, the contractors." (Willoughby 1900: 23, quoting United Garment Workers newsletter from 1896).

Conclusion: Lessons from the 19th century sweating system

The history of the sweating system offers us useful lessons for today. Any strategy to ameliorate the harms of subcontracting must focus on the entities that have the economic power to change the system: the companies that retain the subcontractors. Efforts to regulate the subcontractors themselves will rarely be sufficient because the subcontractors are too numerous, the economic pressures on contractors to compete by undermining labor standards are too intense, and new subcontractors will always replace ones that are put out of business.

Laws, regulations, law enforcement efforts, consumer boycotts, and collective bargaining agreements should attempt to place responsibility for wages and working conditions on the companies that subcontract with labor recruiters and labor contractors. Emphasizing the responsibility of the business that subcontracts, rather than that of the recruiter, will maximize the impact of the limited resources available to prevent substandard employment practices. This approach also benefits those employers that prefer to take responsibility by supervising the labor contractors closely (or not using contractors at all) and by treating their workers well. Companies deserve protection against unfair competition by unscrupulous employers that seek to undermine labor standards and lower labor costs by resorting to labor contractors.

Workers in many occupational settings during the 21st century seem to be fighting the same labor practices that were used to weaken workers' bargaining power and suppress improvements in wages and working conditions during the 1880's. The reform efforts from that time period offer us valuable lessons in struggling against labor contracting abuses. Perhaps we should even start speaking again in terms of the "sweating system."

References

Black, Clementine. 1907. *Sweated Industry and the Minimum Wage.* London: Duckworth Co. p. 23.

Eileen Boris. 1994. *Home to Work : Motherhood and the Politics of Industrial Homework in the United States.* Cambridge, England and New York: Cambridge University Press, pp. 53-54.

Goodchild, Frank M. 1895. "The Sweating System in Philadelphia," *Arena*, Jan. 1895, pp. 261–62.

Gould, Anne, International Ladies' Garment Workers Union. 1938. "Fixing Wage Rates in the New York Dress Industry," Washington, D.C.: Bureau of Labor Statistics.

Hall, Frederick Smith. 1943. *Forty Years, 1902-1942, The Work of the New York Child Labor Committee.* New York: New York Child Labor Committee, pp. 83-84.

Illinois Bureau of Labor Statistics. 1893. "The Sweating System," *Seventh Biennial Report 1892.* Springfield: H.W. Rokker, State Printer & Binder, p. 358.

Lovejoy, Owen R. 1905. "The Test of Effective Child-Labor Legislation," *Program, First Annual Meeting, National Child Labor Committee*, pp. 47, 51, reprinted in Publications of the National Child Labor Committee During 1905 and 1906. 1909. New York, p. 51.

National Child Labor Committee. 1913. "The Exploitation of Tenement Home-workers, *Child Labor Bulletin* 1912-1913. Vol. 1, no. 3, New York, p. 69.

Select Committee of the House of Lords. 1890. *Report of the Select Committee of the House of Lords on the Sweating System.* Fifth Report. London (April 28, 1890) pp. iv, xlv.

William Franklin Willoughby. 1900. "The Sweating System in the United States," in Herbert B. Adams, ed., *Monographs on American Social Economics, Vol. IX, Regulation of the Sweating System.* U.S. Commission to the Paris Exposition of 1900, Dept. of Social Economy, pp. 1, 10, 15, 23.

Part II: The empirical framework: Country and regional experiences

The regulation of recruitment agencies: Experience and good practices in countries of origin in Asia

Nilim Baruah[1]

Introduction

In the 21st century, international labour migration or the movement of people across borders for employment is at the top of the policy agendas of many countries, be they countries of origin, transit or destination. The ILO estimates that there are over 80 million migrant workers. Three key determining factors - the "pull" of changing demographics and labour market needs in many industrialized countries, the "push" of population, unemployment and political crises pressures in less developed countries, and established inter-country networks based on family, culture and history – will continue to fuel this kind of movement for many years yet. An alarmingly large proportion of labour migration takes place illegally, and there is a clandestine industry to abet it. Increasingly, governments at both ends of the migration spectrum are developing regulatory mechanisms to manage labour mobility to their individual and mutual benefit, and that of the migrant.

In Asia it is estimated that every year some 2.6 million workers left their countries under contracts to work abroad over the period 1995-99.[2] The South Asian countries accounted for 46 percent of this outflow.

---

[1] Head, Labour Migration Service, International Organization for Migration (IOM), Geneva. Views expressed are those of the author and do not necessarily represent those of IOM.

[2] Abella, Manolo. "Driving forces of labour migration in Asia," *World Migration Report*, IOM, Geneva: 2003.

Southeast Asians, mainly Filipinos, Indonesians, Thais, Burmese and Vietnamese made up 50 percent. A large proportion of workers from South and Southeast Asia continue to leave for the Arab Gulf States to perform all kinds of service, trade and construction jobs. New patterns of labour migration have also emerged in the region over the last decade. There has been a significant outflow of professionals and technical workers to North America and Europe, largely from India and the Philippines, especially in the information technology and nursing sectors. Intraregional labour migration has also grown rapidly, particularly from Southeast Asia to the developed or emerging East Asian economies.

Labour sending countries in Asia range from those that are experiencing a migration transition, characterized by both labour import and export (e.g., Thailand), established labour sending countries (e.g. the Philippines and South Asian countries) to those that are relative newcomers (e.g. Vietnam) to organized labour migration. Nevertheless, as countries of origin they all face some common issues. Briefly, these are:

- Challenges in ensuring the protection and welfare of vulnerable migrant workers, particularly women, during recruitment and employment, and in providing appropriate assistance to migrant workers in terms of pre-departure, welfare and reintegration services.

- Challenges in optimizing benefits of organized labour migration, particularly the development of new markets and increasing remittance flows through formal channels, as well as enhancing the development impact.

- Building institutional capacity and inter-ministerial coordination to meet labour migration challenges.

- Increasing cooperation with destination countries for the protection of migrant workers, access to labour markets and the prevention of irregular migration.

In response to these migration challenges, Asian countries have responded with a set of policies, structures and procedures that seek to protect their migrant workers and facilitate orderly migration. The main policies introduced by Asian countries to protect their migrant workers focus on curbing abuses in recruitment, setting standards for employment contracts, exit controls, welfare services for migrants, the posting of labour attachés abroad and cooperation with countries of destination. This paper will look at policies and mechanisms to curb recruitment abuses in some of the Asian countries relatively more advanced down this road – namely, India, Pakistan, Philippines and Sri Lanka.

Complaints by migrant workers [3]

Recruitment agencies in countries of origin play a vital role in the placement of workers abroad. They account for a majority of workers placed abroad in the Philippines, Pakistan and Sri Lanka, as well as some other Asian countries. However, given that due to structural reasons (including poverty, unemployment and large wage differentials between countries of origin and destination) the supply of workers in lower skill sectors far outstrips the demand and there are far more workers wishing to work abroad (to earn a livelihood and pursue a perceived better life) than there are jobs, migrant workers can be vulnerable to abuses during recruitment.

This is reflected in the fact that there were 6152 complaints filed on violation of recruitment in the Philippines in 2004. Almost half of the complainants were female. The reasons included: excessive fees, misrepresentation and contract substitution in country of destination. In Pakistan, where overseas employment is not as large, there were 346 complaints made during 2001-2003. The reasons included: excessive fees, failure to fulfil placement obligations, contract substitution and disappearance of agents after collection of fees.

Actions taken by states on the receipt of complaints include suspension and cancellation of recruitment licenses. In India, 24 suspensions and two cancellations were made in 2004. In Pakistan, between 2000-2003, 37 licenses were cancelled and 72 suspended.

A common problem faced by many migrant workers worldwide are high migration costs as a result of excessive (and mostly illegal) intermediation fees.

---

[3] Data on Pakistan and the Philippines is from Mughal, Rashid and L. Padilla. "Regulatory Frameworks for Recruitment of Migrant Workers and Minimum Standards in Employment Contracts: A Comparative Study of Pakistan, the Philippines and Sri Lanka," *Labour Migration in Asia: Protection of Migrant Workers, Support Services and Enhancing Development Benefits.* IOM, Geneva: 2005.
Data on India is from "Economic Migration," Office of the Protector General of Emigrants, Ministry of Overseas Indian Affairs in the Government of India. New Delhi: 2005.

Table I: Number of Licensed Recruitment Agencies in 2003

Country	Number
India	1250
Philippines	1327
Sri Lanka	524

Source: Mughal and Padilla, 2005; Ministry of Overseas Indian Affairs, 2005.

Policy and operational responses in countries of origin

Private recruitment agencies have played a vital role in expanding labour migration in Asia. At the same time, they have been responsible for many of the abuses. This has led states to intervene by controlling recruitment activities as well as other measures by other actors.

Licensing requirements

Most Asian labour sending countries prohibit the recruitment of their nationals by persons or entities other than those licensed by the state to do so. Licensing requirements generally require licensees to be resident nationals in order that they can be held accountable for any recruitment violations. It is now also common for countries to require that licensees put up financial guarantees against claims that may be brought by the government or migrants.

The table below illustrates licensing requirements in Pakistan and the Philippines.

Table II

Requirements	Pakistan	Philippines
National	Yes	Yes
Application fee	USD 16	USD 200
Registration	Sole proprietor, partnership or company	Sole proprietor, partnership or company (with minimum paid-up capital of USD 40,000)
Character certificate	Good conduct certificate	No criminal record
Deposit	USD 5000	USD 20,000
License fee	USD 500	USD 1000
Other		Surety bond – USD 2000
Validity of license	3 years (renewable)	4 years (renewable)

Source: Mughal and Padilla, 2005. Original sums are in national currencies and have been approximated in US dollars by the authors.

Limit on fees

A common practice is to put a limit on the fees that can be charged to migrants by recruitment agencies. In India, the fee is differentiated depending on the type of worker (see table III).

Table III

Type of worker	Fee (in USD)
Unskilled	45
Semi-skilled	65
Skilled	110
Other/Highly skilled	220

Source: Emigration and You: An Information Booklet, Office of the Protector General of Emigrants, Ministry of Labour in the Government of India, New Delhi: 2004. Original sums are in Indian Rupees and have been approximated in US dollars by the author.

In the Philippines, the placement or recruitment fee cannot be over one month's salary of the employment contract, with some exceptions. Seafarers are not required to pay placement fees and in the case of performing artists and entertainers bound for Japan, the fee is paid by the employer.[4]

In response to problems of over-charging by recruitment intermediaries and exorbitant migration costs, some countries of destination have also acted with legislation. Israel is in the process of enacting a decree that will limit costs to the migrant worker to no more than 120 percent of the minimum wage in Israel (which is around USD 900 under current exchange rates).

Information dissemination and empowerment of workers

The important role of information dissemination for potential migrants to make informed decisions about migration has long been recognised and acted upon by various agencies such as IOM. Recently, some Asian labour sending countries like the Philippines have recognised the need for not just pre-departure orientation a few days before departure, but the conduct of pre-employment orientation seminars (PEOS) and intensified information campaigns, especially in rural communities to provide applicants with sufficient information to enable them to make

---

[4] Mughal and Padilla, 2005.

informed decisions. This includes undertaking information campaigns to inform potential overseas workers of safe recruitment, travel and employment procedures - the risks of irregular movement, regular movement options and regulations of both receiving and sending states, including illegal recruitment.

Countries like the Philippines and Sri Lanka have gone further and promoted the empowerment of migrant workers, especially through the formation of community based organizations, to enable their voice to be heard and taken account of in policy development.

Enforcement of legislation to regulate recruitment[5]

The legislation enacted is of course only as good as its implementation. In India, complaints against registered recruitment agencies are looked into by the Protector General of Emigrants (PGE) and Indian missions abroad. Complaints against unregistered entities and individuals (i.e. illegal recruiters) are referred to the police. The PGE has a public hearing twice a week in the capital, New Delhi. 1585 petitions were received in 2004. In the same year, 24 suspensions and two cancellations of licenses were made. Twenty-one employers were "blacklisted".

In the Philippines, the number of illegal recruitment cases has gone up each year since 1999 with 866 cases being received in 2003. In 2004, President Gloria Macapagal Arroyo created a Task Force on Illegal Recruitment. In the first month of its operation, it had led to the investigation of 98 alleged illegal recruiters.

Controlling illegal recruitment remains a challenge in Asian countries, despite the progress made and action taken. In Sri Lanka and Bangladesh, for instance, it is estimated that the number of illegal recruiters far outnumber registered entities.

Self–regulation

Policing by states, while necessary to curb recruitment abuses, by itself will not be sufficient, given structural forces at play (poverty, unemployment, large wage differentials between countries of origin and destination and labour supply outstripping demand in lower skill sectors). Industry associations, such as the Bangladesh Association of Recruitment

---

[5] Data on Pakistan and the Philippines is from Mughal and Padilla, 2005. Data on India is from Ministry of Overseas Indian Affairs, 2005.

Agencies (BAIRA), have been formed and have the potential to develop and enforce voluntary codes of conduct.

Performance based incentives and sanctions

Some countries, such as the Philippines, have made continuation of the license contingent on performance. That is a new licensee or one that has been inactive must deploy or place a minimum of workers or else the license is revoked.[6] At the same time awards are bestowed on best performing agencies, recognising their contribution to national development.

Involvement of public employment agencies and international organizations

While the role of state agencies in recruitment has clearly been overtaken in most Asian labour states by the private sector, an argument could be made for deployment through the state for categories of workers especially vulnerable to malpractice and abuse, such as female domestic workers.

International organizations have wide experience in migrant application processing and services can also be called upon for the selection of workers. For example, IOM is doing so with regard to labour migration to Canada, Italy and Spain.

Skills development

It is clear that abuses in recruitment are less common for skilled occupations where the education and awareness of the migrant worker is usually greater and the jobs have better terms and conditions. Some Asian countries have recognised this and put emphasis on the raising of the skill levels of workers to improve their employment opportunities.

Inter-state cooperation

Given that employment takes place in the country of destination, there are limits to what a labour sending state can do to protect its migrant workers without the active cooperation of states of employment (and coordination with other countries of origin). Such cooperation can take place at the global, regional or bilateral level. At a global level the

---

[6] Training Manual for Labour Administrators (Draft), IOM, Geneva: 2005.

ILO and UN have enacted conventions related to the protection of migrant workers and on employment agencies. Various organizations have facilitated the development of multilateral approaches to the international movement of people, for instance the IOM through the Berne Initiative. However, although world migration pressures have increased, the progress towards a multilateral approach in the area of migration management is far slower than in the management of trade and capital flows.

Where feasible, focused bilateral labour agreements (BLAs) and regional integration agreements are effective in facilitating orderly labour migration and protecting migrant workers. BLAs may be reached to prevent indiscriminate international recruitment in sectors such as health, which have a direct bearing on development in poorer countries. The Philippines and India have reached agreements with the UK on the recruitment of health workers.[7]

Often, focused BLAs are difficult to achieve, for instance with destination countries such as the Arab Gulf States. In this case, non-binding consultative mechanisms such as Joint Commissions on Labour, Regional Consultative Processes and Working Groups are a more effective tool for interstate cooperation.

Regional Consultative Processes are for bringing together migration officials of states of origin and destination to discuss migration-related issues in a cooperative way. Along with other international organizations, IOM has been engaged in promoting dialogue and cooperation in managing migration among countries of origin, transit and destination at the regional and sub-regional levels. A major regional process in Asia is the Ministerial Consultations on Overseas Employment for Countries of Origin in Asia, which since the third meeting in 2005 includes the participation of countries of destination. These Consultations have made specific recommendations on "Regulatory frameworks and allied measures to prevent malpractices and abuses in recruitment".

---

[7] Labour agreements formalize each side's commitment to ensure that migration takes place in accordance with agreed principles and procedures. In OECD countries alone, there are over 176 wide-ranging BLAs in force. Economics or labour market shortages are not the only reason that BLAs are reached. BLAs can underscore friendly relations, be linked to cooperation on managing irregular migration or be development oriented.

Conclusions

Of the estimated 175 million migrants worldwide, more than 80 million are thought to be labour migrants. This figure is much higher if one is to take into account accompanying dependents. An estimated 2.6 million persons left from Asian countries between 1995 and 1999 every year under contract to work abroad. The management of migration flows is crucial given this magnitude and that international labour migration is likely to increase in the future. The main policies that Asian states have put in place to protect their migrant workers focus on curbing abuses in recruitment, setting standards for employment contracts, exit controls, welfare services for migrants, posting of labour attachés abroad, and cooperation with countries of destination. The governments of Asian countries are now committing more technical and financial resources to the formulation and implementation of labour migration policies. Over the last two decades a number of specialized institutions have come up to address concerns around foreign employment. This reflects the importance of labour migration as a national development strategy for Asian countries, both as a means of generating foreign currency through remittances, and to increase employment opportunities for its nationals and to protect its workers from abuses.

Asian labour sending states have been in the forefront of developing policies and mechanisms to protect migrant workers in the recruitment process. This experience, briefly covered in the paper, is a rich source of ideas and information for countries in other parts of the globe and in Asia embarking on a pro-active overseas employment programme. Problems in recruitment however still persist in lower skill occupations and this is partly due to structural factors. Information dissemination, better enforcement of regulations, increase in skill levels, greater employment creation at home and enhanced international cooperation can all lead to less abuse during recruitment.

References

Abella, Manolo. "Driving forces of labour migration in Asia," *World Migration Report*, IOM, Geneva: 2003.

Baruah, Nilim. "Capacity Building and Interstate Cooperation to Protect Migrant Workers and Facilitate Orderly Labour Migration." *Labour Migration in Asia: Trends, Challenges and policy responses in countries of origin.* IOM, Geneva: 2003.

"Economic Migration," Office of the Protector General of Emigrants, Ministry of Overseas Indian Affairs in the Government of India, New Delhi: 2005.

Emigration and You: An Information Booklet, Office of the Protector General of Emigrants, Ministry of Labour in the Government of India, New Delhi: 2004.

Mughal, Rashid and L. Padilla. "Regulatory Frameworks for Recruitment of Migrant Workers and Minimum Standards in Employment Contracts: A Comparative Study of Pakistan, the Philippines and Sri Lanka," *Labour Migration in Asia: Protection of Migrant Workers, Support Services and Enhancing Development Benefits.* IOM, Geneva: 2005.

"Summary of Statements and Recommendations of the Ministers." *Second Labour Migration Ministerial Consultations for Countries of Origin in Asia,* Organized by the Department of Labour and Employment in the Government of Philippines and IOM. Manila: 2004.

Towards a Fair Deal for Migrant Workers in the Global Economy. Report VI. International Labour Conference, 92nd Session 2004. International Labour Organization, Geneva: 2004.

Training Manual for Labour Administrators (Draft), IOM, Geneva: 2005.

Private recruitment agencies in the era of globalization: Challenges and responses The case of the Philippines

Cesar A. Averia, Jr. [1]

Overseas employment has significant economic and socio-cultural impacts

We firmly believe that for a developing country like the Philippines, overseas employment can play a very crucial role in making the local economy more prosperous and our society more dynamic. Based on our own experience, Filipino executives and technical employees who have been sent abroad become seasoned and well-trained professionals. They return as entrepreneurs and managers familiar with cutting edge technologies and best practices learned from the developed countries. Overseas workers and their families who have worked and lived for considerable periods in free and open societies usually bring back new ideas, lifestyles, ideals and democratic principles that can encourage progressive social change and help enrich the local culture.

In the case of the Philippines, the ever important Overseas Filipino Workers (OFWs) who we hail as our modern-day heroes, have served and continue to serve as the economic lifeline to many families and communities in our country. Their remittances do not only serve the personal needs of their dependents and relatives, but also constitute sizable and

---

[1] President & CEO, EDI-Staffbuilders International, Inc., Makati, Philippines. http://www.edistaffbuilders.com

stable sources of external fund sources that have strengthened the country's financial institutions, improved investment climates, and significantly contributed to overall economic growth and development. In fact, even during the worst part of the Asian economic crisis in the late 1990s, it was the OFW remittances which served as the buffer that enabled the Philippine economy to withstand the aftershocks better than some of its neighbors.

Tripartite cooperation is a must for a successful Overseas Employment Program (OEP)

It goes without saying that for any Overseas Employment Program (OEP) to succeed, the entire process of deploying a significant sector of the labor force overseas must have a positive effect on all concerned – the migrant workers, the private recruitment companies and the regulatory government agency in charge of supervising overseas employment.

There are simple indicators of success that can be used to determine whether the principal stakeholders were able to achieve the desired objectives, and whether the process was able to help spread the benefits of development:

- Were the overseas workers able to find gainful employment with just compensation?

- Will their health and safety in the workplace be assured?

- Did the private recruitment companies charge fees that were fully justified and not excessive or exorbitant?

- Was there no connivance between the local agencies and their foreign principals?

- Was there any contract substitution and other forms of fraud?

- Were the job offers or orders genuine and not just contrived?

- Was the government able to curb or minimize the usual fraudulent practices committed by private recruitment agencies?

- Were the job orders verified?

- Were the salaries offered commensurate to the work to be performed?

- What was done to ensure that the stipulated job descriptions would be followed?

A snapshot of the overseas Filipino labor force

The following data provided by the Philippine National Statistics Office for 2002 provide a clearer picture and bring about a better understanding of the OFW phenomenon:

- The number of Overseas Filipino Workers (OFWs) who worked abroad during the period April to September 2002 reached 1.06 million, up by 2.6 per cent from 1.03 million in 2001. Of this total, 990,000 or 93.8 per cent were Overseas Contract Workers (OCWs) or those with existing work-contracts abroad. Their number also went up by 2.7 per cent from 964,000 during April to September 2001.

- Of the 1.06 million OFWs, 554,000 or 52.5 per cent were males while 47.5 per cent were females. Both male and female OFWs increased during the six-month period. Male OFWs increased by 4.9 per cent while female OFWs increased slightly by 0.2 per cent.

- A greater number of OFWs were in the 25–29 age group. The majority of these workers were female. In the 45 and over age group, males outnumbered females at a ratio larger than 2 to 1.

- Of the 1.06 million OFWs in October 2002, 808,000 or 76.5 per cent worked in Asia; about 121,000 or 11.5 per cent worked in Europe; and about 87,000 or 8.2 per cent worked in North and South America.

- About one-third of the 808,000 OFWs in Asia (271,000 or 33.5 per cent) were in Saudi Arabia. Those who worked in Hong Kong accounted for about 122,000 (15.0 per cent) and those in Japan, about 87,000 (11.0 per cent).

- The largest group of OFWs, 342,000 or 32.4 per cent, was laborers and unskilled workers. Trades and related workers came next with about 168,000 workers (15.9 per cent), followed by plant and machine operators and assemblers at about 155,000 workers (14.7 per cent).

Overseas Filipino workers remittances to the Philippines: Some revealing statistics

Again, some 2002 data provided by the Philippine National Statistics Office, demonstrate the significant impact of OFW remittances on the Philippine economy:

- From April to September 2002, the total remittances of OFWs amounted to P67.7 billion. These remittances included cash sent (P46.4 billion), cash brought home (P17.0 billion), and remittance in kind (P4.3 billion).

- The average remittance within the six-month period was estimated at P74,487, an increase of 17.1 per cent from P63,606 the year before. Male OFWs sent higher remittances on the average than female OFWs.

- Of the 853,000 OFWs sending cash remittances, about 597,000 or seven in every 10 OFWs used banks, while about 218,000 or more than one-fourth (25.6 per cent) used door-to-door delivery. Others, 37,000 or 4.3 per cent, remitted through agency or local office, friends, coworkers, or other means.

- Cash remittances sent through banks amounted to P35.2 billion or about 76.0 per cent. Cash sent through door-to-door delivery amounted to P9.0 billion or 19.3 per cent, while the remaining P2.2 billion or 4.8 per cent were either remitted through agency or local office, friends, coworkers, or other means.

- Cash remittances sent by OFWs in Asia reached P31.7 billion, accounting to 68.4 per cent of the total cash remittance. Cash remittances coming from the OFWs in Europe came next (P7.4 billion), followed by those from North and South America (P4.7 billion).

- Among OFWs in the Asian countries, OFWs in Saudi Arabia sent the biggest cash remittances (P12.0 billion or about 37.9 per cent). OFWs in Jordan sent the least with P0.06 billion.

- Among the major occupation groups, OFWs working as plant and machine operators and assemblers shared the biggest cash remittances during the period from April to September 2002. They accounted for 19.5 per cent of the total cash remittances. The next biggest remittances were sent by laborers and unskilled workers, P8.8 billion or about 19.0 per cent; followed by trades and related workers, P7.8 billion or about 17.0 per cent. Special occupation workers (or those with occupation which were not classifiable) contributed the least with P0.02 billion or about 0.05 per cent.

Some "best practices" in the Philippines' private recruitment industry

The private recruitment industry would like to make it unequivocally clear that we have fully and wholeheartedly supported – and will continue to support – all policies, statutes and regulations designed to protect migrant workers, especially female migrant workers, from any form of oppression and exploitation. It is in this light that our company, as one of the major players in the Philippine overseas recruitment industry, has strongly adhered to the fundamental "best practices" that have enabled us to sustain our leadership and hallmark as a world-class service provider.

Best Practices:

1. Putting a premium on investing our resources and manpower in exploring and developing new markets where we can bring the multidisciplinary professions and expertise of the overseas Filipino workers. To successfully accomplish this, we establish strategic partnerships principally with well-known and global business organizations.

2. Niche marketing and thorough research and study on countries with potential recruitment needs involves looking not only for clients with specific needs, but also for clients who share the same principles as EDI. This ensures that candidates will have as ideal a working environment as possible.

3. Continuing the search for new markets and developing them in other countries helps in adapting to the decreased demand in existing markets, and opens up new opportunities elsewhere. Sending executives to establish a presence in these markets sends the signal that EDI is willing to send the most qualified candidates and helps forge global alliances.

4. Setting up branch operations in mature markets further solidifies relationships with markets and businesses in foreign countries. This ensures our continuing presence and accessibility to our workers

and forges global alliances with equally reputable private recruitment companies from various regions and countries. Such actions have paved the way for other countries to deploy their own nationals to undertake job opportunities overseas. This also ensures a steady demand for candidates in these countries, as well as a constant source of gainful, fulfilling employment.

5.   Establishing professionalism in the business and delivering quality service includes maintaining a competent, well-trained and highly motivated consultant staff, which will be able to respond to, and deliver to, the stringent demands of our select client base.

6.   EDI does not charge candidates a placement fee, thus emphasizing their professional value. There is always a client who is willing to pay for the best, most qualified executives, managers and employees, thus encouraging clients to be active participants in the selection of qualified candidates.

7.   EDI has also strived to protect the recruitment industry and its workers by investing in the hotel and tourism industry of Qatar for minimal profit. In doing so, EDI ensured that future employees of this industry have a precedent for gainful employment and that any potential abuses will be pre-empted.

8.   A cooperative, complementary and collaborative relationship with the Philippine Overseas Employment Administration (POEA) is established by following their rules and regulations strictly. This helps establish and reinforce legal precedents in international migrant labor and ensures better employment prospects for future migrant workers. It also serves as an example for other countries involved in the recruitment business.

At the end of the day, our continued success will not solely be measured in the high volume of our deployed workers, the growing client base that we have serviced and the new and emerging markets that we will be able to develop and establish. Our true success will be in the ability of our deployed workers to improve and grow in their respective profession and work environment. To accomplish this goal, we have to be vigilant in safeguarding the interests of our OFWs by ensuring that their employers and host countries shall share our concern for their welfare.

Institutional monitoring of migrant recruitment in Sri Lanka

L. K. Ruhunage[1]

Introduction

Migration of Sri Lankans for foreign employment as overseas contract workers (OCWs) has been a salient feature in the socio-economic life in the country for the last three decades. The annual outflow of Sri Lankans for foreign employment at present exceeds 200,000 by number with a total estimated stock of one million workers abroad. The foreign exchange revenue generated on the basis of migrants' remittances has registered as the country's highest net foreign exchange earning source, equaling 28% of total annual export earnings. The impact of foreign employment on alleviating the growing unemployment problem in the country and narrowing gaps in the balance of payment has been so significant that the country has recently developed new policies. These policies are related to training manpower for overseas jobs and exploring more employment opportunities in non-traditional labour markets, in addition to keeping the current emphasis on the traditional Middle East.

The most striking feature in the labour migration phenomenon of Sri Lankans has been the high participation of women in the process. Their share has stood at between 65%-75% during the last ten years (Table-I). The feminization of the labour migration process in Sri Lanka can be attributed to a few local and foreign factors. Firstly, the segment of women who opt for foreign employment as domestic workers are predominantly housewives who have not held waged employment before

---

[1] Employment and Welfare Counsellor, Sri Lanka Consulate, Dubai, United Arab Emirates.

their migration. Migration and the salary they earn as domestic servants in a foreign country gives these workers the opportunity to support their family affairs directly. While the local situation encourages Sri Lankan women to seek jobs abroad as domestic servants, the international situation has also been favorable to Sri Lankan women since Sri Lanka is the only country in South Asia that officially allows women to migrate for domestic sector jobs without reservations.

Table-I Departure for Foreign Employment (1994-2004)

Year	Male	%	Female	%	Total
1994	16377	27	43791	73	60168
1995	46021	27	126468	73	172489
1996	43112	27	119464	73	162576
1997	37552	25	112731	75	150283
1998	53867	34	105949	66	159816
1999	63720	35	116015	65	170735
2000	59793	33	122395	67	182188
2001	59807	32	124200	68	184007
2002	70522	35	133251	65	203773
2003	77089	35	134714	65	208803
2004	79979	37	133474	63	213453

Source: Sri Lanka Bureau of Foreign Employment

Procurement of Sri Lankan labour for foreign employment

It has been noted that Sri Lankan migrant workers find foreign employment mainly through three channels:

(a)   Through recruitment agencies

(b)   Through relatives and friends

(e)   By direct contacts with the employers

In addition to the afore mentioned avenues, instances have also been reported of direct participation by government departments in placement processes in specific areas of foreign jobs such as deployment of nurses in Malaysia by the Health Ministry and placement of teachers in the Maldives and Mauritius by the Department of Education. Direct participation in the placement of Sri Lankan manpower in foreign employment took place in the early days of foreign employment before

1985, when the Ministry of Labour handled the subject. It was reported that the first batch of officially recruited Sri Lankans for the Middle East market was deployed by the Department of Labour in 1976 (Ruhunage, 1979). Aside from government participation, some private companies took their local workers to their overseas job sites, and in some, cases hired them as apprentices. Due to the high number of workers taken abroad under the label of apprentices, the government made a clause in the Amendment Foreign Employment Bureau Act No. 4 of 1994 to include apprentices under the purview of the Act.

After establishment of the Sri Lanka Bureau of Foreign Employment (SLBFE) in 1985 under the Ministry of Labour, the Bureau carried out direct recruitment as a government entity until 1994. This process was phased out with the establishment of a separate agency under the Ministry of Labour as an independent authority licensed under the provisions of the SLBFE Act.

Dominance of recruitment agencies in manpower placements abroad

Even before the Middle East labour migration syndrome came to surface in the 1970s, statutory requirements existed under the Fee Charging Employment Agencies Act No.37 of 1956 to register suppliers of Sri Lankans for overseas jobs with the Department of Labour. Once Middle East migration began, the provisions of the said Act were developed under the Foreign Employment Agency Act No.32 of 1980 to meet the emerging trends in the industry and to meet the controlling and monitoring requirements of recruitment agents. The Act stipulates that no person or body shall engage in placement of manpower in foreign countries without obtaining a license and approval of the Department of Labour.

However, more specified mechanisms related to recruitment agencies have come into effect after establishment Sri Lanka Foreign Employment Bureau under Act No.21 of 1985. Among the 19 main objectives of the Act stipulated in Section 15 the following objectives were devoted completely to matters related to recruitment agencies:

(a) 15b-To assist and support foreign employment agencies in growth and development.

(b) 15d-To assist licensees in the negotiations of terms and conditions of employment with agencies abroad.

(c) 15e-To regulate the business of foreign employment agencies.

(d)   15f-To issue licenses to foreign employment agencies for conducting the business of recruitment for employment outside Sri Lanka
and to determine the terms and conditions of such licenses.

With the establishment of the Sri Lanka Bureau of Foreign Employment (SLBFE) the activities of recruitment agencies were streamlined and
the number of institutes increased rapidly in the face of growing manpower demands. Further, the SLBFE policy announcement made in
1995 mandating that all migrant workers register with the SLBFE prior
to their departure, brought more licensed agencies to surface.

Table II shows the number of licensed agencies operating during the
last 10 years.

Table-II Number of Licensed Agencies (1994-2004)

Year	No. Licenses issued	Stock at end of the year
1994	136	322
1995	183	477
1996	147	464
1997	109	520
1998	47	385
1999	70	431
2000	74	445
2001	99	528
2002	59	538
2003	88	524
2004	110	580

Source: Sri Lanka Bureau of Foreign Employment (SLBFE)

Table III suggests that the agency share has been about 75% of total
placements in recent years.

Table-III Annual Overseas Job Placements (1999-2004)

Year	Total	Through Agencies	% of Agency Share
1999	179,735	120,627	67%
2000	182,188	127,615	70%
2001	184,007	132,467	72%
2002	203,773	152,974	75%
2003	208,803	154,693	74%
2004	213,453	160,089	75%

Source: Sri Lanka Bureau of Foreign Employment (SLBFE)

Job avenues through relatives and friends

The practice of finding foreign jobs through known parties already employed overseas is more common at the village level, with participants seeking foreign jobs in the domestic and unskilled job categories. This avenue could also be considered as the cheapest way of securing a foreign job, as the prospective migrant worker is not burdened with payment of lump sums for recruitment agents. One could consider this method to be safer since the person arranging the job knows the foreign sponsor or the family members for whom the arranged worker will work. There are less chances of being robbed by unscrupulous job agents during the journey to the foreign employment. Statistics show that around 25% of total Sri Lankan migrant workers find foreign jobs through personal contacts, demonstrating the importance of this stream in the process of labour migration.

Direct contact with foreign employers

Gaining foreign jobs through direct contacts with foreign employers seems to be practiced mostly by middle and professional level workers who can access internet job advertisements of foreign companies and job banks. However, the number of Sri Lankans who migrate using this method is relatively small compared to other channels of migration.

Practices of recruitment agencies and the institutional monitoring and controlling process

The Sri Lanka Bureau of Foreign Employment (SLBFE) is the key institute in governing recruitment agencies in Sri Lanka. Under the vested powers by the Act No.21 of 1985 and the Amendment Act No.4 of 1994, the SLBFE monitors and controls the activities of nearly 600 licensed agencies operating in the country today. Part IV of the Act is completely devoted to emphasizing regulations with regard to governance of foreign employment agencies. Section 24(1) clearly states that other than the Bureau, no person or body shall carry on the business of a foreign employment agency unless the party is licensed under the Act. According to Section 28(1), once an application is accepted by the

SLBFE, before a license is issued, the applicant must enter into an agreement with the Bureau to carry on the business in a morally irreproachable manner and to take all steps possible to ensure that the terms and conditions of any contract of employment between a foreign employer and a person recruited for employment are observed by that employer.

Further, Section 28 enlists that the applicant shall enter into a cash bond with the Bureau, as well as a Bank guarantee to be withdrawn by the Bureau in case of a breach of contract by the licensee. Section 31 of the Act has vested powers to the Bureau to cancel a license, if the licensee has contravened any of the provisions of the Act, or any regulation made there under. The Section has further vested powers with the SLBFE to call for particulars as it may require from an agency or to inspect the documents related to placements. Section 44 specifies the obligations of the agency towards recruiting terms and conditions of a placement it makes. The authority to conduct inquires and to demand compensation for the worker if the agency is found guilty in the relevant complaint is also specified under Section 44.

Section 37 has brought the recruitment of workers for foreign jobs by the agencies under the direct surveillance of SLBFE. Accordingly, a licensee must not issue any advertisement, conduct interviews or take any other action in connection with or incidental to employment without the prior approval in writing of the Bureau. Even after the prior approval and completion of procurement, the agency is not authorized to deploy the worker without final exit clearance of the SLBFE for which the prescribed fees have to be paid by the agency. Such final approval is endorsed in the passport of the worker by affixing a security stamp to prove the correct legal procedures are adopted by the Agent in deployment of the worker. For this purpose separate pages are included in the passport by the Immigration authorities.

The airport surveillance desk, operated since 1995 by the SLBFE, greatly curtails malpractices for outgoing migrant workers and the exploitation of workers by the recruitment agents who promise fake job opportunities.

With an objective of good governance of the affairs coming under the provisions of SLBFE, the Act allows for three delegates from recruitment agencies to be included in its 11 member Board of directors. Therefore, the policies framed on the industry are subject to the knowledge and approval of such representatives of the recruitment agents. Further, under

Section 54, the Act itself has announced an Association of Licensed Foreign Employment Agencies (ALFEA). It states that every licensee shall become a member of the Association, which is criticized by some section of agents who argue such a condition violates their fundamental rights for free association guaranteed under the Country's constitution. The objectives of the ALFEA as envisaged in the Act are to:

(a)   Resolve disputes and disagreement between licensees

(c)   Make recommendation to the authorities with regard to promotion and regulation of the foreign employment industry

(d)   Promote employment opportunities for Sri Lankans outside the country

(e)   Formulate a code of good conduct for licensees and ensure its enforcement.

Participation of Sri Lanka overseas missions in the process of recruitment

In keeping with a series of new policies implemented on recommendations of a Presidential Task Force in 1998, the involvement of Sri Lankan overseas Missions in the labour recruitment process has been increased. Appointment of Labour Welfare Officers to the Sri Lanka Missions in the labour receiving countries and the introduction of a uniform service contract system for domestic sector workers were some of the significant policies framed. Initially, the Mission surveillance was for female domestic sector workers. Under this mechanism every recruitment order and any individual recruitment of domestic sector females are subject to the prior approval of the Sri Lanka Mission concerned. Without such prior approval, no job order is accepted or final approval for departure is granted by the SLBFE from the sending point. This process was recently tightened, bringing more job categories into the scheme, such as female cleaners and garment factory workers. The significance in this arrangement is that the Mission monitoring applies only for female workers but not for male workers. The argument of the authorities in this respect has been that females are more vulnerable for exploitation then men.

With an objective of improved recruitment monitoring of all workers for foreign employment at receiving ends, the Sri Lanka Missions are now required to register all recruitment agencies and companies that look

59

for Sri Lankan labour. Without such registration, foreign parties may not recruit any worker. This policy empowers the Mission to evaluate the status of the concerned receiving agents or the foreign employer and the job opportunities offered by these parties before the procurement is made.

Problems and conflicts in the placement process

After nearly three decades of labour movement for overseas contract jobs, and despite control mechanisms of government, Sri Lanka is still not exceptional or cleared from malpractices or exploitations connected with labour migration. The reported incidents of human trafficking to countries like Italy, Japan, South Korea, Singapore and Cyprus are alarmingly increasing. Smuggling of people using visiting visas based on the promise of providing lucrative jobs has become a commonly reported complaint at the overseas Missions in the Middle East to which such victims report for assistance.

The involvement of sub-agents or middlemen between a prospective migrant worker and the recruitment agency seemed to be a reason for most of these exploitations. The role played by the sub-agent at the initial stage of procurement of job recruitment is such that sub-agents form another level of institutional structure surrounding migration (Gamburd, 2000). It is a pity to note that with all those awareness programmes conducted by the authorities, about 50% of domestic sector females are brought for overseas jobs from the village by sub-agents who operate freely island wide, most without any liability for the agent or the worker. However, some argue that the sub-agent bridges the gap between a prospective migrant worker in the village and the recruitment agent in the town by acting as a coordinator between them and assisting the village woman not only in finding a foreign job but by motivating her for such action.

According to available data, at present there are about 600 recruitment agencies in Sri Lanka that are licensed for the course of recruitment of Sri Lankans for overseas employment. However, the actual fact that can be derived from the practices of these agencies is that most of them are just 'dead agencies' without viable business engagements with foreign counterparts. The majority of further agencies recruit only domestic sector females, which does not require much business expertise or knowledge in market strategies. Competition and 'cut throat' policies reported in the industry to grab job orders from foreign principals have become the factors that stand against a positive development of the industry. Though the Association of Licensed Foreign Employment Agencies (ALFEA) has existed for many years, it is questionable whether it has succeeded in formulating a code of good conduct for its members as required in the Act. Complaints related to exorbitant recruitment charges and ignoring the grievances of workers who have been recruited by individual agencies are commonly heard. Amidst these complaints, the agencies argue that no proper assessment is made by the authorities to evaluate their service to the country. The Ministry of Labour only conducted the rewarding scheme for best performers in the business of manpower recruitment once in 2001, and thereafter the scheme seems to have been discontinued. Although the income earned from foreign employment placements by the agents are exempted from income tax to some extent, the incentives offered to the industry by the government are claimed to be insufficient in the face of a stable job supply by agents and growing foreign revenue earned from such supply.

References

Gamburd, M. R. 2002-Transnationalism and Sri Lanka's Migrant Housemaids. The Kitchen Spoon's handle. Cornell University Press, Ithaca and London.

Premarathna, I. 1986-Foreign Employment Agencies. Ministry of Plan Implementation, Colombo.

Ruhunage, L. K. 1979-Migration of Sri Lankans to the Middle Eastern Countries, Ministry of Plan Implementation, Colombo.

Sri Lanka Bureau of Foreign Employment Act No.21, 1985.

Sri Lanka Bureau of Foreign Employment Amendment Act, No.4, 1994.

Statistical Handbook on Migration, 2003-Sri Lanka Bureau of Foreign Employment, Colombo.

Protection of Bangladeshi migrants through good governance

Tasneem Siddiqui[1]

M igration of labour has been a significant factor in growth and development of many countries. Nonetheless labour migration has become an extremely exploitative and complex phenomenon. International regimes involved in managing voluntary labour migration now highlights the need for development of national and regional policies along with international instruments to make migration a mutually beneficial experience for all parties involved, the receiving and sending countries, and those who migrate.

Bangladesh is one of the major labour-sending countries. Each year, a large number of people voluntarily migrate overseas for both long and short-term employment (Table 1). This paper highlights the challenges that Bangladesh faces in ensuring effective governance of the migration sector as a whole, and of the recruitment industry in particular. It emphasises the need for pro-active migration policy and action by the public and private sectors and civil society, to ensure greater benefit of the state and communities, and protection to those who migrate.

This paper is based on secondary information. Over the last five years, some important empirical studies have been conducted on international migration. A number of conferences, seminars and workshops have also been organized. This paper relies on the findings of these studies and conference proceedings.

---

[1] Professor of Political Science, and Chair of the Refugee and Migratory Movements Research Unit (RMMRU), University of Dhaka, Bangladesh.

Table 1: Percentage distribution of Bangladeshi migrant workers by level of skills (1976- Sept 2003)

Year	Professional	Skilled	Semi-skilled	Unskilled	Total
1976	9.33	29.16	8.92	52.59	6087
1977	11.23	41.00	3.12	44.66	15725
1978	15.15	35.91	4.60	44.34	22809
1979	14.26	28.60	6.88	50.26	24495
1980	6.59	40.60	7.79	45.02	30073
1981	6.98	40.21	4.39	48.42	55787
1982	6.21	32.84	5.21	55.74	62762
1983	3.08	31.98	8.61	56.33	59220
1984	4.66	30.30	9.67	55.37	56714
1985	3.31	36.33	10.07	50.30	77694
1986	3.22	38.30	13.49	44.99	68658
1987	3.00	32.21	13.00	51.79	74017
1988	3.92	37.12	15.99	43.09	68121
1989	5.23	38.16	17.36	39.24	101724
1990	5.78	34.30	20.03	39.88	103814
1991	6.13	31.87	22.16	39.84	147131
1992	6.05	26.94	16.47	50.54	188124
1993	4.54	29.31	27.06	39.09	244508
1994	4.50	32.76	24.97	37.77	186326
1995	3.39	31.94	17.09	47.58	187543
1996	1.51	30.37	16.38	51.74	211714
1997	1.64	28.22	18.85	51.29	231077
1998	3.58	27.91	19.27	49.23	267667
1999	3.00	36.71	16.76	43.53	268182
2000	4.79	44.73	11.88	38.60	222686
2001	3.14	22.62	16.25	57.99	188965
2002	6.41	24.98	15.99	52.61	225256
2003 (Jan-Sept)	6.09	29.53	11.93	52.45	185523
Total	**4.40**	**31.80**	**16.66**	**47.14**	**3582402**

Note: 150,000 Bangladeshi workers legalized in Malaysia during 1997

Source: Prepared from BMET data 2003.

Importance of migration

Migration and the economy of Bangladesh

Remittances are a substantive yardstick of macro level benefits of migration to sending countries. The Bangladesh Bank[2] data show that the remittances sent by overseas wage earners have grown over time (Table 2). Throughout the last 25 years, the remittance flows broadly indicate an average yearly increase of around 10 percent.

Remittance plays a vital role in the economy of Bangladesh. The country has a very narrow export base. Ready-made garments, frozen fish, jute, leather and tea account for four-fifths of its export earnings. Currently, garments manufacturing is treated as the highest foreign exchange earning sector of the country (US$4.583[3] billion in 2003). However, if the earnings are adjusted with the cost of import of raw material, then the net earnings from migrant workers' remittances is higher than that of the garments sector. In 2003, net export earnings from ready-made garments (RMG) were estimated to be between US$2.29 billion and US$2.52 billion, whereas the net earnings from remittances were more than US$3 billion. In fact, since the 1980s, contrary to popular belief, remittances sent by migrant workers have played a much greater role in sustaining the economy of Bangladesh than the garments sector.[4]

During the period 1977-1998, the annual average contribution of remittances to foreign exchange earning was 26.5 percent (Siddiqui and Abrar, 2001). This has been used in financing the import of capital goods and raw materials for industrial development. In 1998-1999, 22 percent of the official import bill was financed by remittances (Afsar et al, 2000; Murshid et al, 2000). The steady flow of remittances has resolved the problem of foreign exchange constraints, improved the balance of payments and helped increase the supply of national savings (Quibria, 1986). Remittances are also important when considered in the backdrop of the country's development budget. In select years in the 1990s, remittances were equivalent to the country's development budget. The Government

---

[2] The central bank of Bangladesh.

[3] US$ 1.00 is equivalent to Bangladesh taka 62.50 at present.

[4] Speech delivered by Professor Wahiduddin Mahmud, Former Advisor to the Interim Government of Bangladesh in 1996, at a conference on 'Streamlining Labour Recruitment Process in Bangladesh for Employment Abroad', 24 September 2001. Quoted in Siddiqui T. (ed) 2002, Beyond the Maze, p. 53.

Table 2. Migration by Country of Employment and Flow of Remittances (1976- 2003)

Country/Year	K.S.A	Kuwait	U.A.E	Qatar	Iraq	Libya	Bahrain	Oman	Malaysia	Korea	S.Pore	Others	Total	Remittances Million US	Remittances (Crore Tk.)
1976	217	643	1989	1221	587	173	335	113				809	6087	23.71	35.85
1977	1379	1315	5819	2262	1238	718	870	1492				632	15725	82.79	125.16
1978	3212	2243	7512	1303	1454	2394	762	2877	23			1029	22809	106.9	165.59
1979	6476	2298	5069	1383	2363	1969	827	3777			110	223	24495	172.06	266.95
1980	8695	3687	4847	1455	1927	2976	1351	4745	3		385	2	30073	301.33	492.95
1981	13384	5464	6418	2268	13153	4162	1392	7352			1083	1111	55787	304.88	620.74
1982	16294	7244	6863	6252	12898	2071	2037	8248			331	524	62762	490.77	1176.84
1983	12928	10283	6615	7556	4932	2209	2473	11110	23		178	913	59220	627.51	1568.76
1984	20399	5627	5185	2726	4701	3386	2300	10448			718	1224	56714	500	1265.49
1985	37133	7384	8336	4751	5051	1514	2965	9218			792	550	77694	500	1419.61
1986	27235	10286	8790	4847	4728	3111	2597	6255	53		25	254	68658	576.2	1752.85
1987	39292	9559	9953	5889	3847	2271	2055	440				711	74017	747.6	2313.94
1988	27622	6524	13437	7390	4191	2759	3268	2219	2			709	68121	763.9	2423.59
1989	39949	12404	15184	8462	2573	1609	4830	15429	401		229	654	101724	757.85	2446
1990	57486	5957	8307	7672	2700	471	4563	13980	1385		776	517	103814	781.54	2691.63
1991	75656	28574	8583	3772		1124	3480	23087	1628		62	585	147131	769.3	2818.65
1992	93132	34377	12975	3251		1617	5804	25825	10537		313	293	188124	901.97	3513.26
1993	106387	26407	15810	2441		1800	5396	15866	67938		1739	724	244508	1009.09	3986.97
1994	91385	14912	15051	624		1864	4233	6470	47826	1558	391	2012	186326	1153.54	4629.63
1995	84009	17492	14686	71		1106	3004	20949	35174	3315	3762	3975	187543	1201.52	4838.31
1996	72734	21042	23812	112		1966	3759	8691	66631	2759	5304	4904	211714	1355.34	5685.3

Part II: The empirical framework: Country and regional experiences

Country / Year	K.S.A	Kuwait	U.A.E	Qatar	Iraq	Libya	Bahrain	Oman	Malaysia	Korea	S.Pore	Others	Total	Remittances	
														Million US	(Crore Tk.)
1997	106534	21126	54719	1873		1934	5010	5985	152844	889	27401	2762	381077	1525.03	6709.15
1998	158715	25444	38796	6806		1254	7014	4779	551	578	21728	2602	267667	1599.24	7513.18
1999	26286	3324	3912	864		239	666	713		136	1000	563	268182	1806.63	8882.74
2000	144618	594	34034	1433		1010	4637	5258	17237	990	11095	1780	222686	1954.95	10199.12
2001	137248	5341	16252	223		450	4371	4561	4921	1561	9615	4422	188965	2068.72	11577.63
2002	163254	15767	25438	552		1575	5370	3927	85	28	6870	2390	225256	2847.79	16484.53
2003	95319	7908	22336	64		1991	3634	2166	7	149	3313	2542	139429	1858.39	10760.5
Total	1826431	332302	429160	92270	66343	51228	92976	229312	257746	13328	103069	39416	3536308	26790.85	116378.13

Source: Prepared from BMET and Bangladesh Bank data 2003

of Bangladesh treats foreign aid (concessional loans and grants) as an important resource base for the country. However, the amount Bangladesh received through remittances in 2003 was twice that of foreign aid.

The contribution of remittances to Gross Domestic Product (GDP) has also grown from a meagre 1 percent in 1977-1978 to 5.2 percent in 1982-83. During the 1990s, the ratio hovered around 4 percent. However, if the unofficial flow of remittances is taken into account, the total contribution of remittances to GDP would certainly be much higher. Murshid et al, (2000) finds that an increase of Taka (Tk) 1 in remittances would result in an increase in national income of Tk 3.33.

Following the phasing out of the Multi-Fibre Agreement (MFA) at the end of 2004, Bangladesh ceased to enjoy any special quota and faces steep competition in the export of RMG. As a result, the country's RMG export is expected to decline sharply. This is likely to result in the large scale loss of jobs and a shortfall in foreign exchange earning. The potential for absorbing laid-off garments workers and compensating for lost export earnings through increased exports of other commodities (e.g. frozen fish, jute, leather and tea) appears rather bleak. It is in this context that labour migration has become a key sector for earning foreign exchange and for creating opportunities for employment. Therefore, the importance of labour migration to the economy of Bangladesh can hardly be overemphasized.

Creation of overseas and domestic jobs

Since the mid-1970s, more than 3 million people have gone abroad to take up employment. It is estimated that at any given time over the last ten years, at least 1 million Bangladeshis are employed abroad. Bangladeshi migrant workers are predominantly men. During the period 1991-2003, women constituted less than 1 percent of those who migrated from Bangladesh officially (Table 3). A large number of Bangladeshis, both men and women, are believed to have gone abroad through irregular channels.

The major countries of destination for short-term migrants from Bangladesh currently include: Saudi Arabia, the United Arab Emirates (UAE), Bahrain, Brunei, Hong Kong (China), Kuwait, Malaysia, Oman, Qatar, Singapore, and the Republic of Korea. Saudi Arabia alone accounts for nearly one half of the total number of workers who have

Table 3: Number and percentage of women migrants in comparison to total flow (1991-2003)

Year	Women Migrants		Total Number
	Number	% of Total	Male and Female
1991-1995	9308	0.98	953632
1996	1567	0.74	211714
1997	1762	0.76	231077
1998	939	0.35	267667
1999	366	0.14	268182
2000	454	0.20	222686
2001	659	0.35	188965
2002	1217	0.54	225256
2003 (Jan-Sept)	1240	0.67	185523
Total	**17512**	**0.64**	**2754693**

Source: Prepared from manually consolidated figures provided by BMET, 2003.

migrated from Bangladesh. However, the labour market for Bangladeshi migrant workers is not static. Destination countries are changing all the time. Bangladesh mostly participates in the low-skilled and unskilled end of the global market. Only a small proportion of migrants are professionals (4.40 percent), 31 percent of them are skilled, 16 percent semi-skilled and 47 percent are unskilled workers.

In addition to direct employment, migration has also indirectly contributed to the creation of employment. Recent studies (Siddiqui and Abrar 2001, Murshid et al 2000) have shown that the family members of migrants have used a portion of their remittances in generating income and employment. Siddiqui and Abrar found that 100 families from Tangail and Chittagong spent 11.24 percent of their remittances in agricultural land purchase, 2.24 percent in either paying off or taking out a mortgage on land for cultivation, 5 percent for investment in micro- and small enterprises and another 3.5 percent in savings, bonds and insurance. A further 7.19 percent of the total remittance went into financing the migration of other household members (Table 4). In addition, the capacity of the migrants' families to buy consumable items helps sustain local small businesses and producers.

Meanwhile, demand for better governance of migration has created jobs in the public sector as well. A new ministry has been created with a

Table 4: Utilisation of remittances by 100 households

Use	In taka	%
Food and clothing	4,466,280	2.45
Medical treatment	703,800	3.22
Child education	600,940	2.75
Agricultural land purchase	2,455,400	11.24
Homestead land purchase	210,000	0.96
Home construction/repair	3,280,000	15.02
Release of mortgaged land	490,000	2.24
Taking mortgage on land	435,000	1.99
Repayment of loan (for migration)	2,304,600	10.55
Repayment of loan (other purpose)	757500	3.47
Investment in business	1,039,200	4.76
Savings/fixed deposit	670,000	3.07
Insurance	72,140	0.33
Social ceremonies	1,980,000	9.07
Gift/donation to relatives	205,000	0.94
Send relative for pilgrimage	200,000	0.92
Community development activities	20,520	0.09
Sending family member abroad	1,571,000	7.19
Furniture	151,300	0.69
Others	227,000	1.04
Total	**21,839,680**	**100.00**

Source: Siddiqui and Abrar, 2001.

state minister, secretary and other associated staff. Forty-eight skill training centres and the Bureau of Manpower, Employment and Training (BMET) are among the major agencies creating jobs in the public sector. The movement of migrants also has relevance in determining the size of the Ministry of Civil Aviation, and Customs and Immigration Departments. Migrants also constitute a majority of the customers of Biman Bangladesh airlines. The presence of airlines of the Gulf and South-East Asian countries has also created jobs for a large number of people. A powerful private sector has emerged, centered around the recruitment industry. Private recruiting agencies, their agents and sub-agents, travel agencies, medical centres and inter-state transportation owners and workers all earn their livelihood through their involvement in processing migration. There are 700 licensed recruiting agencies, 10,000 sub-agents and around 1,350 travel agencies.

One can see that short-term migration has been extremely successful in creating a large number of jobs for Bangladeshis. Along with the employment of workers overseas, it has also created jobs within Bangladesh. In the public sector a few agencies and a new ministry have been created to manage migration. The facilitation of migration has created jobs in the private sector as well.

Governance of migration

Successive governments realised the importance of labour migration and took different measures to govern. They created various institutions, promulgated statutory regulatory orders, framed rules, and tried to negotiate bilateral agreements.

National instruments

Emigration from Bangladesh used to be governed by the Emigration Ordinance, 1922. In 1982, the Government promulgated a new Emigration Ordinance. This is currently the key regulatory instrument in relation to migration. Under the terms of the Ordinance, the government regulates the private recruiting agencies of Bangladesh and provides clearance to those who go abroad for employment. On 11 April 1983, by a notification[5] of the Labour and Manpower Ministry, the Government set up four Special Courts in each of the divisions of the country (Dhaka, Chittagong, Khulna and Rajshahi).

In December 2002, the present Government framed three rules under the 1982 Ordinance: Emigration Rules; Rules for Conduct and Licensing Recruiting Agencies; and Rules for Wage Earners' Welfare Fund. A National Migration Policy is currently being developed. The main principle of the policy is "the government of Bangladesh will provide all kinds of assistance to both male and female workers to freely choose standard and full employment. The government will be committed towards ensuring human rights and rights at the workplace of Bangladeshi migrants in receiving countries.

---

[5] No. SRO 129-L/83/LMVIII/!(11)83.

Institutions

Labour recruitment from Bangladesh involves various government ministries and agencies; private recruiting agents and their local and international intermediaries; and potential migrants and their families.

Ministries

There are five key government ministries which deal with international labour migration: the Ministry of Expatriates' Welfare and Overseas Employment (MoEW&OE); the Ministry of Home Affairs; the Ministry of Foreign Affairs; the Ministry of Finance; and the Ministry of Civil Aviation and Tourism. Until 2001, the Ministry of Labour and Employment was in charge of international labour migration. Then in December 2001, the current Government established a new ministry in response to demands from expatriate Bangladeshis and migrant workers. This new ministry is responsible for implementing the rules framed in 2002 under the Emigration Ordinance 1982 and, accordingly, for promoting, monitoring and regulating the migration sector. Its activities are concentrated in two broad areas: firstly, to create employment overseas and secondly, to address problems experienced by expatriates and to ensure their welfare (Govt. of Bangladesh, 2003).

The role of foreign missions is also extremely important in respect to migration. The functions that Bangladesh missions abroad currently perform regarding labour export are:

(a)   Exploring the potential labour market;

(b)   Attestation of documents pertaining to recruitment;

(c)   Providing consular services for Bangladeshi workers; and

(d)   Ensuring the welfare of migrant workers.

Bureau of Manpower, Employment and Training (BMET)

The BMET is the executing agency of the Ministry of Expatriates' Welfare and Overseas Employment in respect to processing labour migration. The BMET was created in 1976 by the Government. Currently, the BMET is responsible for a wide range of functions including: control and regulation of recruiting agents; collection and analysis of labour market information; registration of job seekers for local and foreign employment; development and implementation of training programmes in response to specific labour needs both in the national and international labour market; development of apprentice and in-plant programmes within existing industries; organizing pre-departure briefing sessions; and resolving legal disputes.

Private recruiting agencies

In the 1970s, the government was responsible for the functions of recruitment. However, since 1981, private recruiting agents have carried out this role, as part of private sector development. The private agencies work under license from the government. On their own initiative, they collect information on demands and orders for foreign employment. After obtaining permission from the BMET, the agencies recruit workers as per the specifications of the foreign employers and then execute the procedures involved in their deployment. Over time, the recruiting agencies became organized under the Bangladesh Association of International Recruiting Agencies (BAIRA). This association was formed in December 1984 with representatives of 23 recruiting agencies. By 2002, the association had a membership of around 700 agencies.

Bangladesh Overseas Employment Services Limited (BOESL)

In 1984, the Government also established the Bangladesh Overseas Employment Services Limited (BOESL) as a limited company to take on a direct recruitment role (Table 5).

Migration under individual contracts

About 55 to 60 percent of recruitment is conducted through individual initiatives and social networks. Usually, persons already deployed in the host countries arrange visas for their friends and relatives through their own contacts. Sometimes these visas are sold to the interested parties. The cost of migration and illicit practices are less when work visas are procured through individual migrants working abroad rather than the private recruiting agencies (Siddiqui ed., 2002).

Bilateral agreements and memoranda of understanding

Bilateral agreements or memoranda of understanding are important instruments through which protection of the rights of migrants is ensured. Successive Bangladesh governments have also sent high-level delegations to various labour-receiving states to negotiate such agreements. However, there has been a general reluctance among labour-receiving countries to sign any bilateral agreements or memoranda of understanding that are legally binding. In response, the government has developed a minimum set of standards for sending labour. When an

Table 5: Percentage distribution of Bangladeshi migrant workers by sending agency (1976-Sept 2003)

Year	BMET	BOESL	Recruiting Agent	Individual	Total
1976	86.73	0.00	4.67	8.61	6087
1977	36.43	0.00	7.45	56.12	15725
1978	27.01	0.00	8.74	64.25	22809
1979	28.40	0.00	12.11	59.49	24495
1980	19.00	0.00	25.85	55.15	30073
1981	10.89	0.00	39.83	49.29	55787
1982	7.14	0.00	39.74	53.12	62762
1983	1.23	0.00	44.44	54.32	59220
1984	0.00	0.28	57.23	42.49	56714
1985	0.00	1.57	50.71	47.72	77694
1986	0.00	2.76	40.58	56.66	68658
1987	0.00	0.46	45.69	53.85	74017
1988	0.00	0.70	50.08	49.22	68121
1989	0.00	0.70	35.89	63.42	101724
1990	0.00	0.42	38.78	60.80	103814
1991	0.00	0.10	44.10	55.80	147131
1992	0.02	0.29	31.76	67.93	188124
1993	0.21	0.23	52.95	46.61	244508
1994	0.13	0.10	51.18	48.60	186326
1995	0.04	0.34	40.60	60.65	187543
1996	0.00	0.19	56.05	43.76	211714
1997	0.01	0.14	37.13	62.72	231077
1998	0.00	0.16	31.87	67.98	267667
1999	0.00	0.12	41.27	58.62	268182
2000	0.00	0.24	41.08	58.69	222686
2001	0.00	0.08	40.57	59.35	188965
2002	0.00	0.10	37.47	62.43	225256
2003 Jan-Sept	0.00	0.22	33.93	65.86	185523
Total	**1.17**	**0.28**	**41.10**	**57.45**	**3582402**

Source: Prepared from BMET data 2003.

understanding is reached with any country for sending labour, the Bangladesh government then hands over a set of standards with the implicit understanding that the receiving country will honour it. However, this does not place the country concerned under any legal obligation.

In the past, Bangladesh has signed agreements with Iraq, Libya, Qatar and Malaysia on sending labour. In these instances, the Government handed over the expected minimum set of standards to the government representatives of those countries. For the first time, in 2003, the Government of Bangladesh signed a memorandum of understanding with Malaysia that contained labour standard issues.

The different steps that have been taken by successive governments show that it has been difficult to effectively manage migration. Management challenges are faced at all the stages, pre-departure, during or after return. In the following I will highlight some of the problems that the government and potential migrants face while participating in the global labour market.

Challenges of governance

Policy challenges

The MoEWOE severely suffers from lack of resources. The total revenue budget of BMET was Tk 112,030,000 in 1997-98, Tk 124,730,000 in 1998-99 and Tk 131,092,000 in 1999-2000. Needless to say, the total government investment in this important foreign exchange earning sector is dismally insignificant.

It is amply demonstrated that labour migration involves different ministries, agencies and migrant workers. Inter-agency collaboration is a pre-requisite for the establishment of programmes and services for streamlining the labour migration process. In 2001, the then caretaker government prepared a strategy document. It recommended for formation of an advisory body. The MoEWOE has established an inter-ministerial committee. However, forming an advisory committee particularly with representation of civil society is not on the agenda. Under these circumstances, coordination is a major problem in governing migration.

Another important policy challenge before the government is to ensure equal access to migration for both men and women. In 1981, the then Government issued a circular imposing a ban on the migration of all categories of female workers other than professionals. In 1987, the ban was replaced by the imposition of restrictions on the migration of women of unskilled and semi-skilled categories. In 1997, a ban was again imposed on all categories of woman workers, including professionals. Later the same year this was changed from a ban to restrictions, from which professionals were excluded. In 2003, the present Government allowed labour migration of unskilled and semi-skilled women over 35. Nonetheless, they are still discriminated against men, as they require written permission from their male guardians. However, those under 35 are still not allowed to migrate on their own. A section of policy makers now realise that women of all age groups needs to be ensured the right to seek employment but hesitate to pursue radical policy changes.

The association of private recruiting agencies of Bangladesh, BAIRA is quite a powerful body in the area of labour migration governance. They are represented in all relevant committees, i.e. Wage Earners' Welfare Management. Many of the members of BAIRA are members of parliament (MP) as well. By taking advantage of being MPs, they are represented in the inter-ministerial committee and the parliamentary standing committee on labour migration. Until now, BAIRA's actions are geared towards ensuring that government policy on migration is recruitment industry friendly. However, it is yet to orient its function towards emerging as a self-regulatory body of the recruiting agencies. The Bangladesh Chamber of Commerce and Industry, Bar Association of Bangladesh, Medical Council and Press Council, all have developed Codes of Conduct for their members. Violation of such codes of conduct leads to different punitive actions by the professional bodies up to the extent of cancellation of membership. One does not witness any such initiative from BAIRA.

There are around 2,500 travel agencies (TA) in Bangladesh. Under their license these agencies are authorised to issue tickets after verification of visas to those who want to travel abroad. The TAs are barred from engaging in recruitment and processing of documents for emigration. However, a section of them illegally engage in these activities. Of course, a section of recruiting agencies, licensed or unlicensed also sometime take recourse to irregular recruitment. Illicit contacts with immigration officials both in Bangladesh and abroad allow them to conduct such activities. Their activities can be termed as human smuggling. In the recent past there have been cases where potential migrants have fallen victim to their fraudulence, some even lost their lives. In some occasion, recruiting agencies are also engaged in such fraudulence.

It has become extremely difficult to regulate such irregular migration. While the Ministry of EW&OE regulates the recruitment agencies, the Civil Aviation authorities regulate the travel agencies. The travel industry in Bangladesh has formed its own organisation, the Association of Travel Agencies of Bangladesh (ATAB). Through ATAB the TAs could have been brought under self-regulation. However, its membership currently stands at around 1,000. That leaves around 1,500 agencies without being under any trade umbrella.

Medical tests are mandatory for those who want to go abroad to work. There are around 35 diagnostic centres that conduct health check ups of the migrants upon requisition of the recruiting agents. A section of the diagnostic centres cheat the potential migrants by conducting unnecessary health check ups. They also manipulate results and, create situation for treatment and further tests. Many of these diagnostic centres are owned by recruiting agencies directly or indirectly. Still today, there is no regulation of diagnostic centres by concerned ministries or agencies.

Operational challenges

Pre-departure

Procurement of work permits: The procurement of a work visa, the recruitment of the worker and receipt of emigration clearance are key steps in processing migration. Bangladesh mainly participates in the low-skilled and unskilled labour market and has recently been facing tough competition from the newly emerging labour-sending countries such as Nepal, Cambodia and Indonesia. Such competition among labour-sending countries is resulting in a continuous lowering of standards in the terms and conditions of work. Moreover, unemployment rates have increased in some of the labour-receiving countries. This has led to the formulation of a policy for the indigenization of the labour force. To discourage dependence on overseas labour, some of these countries have introduced a levy to be paid by the employer when they recruit foreign workers. However, these governments did not, at the same time, raise wage rates in an effort to encourage local workers to take up the unskilled jobs. Therefore local workers do not find these jobs attractive and there is a continuing need to import labour for certain types of work. With competition for these jobs among the labour-sending countries, the employers found they could conveniently shift the government levy to the recruiting agencies of the labour-sending countries. As a result, the recruiting agencies not only receive no commission for supplying labour, they also have to purchase the visa from the employers by paying the fee that the employers are required to pay to the government.[6]

---

[6] Lion Nazrul Islam, E.C member BAIRA, 2002.

The buying and selling of the visa itself has become a profitable business for a certain group of people. A nexus of interest has developed among high-level state functionaries in the labour-receiving countries, their recruiting agents, a group of expatriate Bangladeshis and a section of Bangladeshi recruiting agents. As a result, it has become extremely difficult to secure a visa through what were formerly considered to be the regular channels. Now this nexus is involved in visa transaction through irregular practices. The visas are then put into auction to other agents who have less access to visas. It has become extremely difficult to take action against this group of people, who often hold high places both socially and politically.[7]

System of Dalals (informal agents): Recruiting agencies that purchase visas in turn take their profit margin and then sell the visas to individual migrants. Almost all recruiting agencies are based in the capital city, Dhaka, since it is not financially viable to have offices throughout the country. The agencies recruit through a host of informal agents and sub-agents, who perform two key functions: the recruitment of workers and financial transactions. Recruitment at the grass-roots level is conducted verbally, with even payments made without a receipt. The *dalal* system has not been institutionalized. The *dalals* (informal agents) are not formally registered with the recruiting agents they serve and do not possess any formal identification documents. This has created a situation in which both recruiting agents and their sub-agents can commit fraud and evade responsibility. In the process, a good number of those who wish to migrate are cheated and lose a large part of their assets while processing migration.

Although the 1982 Ordinance empowered the government to cancel and suspend licences and withold repayment of the security deposit if it is shown that the licensee's conduct is improper or in violation of the law and the prescribed code of conduct, in the absence of any documentation, the government is unable to take action. In 2001, the Interim Government prepared a strategy document, which recommended the recruitment of migrants through the establishment of a database, or by registering the *dalals* with the recruiting agents. The current government has undertaken a programme to implement this. However, the recruitment is still done through conventional method and the database is rarely used.

---

[7] Statement of the representative of BAIRA at the Interagency Meeting organized by the Ministry of Labour on 12 August 2001 for the study on Streamlining Labour Recruitment Process in Bangladesh commissioned by the Ministry.

Issuance of passports: Studies have shown that a large number of migrants fall into the low literacy category. In many cases, they rely on the recruiting agents for issuance of their passports. The recruiting agents usually process a large number of passports at any given time. In some instances migrants do not even sign the passport application form. Instead, the employees of recruiting agents sign the forms on their behalf. As a result, migrants often find themselves in trouble in the receiving country, when their signatures do not match the signature in the passport. Meanwhile, some of the recruiting agents or sub-agents commit fraud in procuring the passports. There are occasions when a visa is sold to a worker other than the one to whom it was issued. When the person or his/her father's name does not match with the one in the passport, the migrant, for all practical purposes, becomes an undocumented worker.

Lack of access to information: Lack of access to information prior to migration places migrants in a vulnerable situation. When a person is unaware of their rights, it becomes almost impossible for them to assert those rights. While processing migration, they do not have access to the names of licensed recruiting agents and they do not understand the importance of keeping documentation. Before embarking on short-term contract migration, it is of critical importance that a migrant worker has at his/her disposal specific information about the country of destination: their rights and duties under the legal regime of the receiving country; cultural sensitivities; and the physical environment. However, the migrant worker is either oblivious to these issues or has to rely solely on information derived from verbal interaction with the *dalals*. The BMET conducts briefing programmes for workers recruited for Saudi Arabia, Malaysia, Kuwait and the Republic of Korea. However, these briefing programmes last only two hours and the range of issues covered is limited.

Although there are various instruments and agencies in operation, protection of migrants in overseas jobs has proved to be difficult to achieve. There is a need to streamline the process of recruitment, ranging from procurement of the visa to sending workers overseas.

In the country of destination

Working conditions: A study[8] has been conducted on the working conditions of Bangladeshi factory workers in countries in the Middle

---

[8] 'Work Condition of Bangladeshi Factory Workers in the Middle-Eastern Countries' by Tasneem Siddiqui and Jalaluddin Sikdar, commissioned by Solidarity Center, Sri Lanka.

East. It is based on interviews with 100 recently returned migrants from seven countries: Bahrain, Jordan, Kuwait, Oman, Qatar, Saudi Arabia and the UAE. Of the migrants who have been interviewed for this ongoing study, 40 went to Saudi Arabia, where they worked in factory jobs including garment making, construction, plastics, leather processing, welding, tile-making, printing, glass-making, water purification, packaging and the manufacture of gold items. The average salary was about Tk 10,000 for males and about Tk 6,000 for females. This gives some idea of the wage structure for skilled and semi-skilled migrants.

The study also looks at the regularity of payment of wages for migrant workers. Out of the 100 interviewed, 56 stated that they received their salaries regularly without any delay. However, 43 experienced delays in the payment of wages, varying from 10 days to 180 days. In one extreme case, a female migrant worker in the UAE did not receive any payment of wages throughout the entire year she worked in a garments factory.

The same study also throws light on the practice of overtime worked by factory workers. The nature of jobs was such that 59 of the interviewees had to work overtime on a regular basis, 44 worked up to five hours' overtime and 15 worked up to eight hours. Of the 41 who did not do overtime, only 13 mentioned that either their work did not entail overtime or they chose not to work overtime. The rest (28) reported that they stayed for longer periods at work but that this work was not counted as overtime.

Officially, the interviewees were required to work for six days with a one day break every week – usually on Friday. However, as many as 27 interviewees said that they had to work on most of the holidays and could usually enjoy a weekend holiday only once or twice a month.

The above study gives some idea of wages, overtime and holiday conditions experienced by factory workers in the Gulf States. The situation among unskilled workers of course differed significantly from this. Rahim (2002) and Reza (2002) threw light on the work conditions of unskilled and semi-skilled workers in the Gulf region. In Saudi Arabia, during the early 1990s, the monthly wage for an unskilled worker was Rials 600-800, a rate that has now fallen to Rials 250-400 (Rahim, 2002). In Kuwait, the monthly salary of unskilled workers ranged from KD 8-25 (Reza, 2002). A survey of the list of complaints to the BMET from returnee migrants shows that the majority of complaints were related to non-payment of wages.

Accommodation and food: Large companies and formal sectors provide accommodation to their employees in labour camps on the outskirts of the cities. In Singapore, in a typical situation, a large group of 20 to 25 workers are accommodated in small houses. Those who work in cleaning companies, or those who are on a free visa or self-employed arrange their own accommodation. In most cases, employers provided accommodation for the female garment workers. Women who worked in factories lived in hostels, either within the factory premises or outside. Excessive heat was a major problem for some female migrants. In the UAE, women garment factory workers share their rooms with at least 18 co-workers (Afsar et al, 2000). Some women who worked as domestic workers were satisfied with their accommodation. They were given separate rooms and wardrobes in which to keep their belongings. Others who reported that they were made to sleep in kitchens said they had no privacy at all (Siddiqui, 2001).

In the factories, the employers generally provided the food. In the first few months, most of the workers – in particular the factory workers – had problems with regard to food. The food is usually served to suit the preference of the majority of the workers. As a result, the food served in most of the factories where Bangladeshi female migrants work was either Sri Lankan or Southern Indian. A few of the respondents cooked their own food occasionally (Siddiqui et al, 2004). Some of the domestic workers also faced problems with food. In many cases, the female head of house used to keep strict control over food. While some domestic workers were served stale food, others stated that food was abundant and they were allowed to eat as much as they wanted. In order to solve food-related problems, some employers made efforts to buy items that would allow the domestic workers to cook their own food (Siddiqui, 2001).

Changing jobs: Those who work at the low-skills end receive much lower wages than the national minimum rate. This encourages other employers of the receiving country to try to lure them away with a nominally higher wage rate. To reduce the scope for this kind of job change, the employers withhold all forms of documentation such as job contract, travel documents and passports from the migrant worker. In their negotiations with the government of Bangladesh, the receiving countries ensure that the occupational mobility of the labourers they are hiring is minimal. The 1982 Ordinance treats the return of overseas workers before finishing the contract as a punishable offence. Under such circumstances, the ability of migrant workers to assert rights in the labour market is restrained in many ways. Workers without documents in their possession have major problems in seeking legal redress when employers do not honour the conditions of contracts. The lack of possession of documents also curtails the right of migrant workers to move freely in the city of employment. In Malaysia, in particular, workers are routinely harassed by the law enforcement agencies in the event of a minor offence if they fail to produce any form of identification.

Contract substitution is another measure practised by some employers, which curtails the rights of migrant workers. On arrival in the country of destination, workers are made to sign a second contract which includes reduced wages and lower living and working conditions. In some cases, workers are given a different job than that stipulated in the original contract. In Malaysia, some of the migrant workers end up working on plantations while their original contracts were to work in factories. In Saudi Arabia, workers are often hired as cooks and security guards and then sent to work as agricultural labourers. Because of the extreme hardships faced working on plantations and in the agricultural sector, a considerable number flee these jobs to seek other types of employment. Through the network of Bangladeshi workers, some of the migrants manage to obtain jobs with better terms and conditions. However, having left the jobs for which they had obtained visas, they become undocumented workers and vulnerable to many additional forms of exploitation.

The majority of unskilled and semi-skilled Bangladeshi workers did not have any knowledge about the labour laws of the countries to which they migrated. As a result, it is easy for employers to violate existing laws relating to wages and working and living conditions.

It can be concluded that compared to unskilled workers, formal sector factory workers enjoy relatively better working conditions. However, there is still a large gap between the wages of male and female migrant factory workers, with studies showing that female workers receive much lower wages than their male counterparts. The salary of unskilled workers has fallen drastically both in the Gulf region and in South-East Asia. In addition, a considerable number of workers do not receive their wages on a regular basis and freedom to move from one job to another is restricted for both skilled and unskilled workers.

Measures in ensuring protection

Government

Policy

The government should commit adequate resources to the migration sector. The Ministry of Expatriates' Welfare and Overseas Employment should propose to the relevant ministry for the allocation of resources equivalent to the value of 5 percent of the annual remittances in order to organize services for migrant workers.

The 1982 Ordinance should be replaced by rights-based legislation reflecting the 1990 UN *Convention on the Protection of the Rights of All Migrant Workers and Members of Their Families* and relevant ILO conventions.

The Bangladesh government has signed the 1990 Convention and, as a labour-sending country, it is in Bangladesh's interest to accede to this and ILO instruments forthwith and to frame the necessary enabling national legislation.

To ensure equal access for men and women to overseas employment, government restrictions on the migration of unskilled and semi-skilled women workers below the age of 35 should be rescinded.

Vocational training should be incorporated into mainstream primary and secondary school curricula and textbooks should include chapters on migration. In order to help improve communication skills, English should be introduced as a second language from the first grade.

The existing training institutes of the BMET should be upgraded in order to help increase skilled migration. The BMET also needs to extend its training outreach through joint ventures with non-governmental organisations (NGOs) and private training institutes. In this respect, the BMET should disseminate information on the labour market to organizations that provide training and to NGOs. To ensure that the poor, both men and women, have access to such training, special scholarship programmes should be established. These measures will require a major allocation of resources.

Actions

While processing migration: The Bangladesh missions in Saudi Arabia, Malaysia, the UAE and Kuwait should seek to draw the attention of the authorities to the negative consequences of work visa manipulation on both parties and urge them to take the necessary steps to halt this practice. The Ministry of Expatriates' Welfare and Overseas Employment should take the necessary legal and administrative actions against identified Bangladeshi procurers and middlemen engaged in the visa trade.

In order to curb illegal practices the Government of Bangladesh will have to play a proactive role in visa procurement. With this aim it should continuously strive for signing MoUs and other bilateral agreements with labour receiving countries. Bangladesh missions in receiving countries, particularly in the Middle East, should act as the prime facilitator of procurement. In doing so, missions will gather information on labour needs for the foreseeable future from the concerned government agencies and the private sector, and negotiate with them.

BMET should refrain from issuing a recruiting licence to anyone who is staying abroad on a work-permit. Existing standards for securing a licence should include a clause that a person holding a work permit in a destination country cannot apply for a licence. If he wants to apply for a licence, then he will have to surrender the work permit. If a person is found holding a licence violating the rule, his licence will be cancelled immediately and the authority will seized the security deposit.

Following the recommendation of the Interim Government of 2001, an advisory committee should be established forthwith. This should act as an inter-ministerial/inter-agency watchdog with legal authority to monitor the management of the migration process.

In an effort to reduce fraudulent practices experienced by migrants before departure, there is a need to either create an employment exchange bureau or to regulate the *dalal* system through mandatory registration.

The renewal of the licence of recruiting agencies should be contingent on performance. The BMET should renew the licences of those recruiting agencies that are able to process at least 50 cases in the previous year. At present, only government officials can lodge complaints against recruiting agents for violation of the provisions of the 1982 Ordinance. This should be changed to ensure that migrant workers have the right to seek redress directly.

Steps should be taken immediately to look into allegations against the diagnostic centre based cartel. For proper monitoring, diagnostic centres have to register with the BMET.

The BMET should concentrate on the regulation and monitoring of the international labour migration sector, rather than on implementing specific programmes.

Before embarking on short-term contract migration, migrant workers should receive pre-departure orientation training. Instead of providing this training itself the government may decide to encourage selected specialized agencies, NGOs and migrant support groups to provide residential, pre-departure orientation training in different migrant-prone areas on a decentralized basis.

In destination areas: The role of foreign missions in the labour-receiving countries should be redefined. Protection of the rights of migrant workers should be considered a priority concern. The government should consider establishing a migrant workers' resource centre (MWRC) in each of the major receiving countries within the premises of and under the administrative jurisdiction of the Bangladesh missions.

The concerned officials of the Ministries of Expatriates' Welfare and Foreign Affairs will conduct an annual review of the performance of labour attaches in various countries, identify the problems encountered, suggest remedial measures and set targets for the following year.

Social protection measures relating to health, security and accidents should be specified in the job contracts of semi-skilled and unskilled workers. The pre-departure orientation training should explain in detail to the migrants all such entitlements.

The Bangladesh missions should inform the authorities of the receiving countries about the difficulties faced by claimants in view of the stringent conditions in place in certain countries with respect to claims for compensation. This issue needs to be pursued in liaison with other labour-sending countries.

The government of Bangladesh should also negotiate with the receiving countries ways of simplifying the procedure for receiving benefits that fall due at the end of the contract period, so that the migrant can begin to process the claim well in advance and collect the amount before his/her departure.

The current practice of forced repatriation of migrant workers who contract a disease such as HIV/AIDS should be discontinued. The sending countries should jointly seek to convince the receiving countries that the cost of medical care should be borne by employers when such diseases are contracted in the destination country.

Upon return: In an effort to ensure continuous employment and earnings on their return to Bangladesh, migrants should be informed about the need to save. To encourage small savers, proper incentive programmes should be established. This may involve offering bonds, shares and mutual funds at attractive rates. Migrant workers should also be informed about the various forms of saving instruments offered by government, non-governmental and private agencies. In this regard, existing legal requirements may be relaxed so that selected micro-finance institutions can mobilize the migrants' savings without providing credit.

The BMET should encourage NGOs and the private sector to offer special programmes for the economic reintegration of the returnees. This may include helping them gain access to: the formal banking sector; credit agencies for soft loans; land allotment on moderate terms; insurance schemes; and access to schemes organized under the Wage Earners' Welfare Fund.

Private Sector

Policy

BAIRA should develop a Code of Conduct for its members to bring order in the recruitment sector. A research body should be responsible for helping BAIRA to prepare such the code of conduct. The research body should form an expert committee consisting of BAIRA representatives, government functionaries and representatives of migrant workers' association. This committee will identify the core areas to be covered in the code of conduct and monitor the preparation of the document.

To curb the activities of visa manipulating syndicates based in destination countries BAIRA have to demonstrate their commitment. BAIRA should take necessary legal and administrative actions against identified Bangladeshi procurers and middlemen engaged in visa trade. Based on the code of conduct, it should renounce membership of the agencies engaged in this practice.

The *Dalal* system should be regulated by BAIRA. The recruiting agencies should be obliged to register their intermediaries on their own and send the list of intermediaries to the manpower authority. The *dalals* will have their geographical area of operation specified. Each of them will have to be issued with a photo-identity and their names will be displayed at local level government offices, including thana, TNO and Union Council offices. It will be a penal offence for individuals to work as intermediary without being registered with a recruiting agency and likewise for recruiting agency to avail services of an individual who is not registered with it. All transactions should be made through banks and *dalals*/agencies have to be required to issue receipts for any transactions made.

Membership to association should be made mandatory to the travel agents. The association/s should develop their code of conduct to regulate the members. Institutional mechanism for coordinating the ministry of civil aviation and ministry of EW&OE should be established.

Diagnostic centres should be brought under the coordination of BMET. GAMCA is the association of the diagnostic centres. It should also bring its members under self-regulation that will include incentives for good practices and penalties for violation of the code of conduct. The current practice of recruiting agencies owning diagnostic centres should be forbidden.

Civil society

In order to reduce exploitation and violation of human rights of the migrants, NGOs, migrant workers' associations and trade unions can play an important role. In Bangladesh, returnee migrants' associations have performed extremely well. There is a need to strengthen their institutional capacity so they can have an even greater impact.

Trade unions are not well informed about migrant issues. Expert bodies and associations of migrant workers should organize consultation meetings with local trade unions to familiarise them with the issue. Subsequently the trade unions of Bangladesh may make concerted efforts to develop links with the trade unions of the receiving countries. They can use international fora to campaign for the membership of migrants in the trade unions of the receiving countries.

In order to fill the gap of information and counter misinformation of vested groups a concerted and vigorous awareness campaign has to be organised. The civil society (NGOs, migrant workers' associations and trade unions) should be the major actor in this respect. Awareness campaigns have to be launched both in Bangladesh and in destination countries.

Measures for implementation of an awareness campaign within Bangladesh include (a) media campaign, (b) awareness campaign through community leaders and development practitioners, and (c) pre-departure orientation training to the migrants. In the media campaign both print and electronic media have to be used. As the bulk of the aspirant migrants and members of their families are semi-literate or illiterate, radio and television will constitute important channels of dissemination. A parallel campaign is to be launched to develop a conscious and vigilant group at the grassroots. They, on the one hand, will be the conduits of information, and, on the other, will act as a network of civic group to pre-empt fraudulent practices.

Before embarking on short-term contract migration it is of immense importance that a migrant worker has at his disposal specific information about the destination country, general job condition, rights and duties under the legal regime of the receiving country and under international law. The Philippines and Sri Lanka have been at the forefront in managing labour migration. Both these countries have identified pre-departure orientation training as one of the most effective tools in protecting the rights of migrant workers and curbing fraudulent practices from this process. Specialised training NGOs should provide such training. Returnee migrants can be used as trainers.

Once a migrant worker takes up employment in the host country, it is of immense importance that the Bangladeshi missions abroad are in close contact with him/her. Two methods have been suggested in this regard: (a) periodic meetings with the migrant population, and (b) production and distribution of audio and video materials.

Periodic meetings with migrant workers may be organised by the Bangladeshi missions in destination countries. Such meetings have to take place near the work concentrations of Bangladeshi migrants. Taking into account the resources and manpower available, each of the missions will be assigned with a target to organise such meetings. The purpose of the meeting will be to disseminate information on issues pertaining to the needs of the migrant workers. This may include banking facilities, health matters, cultural practices, etc. Members of the Bangladeshi long term emigrant community can act as resource persons in these sessions. Those meetings can be rounded up with films and video shows.

Country specific audio and video materials have to be developed for the migrant population. They will serve both as sources of information and entertainment. Bangladeshi missions will facilitate the distribution of the materials through local ethnic convenience stores that are frequented by the Bangladeshis and big employers of Bangladeshi labour.

The External Publicity Department of the Ministry of Foreign Affairs may be assigned with the task of distribution of the materials. However, the NGOs will help in producing those materials.

Conclusion

Labour migration plays a vital and indispensable role to the economy of Bangladesh. It is true that some of the problems faced by the labour migrants are beyond the jurisdiction of the Bangladesh state. Nonetheless, some of the hardships are caused by the actors within the state. The government can adopt different policies and take actions in making the various actors accountable and protect the migrants The private sector also needs to act responsibly and make efforts to streamline recruitment. The civil society institutions can play a major role in promoting the rights of the migrants through advocacy and training.

References:

Afsar R.,Yunus M. and Islam S. (2000): 'Are Migrants Chasing after the Golden Deer: A Study on Cost Benefit Analysis of Overseas Migration by Bangladeshi Labour,' IOM (mimeo).

Govt. of Bangladesh (2003): *Annual Report-2002 Ministry of Expatriate Welfare and Overseas Employment.*

Murshid K.A.S., Kazi I. and Meherun A. (2000): 'A Study on Remittance Inflows and Utilization', Dhaka, IOM (mimeo).

Quibria M.G. (1986): 'Migrant Workers and Remittances: Issues for Asian Developing Countries', *Asian Development Review*, Vol. 4.

Rahim A.B.M (2002): 'Future of Labour Export to Saudi Arabia', in Siddiqui T. (ed) op.cit., pp. 104-107.

Reza S. (2002): 'Labour Situation in Kuwait', pp. 120-126, in Siddiqui T. (ed.) op.cit.

Siddiqui T. (2001): *Transcending Boundaries: Labour Migration of Women from Bangladesh*, Dhaka, UPL.

Siddiqui T. (ed.) (2002): Beyond the Maze: Streamlining Labour Recruitment Process in Bangladesh, Dhaka, RMMRU.

Siddiqui T. and Abrar C.R. (2001): 'Migrant Workers' Remittances and Micro-finance Institutions', ILO (mimeo).

Siddiqui T., Sikder M. J. and Hossainul Haque K. N. M. (2004): 'Work Condition of Bangladeshi Factory Workers in the Middle East', ACILS (mimeo).

Australia: 'Good practice'!

Alan Matheson[1]

Preamble

"Good/best" practice is always in "the eye of the beholder". "Migration systems", labour market systems and industrial systems are dynamic and evolving. Migration policy and programs are complex; Australia for example, has 70 types of visas, nine migration acts together with innumerable regulations, with 14 major legislative changes in the past two years.

Triangular dynamics

The "triangular relationship" between worker, "merchant of labour" (labour hire, private employment agency, contractor subcontractor, or hire company) and employer needs to be understood within three standards/processes of the ILO.

These processes include:

- Migration: ILO Conventions including those related specifically to migration but also those related, for example, to issues of equality

- Merchants of Labour: ILO Convention 181

- Employment: ILC 2006 "The Employment Relationship" Report V (1)

---

[1] Australian Council of Trade Unions (ACTU).

Context

As well as the increasing significance not only in terms of numbers of workers moving across borders, there are labour market dynamics and developments and industrial systems, which provide a context for this discussion. Currently, in response to labour hire developments (outsourcing, contracting out, corporatisation and privatization of government utilities and businesses, as well as casual and temporary work), the Australian Parliament's House of Representatives, Employment, Workplace Relations and Workforce Participation Committee is involved in an "Inquiry into Independent Contracting and Labour Hire Arrangements".

Labour market issues

Labour market issues include:

* Skills shortage and responses: training policies, programs and budgets; population dynamics – ageing demographics; extension of retirement ages linked with social policies – pensions, superannuation; push for increased workforce participation of disabled persons, lone parents etc.

* Utilisation of global student mobility, e.g. Working Holiday Makers (WHM) and privatization of university education and trade training.

* Growth and diversity of casual and temporary work.

The international roll out of the temporary staffing industry resembles a textbook case of corporate globalisation: a small number of large firms are leading an aggressive global push, unlocking once-protected national markets through a sustained and cumulative process of regulatory liberalization. [2]

Trade unions, labour market and migration

The Australian Council of Trade Unions (ACTU) checklist for determining whether the use of skilled migrant workers is appropriate reads as follows:

* It is agreed that such labour is not the solution to the skills shortage but rather a means to overcome an immediate and pressing need;

---

[2] Geographies of the Temporary Staffing Industry Research Program Working Paper 5: "Constructing markets for temporary labour: employment liberalization and the internationalisation of the staffing industry," J. Peck, N. Theodore, K. Ward, September 2004 P.27.

- The employer has demonstrated that all avenues of upskilling of existing workers and recruiting local workers have been exhausted;
- Those workers are subject to the same award or agreement terms and conditions as the permanent workers at the site;
- The employer has in place an agreed training plan with the union and is making an acceptable contribution to training;
- The workers are not to be exploited through the recruitment, travel or accommodation procedures and recruitment is only undertaken by accredited recruitment agencies;
- That there be an agreement with the union on the number of workers and the length of time they may be employed in particular workplaces;
- Those workers employed continually in Australia for more than a year are to be offered permanent residency.

The international union movement is committed to the development of the "ILO plan of action for migrant workers" based on a "rights based approach, in accordance with existing international labour standards and ILO principles, which recognizes labour market needs and the sovereign rights of all nations to determine their own migration policies, including determining entry into their territory and under which conditions migrants may remain".[3]

Such a plan would be based on the following principals:

- Expand avenues for regular labour migration
- Promotion of management of migration
- Licensing and supervision of recruitment and contracting agencies
- Promoting decent work including the promotion of human rights of migrant workers
- Combating irregular labour migration
- Guidelines for ethical recruitment
- Manage remittance flows
- Accreditation and recognition of skills
- Promotion of social inclusion

---

[3] Resolution concerning a fair deal for migrant workers in a global economy, ILC 2004.

A fundamental issue for this policy dialogue is the employment relationship and in particular the "regulation of triangular employment relationships". [4] The issue is complex and has been on the agenda of the ILO for a number of years. One of the challenges of the ILC 2004 resolution on migrant workers is positioning its implementation within other significant policy developments in the ILO. For example, this policy dialogue rightly focuses on "the merchants", and the ILC has focused on "recruitment agencies" in discussions on labour migration and the ILO office and the GB are involved in developing 'a framework' which will include attention to the "licensing and supervision of recruitment and contracting agencies for migrant workers". However, it is disturbing to note that neither the questionnaire nor the introductory document prepared for the ILC 2006 on "The Employment Relationship" makes any reference to migrant labour. Yet the "employment relationship", and "triangular relationships", are keys to "good practice", as they relate to the regulation of the movement of workers across borders.

The Australian "merchants of labour"

There are a number of distinct yet overlapping agencies and individuals involved in the identification, recruitment and employment of workers from overseas, in Australia. Included are:

- Employers: defined, identified and Government "recognized as sponsor"

- Provincial (State) and regional cities/regions: with the status of "recognized to sponsor"

- Labour hire, including Government defined "normal recruitment companies"; "labour hire companies" (contracted by companies to fill short/long term vacancies from either domestic or international labour market); and "contract management companies" (involved in recruitment – either domestic or international, and then on selling workers)

A core issue for Government (and for unions) is "the employment relationship" – who is the employer? Such a clarification would then define accountability and responsibility for issues such as wages and

---

[4] See The Employment Relationship Report V (1) ILC 2006, p.42ff.

working conditions, occupational health and safety, as well as training and skills development. For example, why shouldn't ADECCO or other recruitment agencies be contributing to training and skills development? It also contributes to ensuring that such arrangements are administered and regulated within the national industrial system.

Associated with this movement is the "migration agent". While specifically excluded by both legislation and a code of ethics, from being directly involved as 'an employer' in the migration process, the agent within the Australian context is involved, as an employee or subcontractor of a company/agent recruiting and moving workers into Australia. There is evidence of agents involved in the recruitment of workers overseas and on selling them on their arrival.

Agents must be registered (upon passing a qualification examination) by the national, legislative based, Migrant Agents Registration Authority (MARA). The Migration Institute of Australia (a membership body of registered migrant agents) is responsible for the operation of MARA on the basis of an MOU between it and the Government.

A major issue for self-regulation of "migration agents" is the stability of the industry (or profession). There are some 3,000 registered agents in Australia; 12% of agents have more than 10 years experience, with nearly a half having less than 3 years.

While recognizing self regulation, the Government (Department of Immigration and Indigenous Affairs – DIMA) actively complements this regulation by:

• Monitoring the performance of MARA in relation to registration, complaints handling and financial management.

• Investigating criminal offences allegedly committed by agents.

• Preparing, referring (where appropriate) and arranging carriage and prosecution or defence of any litigation arising in relation to the MARA functions.

In addition to employers and state/regional authority direct sponsorship, there are also the three agencies as noted above. Within the current Parliamentary inquiry into labour hire in Australia the issue of licensing of such agencies involved in domestic recruitment and employment, is being raised. The ACTU's position as outlined in its submission includes:

(I) A code of practice for labour hire and contracting out

(1) Labour hire should primarily be used to supplement rather than replace existing labour.

(2) Labour hire operators should not seek to place workers on artificial contractor arrangements to avoid employment responsibilities.

(3) Labour hire as a form of cost reduction should not be supported. Labour hire workers should receive rates of pay and conditions of employment equivalent to their non-labour hire counterparts.

(4) Labour hire work should be covered by appropriate awards and agreements.

(5) Labour hire operators should provide access to training and skills development for their workers.

(6) Labour hire operators and clients should share responsibility for occupational health and safety obligations.

(7) Labour hire operators should ensure that their workers are able to decline work for the purposes of sick leave, family leave or recreational leave without adverse consequences or discrimination.

(8) Labour hire workers should be given the opportunity to raise concerns about their work with the client or the labour hire operator, or both.

(9) Labour hire operators should ensure that all legal employment obligations are met in respect of their workers.

(10) Work that is contracted out, whether to a labour hire operator or another employer, should be subject to the same rates of pay and conditions as well as consultation with affected employees.

(II) Licensing schemes for labour hire operators:

Licensing schemes should be established at the state and/or federal level to ensure that all labour hire operators are subject to the same regulatory framework, and to minimize unfair competition on the basis of substandard provision of wages, conditions, training and other matters. Any licensing scheme should include requirements for initial accreditation, subsequent regular reporting, professional standards, referral of matters to appropriate compliance authorities and penalties for non-compliance with license conditions.

Labour hire operators should be required to report on the following matters as part of any licensing scheme:

- Wages and entitlements: Labour hire operators should:
  - Specify which, if any, awards apply to workers engaged by them, and should commit to observance of those awards;
  - Advise of their payment or non-payment of 'site rates' – i.e., rates equivalent to those provided to equivalent non-labour hire employees at a client firm;
  - Advise of their policies in respect of workers not accepting shifts for the purpose of sick leave, family leave or recreational leave; and
  - Advise of their payment of taxation, superannuation and workers compensation premiums.
- Training: skills development and safety training programs.
- Occupational health and safety: risk assessment strategies, induction, provision of personal protective equipment and return to work plans, and policies to ensure that all injuries are reported.
- Discrimination: compliance with anti-discrimination laws.
- Code of practice: adherence to an agreed industry code of practice.

Within the existing situation of the three types of agents/companies involved in recruitment and movement of workers, note the following issues.

In terms of monitoring and supervision there is a paper report required by DIMA, of all agencies; this is complemented by site visits of a quarter of all sponsors. Audits or 'veracity checks' particularly target:

- High risk areas: hospitality and construction
- New companies
- Borderline applications
- All labour hire firms are subject to site visits

Probably upwards of 60% of companies and agencies, employ a MARA agent.

Sanctions include either withdrawal or barring of any further and future sponsorship.

The movement of temporary workers, tourists, increased numbers of students/workers on Working Holiday Maker Visas (12 months with permission to work for 3 months; now extended to a further 12 months if it can be demonstrated work has been in agriculture; with the possibility of a permanent visa if skills are in demand), as well as increased numbers of international students in higher education and trade training, provides fertile ground for labour hire companies and exploitation of these workers by recruiting and labour hire companies.

It is of passing interest to note the significance of the extent of this movement of temporary "workers," but also the role it plays. The Government announced substantive extensions to the WHM scheme on the basis that 'guest workers' particularly in agriculture were open to exploitation. The assumption that WHM (and students) were not open to exploitation, is not in accord with reality.

Principles of good practice

The following principles are essential elements of good practice:

- Effective national licensing, regulation, inspection, monitoring and ongoing analysis, and a sanctions regime.
- National legislative framework of licensing based both on national law and practice, and international ILO standards.
- Positioned within the industrial relations system covering issues such as wages and working conditions occupational health and safety and qualification recognition.
- Transparency e.g. the employment relationship should be clear and unambiguous.
- Fundamental rights of workers ensured.
- Recognizes and takes measures to address the ethical dimension of recruitment and selection of workers from overseas countries.
- Tripartite participation and involvement as well as consultation with migrant workers.

References

MARA (Migrant Agents Registration Authority), www.themara.com.au

Australian Government, www.immi.gov.au (nb:Information kit on migration agents), www.immi.gov.au/agents/index.htm

Parliament of Australia, House of Representatives Study Committee on Employment, Workplace Relations and Workforce Participation, Inquiry into Independent Contractors and Labour Hire Arrangements, http://www.aph.gov.au/house/committee/ewrwp/independentcontracting/index.htm

Management of foreign workers in Singapore: Regulation of employment agents

Ng Cher Pong[1]

The need to manage foreign manpower well

Determining the appropriate regulatory and enforcement approach to take towards employment agencies is a major challenge, amidst an increasingly globalised and connected labour market – one in which economic and employment opportunities have driven the movement of people across national borders. According to the United Nations Population Division,[2] the total number of international migrants surpassed 175 million in 2000 and continues to grow. Set against such an external environment, how employment agencies are being licensed and regulated will become even more crucial.

This is particularly so for Singapore because this country has historically maintained a very open labour market. Singapore's economic progress since the early nineteenth century – from the days as a sleepy obscure fishing village to where we are today – has been largely driven by migrant workers from both North and South Asia, most of whom eventually stayed on permanently to form the nation.

The principle of embracing international migration continues to be a major tenet of our public policy today, with migrant workers constituting more than one quarter of our total workforce. However, migrant workers are not homogenous and for the purposes of this discussion, they can be broadly classified into two groups. The first group comprises

---

[1] Divisional Director, Foreign Manpower Management Division, Ministry of Manpower, Singapore.

[2] United Nations Department of Economic and Social Affairs, World Economic and Social Survey 2004, page 25.

highly skilled and educated professionals, who are very mobile and able to fend for themselves in their employment relationships. The second group includes workers who are not as highly skilled and work, for example, as production line operators, bus drivers and marine workers. It is this latter group where the potential for abuse and exploitation exists because these migrant workers are not as educated about their rights. Financially, most of them are also in a precarious position because they took out substantial loans when they left their home countries in search of better economic opportunities. In short, the employment relationship is a highly asymmetrical one and the migrant workers become highly vulnerable.

This is why there are many stories around the world of such foreign workers being exploited by unscrupulous employers and employment agents, who may endanger the lives of the migrant workers, cheat them of their rightful salaries, and even illegally "traffick" them across national boundaries. But a common thread is that such exploitative and abusive behaviours are known to have happened in many countries across different continents. Thus it is not an isolated problem involving a handful of countries, but a global one confronting many countries.

Singapore's approach towards foreign worker management

In Singapore, we have similarly witnessed cases of migrant workers being cheated by their employment agencies, those who were physically abused or owed salaries by their employers and even workers who were housed in unacceptable living conditions. While the proportion of migrant workers affected by such problems may seem small relative to the size of the migrant worker population in Singapore, one case of abuse or exploitation is one too many. As a migrant society, such behaviour is an affront to our belief that foreign workers have much to contribute to our development and should be accorded equal protection as Singaporeans.

Recognising the importance of protecting the well-being of foreign manpower in Singapore, in 2003 we set up a Foreign Manpower Management Division within the Ministry of Manpower. The main role for the Division is to review the framework for providing a conducive environment for foreign workers living and working in Singapore, especially the lower skilled ones who are more vulnerable to exploitation and unfair treatment. This is very much in line with the Ministry's vision of creating a Great Workplace for all workers, both local and foreign.

Generally, there are three key stakeholders involved – the employment agents, the employers and the foreign workers. The government's role is essentially to define the obligations and responsibilities for each stakeholder and to develop a regulatory framework to ensure that each stakeholder fulfils its responsibility. The desired outcome is to ensure that the interests and well-being of the foreign workers are not compromised by unscrupulous individuals who take advantage of the asymmetrical relationship. It is, therefore, necessary for the government to act firmly against errant parties who flout these rules and regulations so as to uphold the integrity of the regulatory framework.

Employers of migrant workers are the main beneficiaries of being able to tap the economic contributions of these workers and they should be made primarily responsible for the management of foreign workers. This includes internalizing the cost of handling the migrant workers, such as making sure that the workers are correctly deployed to approved occupations, paying their salaries punctually, providing a safe working environment, proper housing, medical coverage and acceptable employment terms, as well as buying return air tickets for the workers when their term of employment ends. Irresponsible employers cannot be allowed to externalize the cost of their errant behaviour and expect the migrant workers, other employers and the society at large to bear such cost on their behalf.

On the other hand, employment agents are labour market intermediaries who match employers and migrant workers and facilitate their employment relationship. While some may view employment agents in a more limited role as acting on behalf of the employers, we believe that the responsibilities of employment agents are much wider. Fundamentally, this is an industry involving human relationships, which, unlike goods and services, should not be traded as a commodity. Employers cannot outsource or delegate their responsibilities to employment agents. Nor can the agents act solely on behalf of one party at the expense of vulnerable migrant workers. Therefore, we believe that employment agents have dual responsibilities. First, they help employers recruit workers who meet their needs and satisfy national foreign worker entry requirements, and in some instances, they manage the workers. Second, they also have a responsibility towards the foreign workers of helping them secure suitable employment. The Ministry's regulations penalize agents who act to the detriment of workers, and require employment agents to bring in only workers who meet the government's entry requirements. The Ministry's approach towards regulating employment agents will be elaborated in a later section.

Finally, migrant workers are expected to take some personal responsibility in safeguarding their own interests against exploitation by employers or employment agents. While it is necessary for the government's regulatory framework to be somewhat lopsided in the favour of foreign workers to address the power imbalance within the employment relationship, we should not go over-board to the extent that foreign workers become disengaged and rely entirely on the government to protect their well-being and to address their woes. A fine balance needs to be found somewhere in between these two extremes. Migrant workers are also expected to comply with the laws and employment-related regulations during their stay in Singapore. To facilitate this, the Ministry has made various orientation courses mandatory to educate workers on their rights and obligations, as well as embarked on outreach programmes to continually reinforce these messages among the population of migrant workers.

This is illustrative of the multi-pronged approach that has been taken in Singapore's management of foreign workers. To succeed, we believe that it is necessary to move beyond proposing increased penalties against errant behaviour within the existing legislation. The Ministry's target is to develop a self-sustaining eco-system for the stakeholders involved through a range of regulatory levers and enforcement tools so that all the stakeholders not only are able, but have a strong incentive to discharge their roles and responsibilities outlined above. Such an eco-system is also strengthened by the network of strategic partnerships that the Ministry has built up with other parties such as the unions, industry associations, voluntary welfare organisations and non-government organizations. These external parties are usually better positioned than the Ministry to reach out to workers and key stakeholders involved in their management.

Employment agency regulatory and enforcement framework

As for the regulatory and enforcement framework for employment agencies in Singapore, we shall now outline some of the key strategies that we have adopted, the rationale for our policy choices, and some of the major challenges that we face.

As at the end of 2004, there were more than 1,200 licensed employment agencies in Singapore, of which about 800 were involved in placing low- to semi-skilled migrant workers. In regulating such agents, we seek to achieve our three main desired outcomes.

First, employment agents should be professional in matching both local and foreign workers with employers. Those who do so will minimize subsequent problems associated with the mismatch of employment relationships. They should therefore not be solely driven by commissions and should not place workers into vacancies that are not a suitable match.

Second, when employment agents are expected to discharge responsibilities in managing the migrant workers on behalf of employers, they should not cut corners and must be reliable in doing so. This includes the provision of proper accommodation and repatriation of foreign workers who wish to return to their home countries.

Third, employment agents must act in a fair and ethical manner as they broker the employment relationship between two parties who may have very unequal bargaining power. They should not profiteer at the expense of the vulnerable workers.

Driven by these desired outcomes, the Ministry has been steadily expanding its suite of regulatory tools that are being used. These can broadly be categorized as legislation and licensing, accreditation, as well as enforcement actions.

Legislation and licensing

Singapore relies on the Employment Agencies Act to regulate employment agents, with the primary aim of protecting vulnerable workers. All persons providing recruitment and placement services to other employers in Singapore are regulated by the Act. The Act contains provisions for all such persons to be licensed by the Ministry. All licensed employment agents are governed by the licensing rules, regulations and conditions, which include prohibiting agents from placing foreign workers in occupations for which they have not been approved and a provision of proper housing before migrant workers are placed. The Act also prescribes the maximum penalties for persons who have committed various types of offences, which are currently a fine of up to S$10,000, or imprisonment of up to 2 years, or both. Errant agents also risk having their licenses revoked and their security deposits with the Ministry forfeited.

The Ministry carefully screens applications for employment agent licenses to ensure that employment agents do not act in a manner detrimental to any person's interests. Licenses will not be issued to applicants who have had records of convictions that are likely to have an adverse impact on their clients, such as the Women's Charter, the Children and Young Persons Act and the Penal Code. Applicants are also required to be sufficiently familiar with Singapore's employment laws before they are issued an operating license. To achieve this, a post-secondary education institution runs a Certificate in Employment Agencies Course and achieving this certificate is a pre-requisite for applicants placing low- to semi-skilled migrant workers. In addition, licenses are renewed on an annual basis, which allows the Ministry to perform regular screening of the licensees.

Accreditation for employment agents involved in placing foreign domestic workers

Unlike business employers, domestic employers are generally more reliant on employment agents. Similarly, the well-being of foreign domestic workers is also more dependent on the professionalism of employment agents. From a foreign worker management perspective, how such employment agents fulfill their responsibilities becomes even more critical. In recognition of this, we have set more exact standards for employment agents involved in placing foreign domestic workers. Since June 2004, such employment agents are required to be accredited by independent bodies before their licenses can be renewed. Besides increasing the protection of the welfare of the foreign domestic workers, the accreditation scheme also aims to offer basic protection for domestic employers who may be misled by unscrupulous agents. To be accredited, employment agents are required to meet several requirements.

First, to enhance the protection of foreign domestic workers, the employment agents must:

- Prepare the domestic workers adequately through appropriate orientation and training programmes before they are placed;
- Ensure that all the placed workers are aware of the contact numbers of the employment agents and other organizations that may assist them when they are in need of help;
- Facilitate written employment contracts between each worker and their employer; and
- Conduct periodic follow-up calls to check on the well-being of the workers during their initial period of employment.

Second, to protect the interests of the employers, employment agents must:

- Place workers with the competencies and skills that have been mutually agreed upon with the employers;
- Be truthful and accurate in their communications, including advertisements and provision of worker resumes; and
- Maintain a system for complaint resolution, including specified timeframes and recourse actions.

Two independent bodies appointed by the Ministry administer the accreditation scheme. To date, the scheme has been successful in raising the professionalism of such employment agents and the Ministry plans to continue to strengthen the accreditation scheme.

Enforcement actions

Enforcement is the key component underpinning the regulatory framework, without which employment agents will not take the licensing rules and conditions imposed seriously. Without effective enforcement by the Ministry, unscrupulous individuals will be emboldened by the fact that they stand a very high chance of getting away with exploitative behaviour. There will not be a level playing field within the industry, which in turn creates a vicious self-sustaining cycle – even bona fide employment agents will find it necessary to profiteer at the expense of vulnerable workers in order to stay competitive. The legislative and licensing framework is, therefore, only as good as its enforcement.

The Ministry takes a very tough stance against errant behaviour by employment agents. We investigate all complaints lodged against employment agents for compromising the interests of foreign workers, and take stern actions whenever the allegations are found to be substantiated. Such actions include prosecuting errant individuals and revocation of licenses.

Cross-border challenge of regulating employment agents

While attempts have been made to regulate and to professionalize employment agents operating in Singapore, we note that the system is not a fool-proof one. The limitations are due primarily to the industry practice whereby employment agents in the host country typically work with their counterparts in the various source countries. While the Ministry can take enforcement actions on employment agencies in Singapore, migrant workers may still be exploited by those in the source countries over which we have no regulatory control. One common challenge is the regulation of recruitment fees imposed on the foreign workers. While many rules could be put in place to prevent the foreign workers from bearing any unreasonable expenses associated with their employment in Singapore, employment agents in the source countries are known to openly impose excessively high fees, which increases the indebtedness of such workers by the time they come into contact with an employment agent in Singapore. This undermines the regulatory controls that are designed to protect the well-being of the foreign workers.

Therefore, in view of the cross-border nature of the work of employment agents, the regulatory and enforcement efforts of different governments will be fully effective only if both host and source countries are equally committed to introducing and enforcing rules to govern the behaviour of employment agents.

Conclusion

In conclusion, foreign workers have always been an important driving force in Singapore's economic growth, and will remain so in the foreseeable future. To continue harnessing their contributions, Singapore recognizes that it is critical to manage these workers effectively, and to ensure that their interests are protected within a highly asymmetrical employment relationship. This requires us to establish a comprehensive regulatory framework to ensure that all the stakeholders in this area fulfill their obligations and responsibilities. In particular, as employment agents play an important role as labour market intermediaries, Singapore has used a combination of regulatory tools, including legislation and licensing, accreditation and enforcement. In view of the transnational nature of the industry for placement of migrant workers, there is also scope for cooperation between the source and host countries in regulating employment agencies.

What can we learn from Bahrain's labour market reform?

Mohammed Dito[1]

Labour markets reforms became a process that has gained real global dimensions in recent years. Despite the diversity of socio-economic and political factors driving the reforms in many parts of the world, the core element remains: balancing social justice with economic development. From South Africa to Latin America and from South East Asia to the developed industrial world, this is the challenge that faces policy makers worldwide. Indeed this is the task that will define the direction and content of social progress in different societies and for many generations to come.

International labour migration became one of the distinctive characteristic of globalization. Its effect on internal functioning of labour markets has reached new qualitative and quantities levels, demanding a new and creative policy paradigm, that seeks integrating labour migration as a driving force for enhancing competitiveness and efficiency of national economies without endangering job prospects for the local citizens.

The Gulf Cooperation Council (GCC) states (Bahrain, Kuwait, Oman, Qatar, Saudi Arabia, and the United Arab Emirates) have been struggling for decades to come to terms with dealing efficiently with the existence of and demand for foreign workers on one side and employing their young nationals in productive and decent jobs in the growing private sectors, on the other side. The issue of the role and the size of foreign workers in the GCC states has been a subject for a long discussion and debate over the past three decades among the public as well the policy

[1] Policy Development Manager, Bahrain Economic Development Board; formerly Head, Employment Services Bureau, Ministry of Labour and Social Affairs, Bahrain.

makers. The main concerns can be summarized in two issues: first, the impact of the large number of foreign workers on the demographic and socio-political situation of the societies. Second, the growing unemployment rates that face the local workforce and its relation to the existing pool of expatriate workers.

Although there have been different policies and programs to tackle the unemployment problem among the citizens, only limited success has been achieved so far. Real efforts are currently being undertaken to review the course of action of labour market policies, especially with the increased influence of external factors (free trade agreements, human rights, etc.) as well as internal factors (high rates of unemployment, especially youth unemployment, privatization of public sector, etc.).

Why it is no longer possible to continue past policies in managing the labour market in this important region of the world? There are a number of reasons, mostly of a complex socio-political nature, but we can highlight the following six interrelated factors:

Repeated attempts to solve the problems with the same paradigm and level of thinking have not been successful. Basically there is a wrong approach taken toward expatriate workers: a mixture of denial of the real need for them and perceiving their presence as a threat while continuing the dependency on them at the same time.

The mode of job-creation in the private sector has depended on cheap unskilled labour without giving expatriate workers actual labour rights, combined with very restricted mobility in the labour market, and the possibility of exploiting the "kafala" sponsorship system to generate a "renters mentality" among a vast number of local businesses. The impact on the labour market is "catastrophic"! The underemployment that has resulted from employing cheap foreign labour without rights under bad working conditions has affected the local workers employed in the private sector. Underemployment became a "firewall" against effective integration of nationals in the private sector labour market.

Focusing on policies addressing the supply side without a parallel and balanced approach to improving the demand side of labour has created unrealistic and unfair expectations by both sides (employer and workers). Proper education and training programs are of critical importance for the success in any labour market. However, adaptability for higher productivity is not an objective for employers or workers alone: it is a challenge and a task for both.

The gap between government and private sector employment creates the essence of labour market distortion and has further complicated the integration of nationals in the private sector, especially with officially declared policies of giving the private sector the lead role in job creation.

The need of improving the performance of labour markets goes hand in hand with improving labour administration institutions. Placing the whole burden of tackling such a complex and large scale problem on the Ministries of Labour alone has not helped achieving this goal. Short-term solutions and policing the labour market have become a common feature of policies adopted by many Ministries of Labour in the GCC states.

The lack of a proper and genuine social dialogue has been a factor that contributed toward the failure of the labour policies in addressing acute problems.

The situation in the GCC countries suggests that the pattern of importing cheap unskilled labour is reproducing itself. Though it is perceived and treated as temporary migration, it is in fact a permanent and stable factor, and it negatively affects the general level of wages and the improvement of productivity.

Low wage foreign unskilled labour, low productivity and high unemployment rates among nationals can create a social mixture of a highly explosive nature. A solution to these problems can only be based on a long term vision: what do we want to be?

This was the question raised by H.H. Sheikh Salman bin Hamad Al Khalifa, Crown Prince of the Kingdom of Bahrain, in his opening speech for the Multi-stakeholders workshop held in Bahrain on the 23rd September 2004. The workshop was an event of a national scale and was comprised of representatives from different segments of the society: Employers, Workers, intellectuals and policy makers. Reforming Bahrain's Labour Market was at the center of discussions between the participants. For the first time in Bahrain's history a rigid and solid scientific analysis of major problems in the labour market and their root causes were explained, discussed in detail and a specific set of policy options were proposed. A constructive "self-criticism" of government policies in the past was combined with a clear strategic action plan for the road ahead. In many ways the workshop represented an act of wisdom and courage from the highest political authority in Bahrain, and an assertion to continue the Reform Project launched by H.M. the King Sheikh Hamad Bin Isa Al Khalifa in 2000.

The Policy Recommendation Package of the reform included a set of policy leverage to tackle the deficiencies in the labour market:

- Imposing a system of labour fees and quota ceilings for expatriates to restrict the supply of labour across the entire economy,

- Subsidising basic work readiness training programmes for Bahrainis and providing incentives for Bahrainis to work in the private sector,

- Increasing mobility of expatriates by allowing those with a valid work visa to switch employers,

- Raising working standards for all employees by adopting and enforcing regulations adhering to ILO standards and implementing clear and predictable termination processes for all employees and install efficient and effective arbitration panels and/or labour courts.

Two main objectives were defined for the reform process. The first is to encourage the private sector to become the engine of growth. The second is for Bahrainis to become employees of choice.

Several activities and meetings with employers, trade unions and others have followed the September workshop and it is expected that mid 2006 will be the starting date for implementing the reform policies. Achieving this vision requires substantial progress along three dimensions: economic, education and labour market reform. The approach is to integrate three main processes: first, eliminate labour market distortions to make education and economic reforms effective, stimulate private sector job creation, especially in the medium and high wage job segments and improve Bahraini skills through education and training to better meet job market demand.

What we can learn from Bahrain's labour reform at this stage is rather a matter of gaining insight than judging the results. A comprehensive rational policy design, participatory and transparent in nature, is a tested methodology for success. The reform policies confirm the basic and simple truths we find on national as well as international labour markets. In sum, the Bahrain labour reform shows that:

- Bad conditions for expatriate workers are, and will continue to be, a basis for worsening conditions for locals,

- Improving workers rights should be combined with improving labour productivity and the work-environment,

- Cost competitiveness based on a lack of rights, instead of equal market conditions, which regulates the type and number of migrant workers admitted, will lead to undesirable social and economic consequences,
- Bureaucratic expatriate management systems can lead the way for corrupt practices,
- Employment needs for business must be based on fair competition between labour supply (locals and migrants), and finally
- Proper information systems, good governance and the active participation of the social partners are three fundamental bases for effective migrant management policies.

Merchants of labour in the Middle East and North Africa: Egypt as a case study

Ibrahim Awad[1]

Introduction

Egypt is at the intersection of the two systems of labour migration operating in the Middle East and North Africa. To the east and southeast, its workers have temporarily migrated for employment to Jordan, Saudi Arabia, Kuwait and other Gulf States over the last 40 years. To a much lesser degree, they have followed the path previously traced by their companions from Algeria, Morocco and Tunisia, seeking employment to the northwest, in Italy, Greece, France and other countries of the European Union (EU). The two systems are like communicating vessels. When foreign labour demand stagnates in their main external markets, i.e. the Gulf States, as has happened in the last two decades, Egyptian workers increasingly try to access Mediterranean and other European labour markets. Naturally, Libya is the third labour market of great importance to Egyptian workers.

An essential difference exists between the status of Egyptian migrant workers in the Gulf and in Mediterranean Europe and beyond. In the first case, they overwhelmingly are regular, documented, workers responding to expressed demand. In the latter, they essentially are irregular migrants crossing the common sea to meet unexpressed, diffusedly analyzed and perceived demand. In the particular case of Libya no entry visas are required and access to, and stay on, the Libyan territory is

[1] Director, International Migration Programme, ILO. The author wishes to express appreciation for valuable research assistance provided by Ms. Shahdan Arram, ILO Sub-Regional Office for North Africa, Cairo.

regular. But once there, Egyptian workers join the informal economy where their employment is out of the purview of labour legislation.

The only two surveys on Egyptian labour migration were carried out in the mid and late 1980s. No reliable figures now exist on the volume, demographic and socioeconomic characteristics, and employment distribution and remuneration of Egyptian workers. Naturally, no information is available either on their recruitment for external employment and, as a result, the role played by 'merchants of labour'. For purposes of this note, 'merchants of labour' are essentially private recruitment agencies, but can also be public employment services engaged in meeting external demand for labour in implementation of bilateral agreements.

In the following section some observations are formulated with regard to the functional importance of 'merchants of labour'. A review of regulations governing recruitment undertaken by public services and private recruitment agencies is also carried out. Thereafter, the recruitment function undertaken by the governmental institution and a sample of private recruitment agencies is examined. Finally, some conclusions are drawn.

Access to external employment: The reality and the regulation

The irregular status of Egyptian migrant workers in Mediterranean Europe leads to a safe assumption about the absence of a role for merchants of labour in their recruitment. In the Gulf, the vast majority of migrants find their way to employment through their personal contacts and relations. In certain cases, as in the medium and high ladders of public employment, such as educational, judicial and academic posts, Egyptian civil servants, judges and professors move through implementation of bilateral agreements. However, even among these categories of workers, some also use their personal efforts. Methods of access to the Gulf States also apply to the Libyan labour market. In this particular case, territorial contiguity and absence of visa requirements allow unskilled and semi-skilled workers to be physically present and to search for employment in the informal economy. In both cases of the Gulf and Libya, some room exits for private recruitment agencies.

The Labour Law enacted in 2003, and the Ministerial decree providing for its implementation, envisages all public and private institutions that can engage in the external employment of Egyptian workers. [2] These are: the very Ministry of Manpower and Migration (MOMM); other Ministries and Public Agencies; the Egyptian Trade Union Federation (ETUF); State-owned enterprises and private sector companies in their fields of activity and in implementation of contracts with foreign parties; private recruitment agencies licensed by the MOMM; and professional associations with respect to their members only. Even international organizations are mentioned among this set of institutions. This most probably stems from confusing institutions that can recruit Egyptians for employment in external labour markets with those that can directly employ them. It also overlooks the fact that such organizations, in employing Egyptians, cannot be considered external, inasmuch as Egypt is, like other member States, one of their constitutive parties. Only licensed private recruitment agencies are allowed to charge the worker up to two per cent of his/her wages for the first year of employment.

The regulatory framework is satisfactory for labour migration to the Gulf labour markets, which, as pointed out, is overwhelmingly regular. That the vast majority of migrant workers to these markets do not use the services of institutions the law lists is not a weakness in its provisions. After all, even in domestic markets, labour demand is essentially met without the intervention of public or private employment services.

The regulatory framework may be considered amiss for purposes of the European and Libyan markets. But this observation is not warranted. If Egyptian migrant workers are irregular and/or informally employed, this is essentially explained by the functioning of receiving labour markets in Mediterranean Europe or contiguous Libya. Naturally, the large informality of the Egyptian labour market also rationalizes for workers the irregularity of their external migration and employment.

The recruitment function undertaken by public and private institutions

The public institution responsible for placing Egyptian workers in external labour markets is the General Directorate of External Employment and Representation (GDEER) in the MOMM. The recruitment process it manages is comprised of several steps. Workers wishing to use

---

[2] Law No. 12/2003 and Decree of the Minister of Manpower and Migration No. 135/2003.

the services of GDEER fill out application forms and submit them personally, by post or through the MOMM's website. Applications are checked and classified in a register in accordance with occupational categories and dates of receipt. When the GDEER receives external requests for workers, it selects from the register applications that meet the characteristics of demand. Candidates are then interviewed and tested by technical committees, under the supervision of GDEER and in presence of representatives of external employers. Selected workers are recruited and contracts are made and approved by the GDEER after checking their provisions.[3]

In addition to its operational recruitment and placement function, the GDEER is also the regulatory body that licenses, supervises and controls the activities of private recruitment agencies. Private agencies wishing to be licensed have letters of guarantee emitted in favour of the MOMM. However, in an institutional setup that effectively protects the rights of migrant workers and provides them with the best services, these two functions should be separated. This is all the more necessary since malpractice, fraud and deception, of which workers are victims, are still common.

In matching external demand for specific labour with domestic supply, licensed private recruitment agencies expectedly advertise job availabilities, screen orders and applications, conduct interviews, check documents, test workers, draw up contracts and have them validated by the GDEER, process visas and organize transport. But these functions are not uniformly carried out by different agencies. Segments of the labour market to which they cater determine their modes of operating. The effectiveness and efficiency of agencies increase as the segments of the labour market rise. Effectiveness and efficiency are also correlated with the skills and socioeconomic characteristics of the workers they recruit.

For purposes of this note, visits to and interviews with the owners/managers of two well reputed recruitment agencies were undertaken. One is specialized in health professions, such as medical doctors and paramedics, where 95 per cent of its clients are well funded public and private health care facilities. Women represent five per cent of the workers it places. Ninety per cent of the volume of work of this agency is carried out in Saudi Arabia, the remainder taking place in Bahrain,

---

[3] Note provided to the author by the Director, GDEER.

Kuwait, Qatar and Egypt itself. The facilities it supplies workers to are large hospitals, including joint ventures with European partners. It does not charge workers for recruiting them, but rather the employers. Having made a name for itself this agency expanded its services to other sectors and countries. The clients are still prominent, large companies at the highest levels of the labour market. One problem faced by this agency is that it could not always meet specific demand for certain medical occupations, unavailable in the Egyptian market. This agency reportedly devotes great attention to the living and working conditions of the workers it supplies to its clients. It checks on them *in situ* and ensures that provisions of employment contracts are respected. Content workers are productive and their working relations are smooth. This is a matter of satisfaction for employers, which reinforces their confidence in the agency. The causality links between the provision of services and client satisfaction are logical. Therefore, the owner/manager of the agency being the source of the story does not detract from its credibility. It is worth highlighting that the owner/manager is himself a medical doctor. He was previously a migrant worker, employed by his now largest client. This brings out the important factors for the success of a private recruitment agency: knowledge of the origin and destination labour markets, knowledge of the sector and occupations it deals with, satisfaction of both migrant workers and foreign employers. Other factors, made possible by the specialization of this particular agency in high-level occupations, are the computerization of its work and databases, its development of a website, a well-educated and relatively large staff and the provision of training to candidates.

The second agency's clients are enterprises of diverse sizes in the same Gulf countries serviced by the former agency and in Libya. It is not specialized but rather supplies workers in such varied sectors and branches of activity as accounting, marketing or construction. Workers are skilled and semi-skilled. As in the former case, women do not make up more than five per cent of recruited workers. Here too, the agency reportedly follows up on the living and working conditions of the migrant workers it supplies. However, extended working relationships with specific clients, like in the case of the previous agency, do not exist. The owner/manager travels in search of clients. He too used to be a migrant professor in Saudi Arabia, which familiarized him with the labour market of this country. Working methods in the agency are orderly but not advanced and computerized like in the first one. The staff is far leaner. Rather than providing training, it offers vocational guidance to

119

candidates leaving them to acquire demanded skills. This agency strives to please migrant workers and satisfy external employers. Its survival in the market may be an indicator that it is to a certain extent successful in achieving these objectives. However, the fact that it provides fewer and lower level services, reveals that it is far less developed than the previous agency. The determining factor for an agency's success seems to be the segment of the labour market it is involved in and the type of workers it deals with.

Conclusions

The effectiveness and professionalism of private recruitment agencies seem correlated with the levels of labour market segments and occupations with which they deal. Informal labour markets do not lend themselves to the intervention of recruitment agencies. Effective agencies in origin countries can greatly contribute to ensuring healthy functioning of the high level segments of destination labour markets. Therefore, a first effort should be geared towards ensuring a larger role for recruitment agencies in matching supply and external demand for labour in these segments. Naturally, the supervisory and control functions performed by public institutions over agencies should be proportionately reinforced. These supervisory and control functions should be separated from any operational or recruiting functions that public institutions may perform. This effort can then gradually move down to lower levels of the market.

Combating irregular migration and informal employment by migrant workers commands that destination countries modernize their economies and labour markets. In parallel with advances in this process, recruitment agencies may intervene to meet demand in the progressively modernizing segments of the labour market. This intervention will also contribute to the modernization process. In the case of Egypt, a first attempt can be made with countries in Mediterranean Europe in which specific sectors, such as agriculture, construction and hotels and restaurants, pull migrant workers in a diffused manner. Modernization and the intervention of agencies would curb irregular labour migration, on the one hand, and ensure protection and decent terms and conditions of employment for migrant workers, on the other.

The South African experience

Rajendra G. Paratian[1]

Introduction

This paper draws on the South African experience, a major migrant receiving country in the Southern Africa region, in an attempt to show the extent to which all aspects of migrants' control in post-apartheid South Africa have been governed by an outdated and irrelevant piece of apartheid legislation – the Aliens Control Act – at odds with internationally accepted human rights norms and the South African constitution, until it was repealed in September 2002. In fact, prior to this date, South Africa has had an immigration policy of all sorts, subject to a dual system of control known as the "two gates" policy, but no coherent migration policy as such. The two gates were the Aliens Control Act of 1991 and various bilateral labour agreements between South Africa and the governments of Mozambique, Botswana, Lesotho, Swaziland and Malawi.

This long development process towards a more modernized immigration policy, answerable to the present needs of South Africa, can be interpreted as a "best practice" example. However, the specificities of the South African experience, from a historical perspective, dictate otherwise, rendering the "best practices approach" in this case questionable and problematic. In the present economic environment of South Africa where unemployment is soaring, there is always the risk that the new immigration legislations under the Immigration Act of 2002 – although

---

[1] Senior Labour Market Policy Specialist, International Labour Organization, Sub-Regional Office for Southern Africa, Harare, Zimbabwe.

121

commendable – will continue to be used as a threat against migrant workers by unscrupulous employers, taking into consideration the draconian nature of the enforcement strategy envisaged in the legislations. Coordination and harmonization with other Acts is essential to the development of a workable migration policy and legislation. Time will tell how the stated policies are going to be translated into practice and implemented.

Two other specificities of South Africa come to the forefront. First, South Africa does not have the large-scale, organized "guest worker" or "temporary employment" schemes characteristic of other parts of the world where private agents play a determinant role. The unregulated character of foreign worker involvement in the temporary sector poses a particular challenge for regional governments, organized labour and NGOs seeking to improve working conditions and to develop a more humane temporary employment regime. Second, the whole issue of temporary employment in South Africa is inextricably intertwined with the broader issue of undocumented migration. How the South African government responds to this broader challenge is a critical factor in determining the status and security of temporary workers from outside the country. This in turn impacts on how and whether temporary work can or ought to be regulated and managed. The enactment of the Immigration Bill in September 2002 and the repeal of the repressive and obsolete Aliens Control Act is a major policy turning point. The question remains whether in terms of its implementation the government will be preoccupied with control and enforcement as opposed to the Draft Green Paper, which proposed that international migration be refocused as an issue of growth and development.

The context of migration flows in South Africa in the pre and post apartheid era

Exposure to border crossing

Many migrants choose to enter South Africa clandestinely by "border jumping". This is not surprising given that South Africa has 7,000 km of borders with six of the Southern African Development Community (SADC) states, and that these borders are extremely porous, in spite of the installation of electrified fencing, as in the case of Mozambique, and along the northern border with Zimbabwe, where a 137 km electric fence was erected in 1986. Electrified fencing in itself is not an effective deterrent, as it appears to be relatively easy to gain access through or under the fence. South Africa also shares a virtually unguarded 250 km border with Swaziland and a 1,000km border with Botswana. Land-locked Lesotho also shares a permeable boundary with South Africa. Access by non-South African temporary migrants to South Africa is, in reality, virtually unrestricted and probably uncontrollable.

Historically, many of the countries of Southern Africa have supplied or continue to supply contract workers to the mines in South Africa. Three types of suppliers of labour characterize migration flows into South Africa. Mozambique, Botswana, Lesotho and Swaziland are longstanding suppliers with relatively consistent numbers. Malawi and Zimbabwe are the episodic suppliers with fluctuating numbers over time. Zimbabwe withdrew its workers at independence in 1981 and the Malawians were thrown out of South Africa in 1988 following false accusations that they were responsible for spreading AIDS in South Africa (Migration Policy Series No.1). Zambia, Tanzania and Angola were once steady supplier of labour but have only occasiaonally supplied labour since the 1960s.

The South African migrant labour system through contract employment became most dependent on the longstanding suppliers. These countries were, and are, firmly integrated into the regional mine labour market. Importantly, national and household economies of these countries have been, and continue to be, heavily dependent on the system of contract labour. This indicates that their withdrawal or expulsion from the system could adversely affect them.

The migrant labour system, influx controls, single-sex compounds, colour bar, anti-unionism and low wage policies were all characteristics of the South African mining industry, symbolizing some of the central repressive institutions of white domination in South Africa. The citizens of the longstanding suppliers of mineworkers to South Africa have been exposed to rural economic impoverishment, social and family disinte-gration, alarming health problems, and racial oppression that were endemic to the contract migrant labour system.

Prior to 2002, workers from the Southern Africa region entering South Africa legally were subject to a dual system of control, the so-called "two gates" policy mentioned above. The Aliens Control Act, passed in 1991, amended in 1995 and repealed in 2002, was a direct legacy of the apartheid era and was both ideologically and practically ill-suited to

123

present-day realities. Its origin was deeply racist and anti-semitic. It was originally passed in 1937 to exclude German Jews fleeing Nazi persecution from coming to South Africa. It was based on the principles of exclusion and expulsion. Non-South African temporary workers, having few legal modes of access to the South African labour market and being unprotected by law, were vulnerable to the sanctions of the Act. Penalties included criminalization, arrest, imprisonment and summary deportation. However, the Aliens Control Act provided specific exemptions, which made legal and administrative room for labour treaties with other countries and temporary employment schemes for non-South African workers.

The "two gates" policy was discriminatory for two reasons. First, the policy favoured employers of the mine industry over other employers. The mining industry has always enjoyed "special status" as an employer in South Africa. It has always operated outside normal immigration legislation and has not had to be held accountable for its labour sourcing policies like other employers – with the possible exception of commercial farming. The "two gates" policy is a good example of the special status of this employer. Some employer groups, such as the mines and the farms, have continued to enjoy special dispensations to recruit and employ foreign migrants virtually at will and the sectors where temporary workers are concentrated remains largely unregulated. Second, it discriminated against miners who remained perpetual contract workers, who are denied the right to more permanent residence and employment, as envisaged by the Aliens Control Act. Within the regional context, the bilateral accords also provide different terms of access to South Africa for migrants from traditional mine sending areas and other countries such as Zimbabwe, Zambia and Namibia – with which there are no bilateral agreements.

The inter-governmental treaties specify a series of conditions and obligations on the part of both South Africa and the sending countries on the issues listed down in Table 1.

Undocumented migration in South Africa

In South Africa significant numbers of foreign workers, both legal and undocumented, are engaged in temporary work in the mining, commercial agriculture and construction sectors in Gauteng, Northern Province, Mpumalanga and KwaZulu/ Natal. Foreign migrants and immigrants in the service and tourism sectors are performing an increasing proportion of temporary work. The actual numbers involved are

Table 1: Conditions and obligations specified in inter-governmental treaties

Recruitment	Right to recruit, length of contract, length of time between contracts, quotas, payment of recruiting fees, the need for written contracts, and provision of facilities for recruiting and processing contracts.
Contracts	Including identification of employer and employee, home address of recruit, place of employment, contract length, minimum wage, food and in-kind provision by employer, transport to and from work, and written contracts.
Remittances and deferred payment	Provision for compulsory deduction of a proportion of wages and transfer to the home country.
Taxation	Exempting contract workers from paying tax in South Africa.
Documentation	Including valid contract, passports and vaccination certificates; endorsement in passport to show purpose and period of entry; employment record books.
Appointment of labour officials to be stationed in South Africa	The labour offices are nominally responsible for inter alia "protecting the interests of workers," registration of undocumented workers, transfer of money, providing information on conditions of employment, and consulting with the South African government on repatriation of sick or destitute workers.

unknown given that the existing systems of data collection do not capture such entries. The operation of South Africa's temporary employment labour market and the role of non-South African workers is poorly documented and understood. Evidence is partial, fragmentary and unsystematic. It is difficult to determine accurately the number of undocumented migrants, and the participation rates of non-South Africans in temporary employment. There is no systematic collection of employment data by the government in the sectors in which temporary workers tend to be concentrated. Employers tend to be individuals, small companies and contractors. There is no obligation for them to report employment records, and no obligation to distinguish the place of origin of those workers. In the temporary employment sector there are no centralised employment records as there are, for example, for the mining industry.

Non-payment is common on some farms. Conditions are worse for undocumented female and child labourers from Mozambique. The magnitude of unpaid work in South Africa is impossible to figure out with any accuracy. There are no estimates at all for the numbers working in other temporary employment sectors such as construction, transport, tourism and services industries.

Much of temporary work by non-South Africans takes place outside any formal regulatory framework. Temporary employment – of a daily, weekly or seasonal kind – is individualized and "hidden" with little overt monitoring or regulation by government, employers' organizations or unions. The primary reason for this is that many temporary workers within South Africa are undocumented "illegal" migrants.

A significant proportion of the temporary labour force is mobilized through brokers and involved in sub-contracting employment arrangements. Sub-contracting has been growing rapidly in all of the major sectors in which foreign migrants are employed, especially in agriculture, construction and mining. The long-distance formal and sub-contractors extend well beyond South Africa's borders. The purveyors of temporary labour are also particularly well integrated into local urban and rural markets and are able to tap the informal, underemployed labour pool of unskilled and semi-skilled South African and non-South African workers waiting for work on the margins of the formal urban labour market.

Under the former Aliens Control Act, based largely on principles of control, exclusion and expulsion, temporary workers were not only unprotected by law but were vulnerable to its sanctions. It is widely accepted that the flow of both legal and undocumented migrants of the country from the Southern African Development Community (SADC) region and beyond has grown markedly since 1990. Many employers in the temporary work sector are able to find sufficient foreign labour on site or in the vicinity, and do not need to recruit cross-border through recruiting organizations and/or temporary employment schemes. Undocumented migrants are in a vulnerable position since their illegal status puts them beyond protective reach of the law; thus, they are particularly open to exploitation and abuse. The pertinent question in the South African context is, therefore, not how existing temporary employment schemes can be better regulated but whether temporary employment schemes might be an instrument for regularising and legitimising the status of temporary workers who are, at present, without any significant protection.

Since the early 1990s, many mines are increasingly using sub-contractors to organise production sections and to do specialised tasks. Sub-contractors recruit labour from within South Africa but also from Mozambique and Lesotho. They do so with or without Teba's (Employment Bureau of Africa) assistance, which is the largest and most organised broker, now an independent company with a historical monopoly over mine recruiting in all the various states of Southern Africa.

The number of workers employed by mining sub-contractors grew substantially in the early 1990s as well as sub-contracting in coal mining. Already in the 1980s mines have progressively out-contracted non-core functions such as catering and cleaning. In the early 1990s subcontractors became involved directly in production including stopping, sweeping, haulage, meshing and lacing. Contractors have a decided preference for labour from Mozambique and Lesotho. They obtain workers through two sources: a) through recruiting agencies such as Teba which recruit workers to order on non-renewable contracts of varying length; and b) through engaging undocumented migrants (often ex-miners) within South Africa. The exact numbers of subcontract recruits are unknown.

Casual labour and temporary employment is not new in many sectors of the South African economy. A recent feature had been the explosive growth of labour broking. It is estimated that over 100,000 temporary employees are hired through these brokers, of which there were over 3,000 agencies in 1995. Labour brokers have networks that extend well outside South Africa either recruiting them or "sub-letting" them to recruiters. Conditions of recruitment and employment are governed by a series of bilateral labour treaties between South Africa and the surrounding states, and all mine contracts are subject to the conditions and obligations laid out in these accords, as shown in Table 1. Temporary work with mine contractors, unlike in other sectors, is largely governed by bilateral accords and the contract system of the mining industry.

Although miners would once have been classified as "temporary workers," in the last 25 years most have become "stabilised", working continuously on the mines, renewing their contracts each year after a fixed period of leave. Contract labour to the mines falls outside the scope of temporary employment as defined by the ILO (Migration Policy Series No. 1).

All mineworkers recruiting by Teba falls under, and should be consistent with, the treaties as amended from time to time. These conditions are summarised in the standard annual Teba contract for foreign miners. Teba uses a variant of this contract for recruiting temporary workers within the mining industry, particularly sub-contractors' labour. These contracts specify certain minimum levels of remuneration and working conditions. They also underwrite the system of contract migrancy by allowing for the recruitment of single men only. Miners' dependants cannot accompany their spouses to South Africa and miners are contractually committed to return home on expiry of the contract. Most miners are on fixed annual contracts. In case of sub-contracted labour, employer flexibility demands verifiable contract lengths. The labour accords specify maximum contract lengths for all contract workers. Recruiting for contractors by other smaller recruiters, such as Algos and Atas in Mozambique and Ramsdens and Actol in Lesotho, is nominally bound by the terms and conditions of the labour accords. Workers signing these recruiters' contracts can generally expect less favourable terms and treatment than those recruited by the more organised and visible Teba organisation. Sub-contract labour recruited through Teba is subject to the normal terms and conditions of Teba contract, although this offers them little wage protection and no direct protection at work.

The growth of temporary work on the mine through sub-contracting of non-core and core functions has had very direct implications for working conditions in that sector. The National Union of Mines (NUM) claims that subcontracting represents a new path to poverty and oppression. Contractor's labour is temporary labour, generally not unionised and exempted from wage rates negotiated between the NUM and the Chamber of Mines. In 1995, the NUM and the Chamber agreed that all subcontractors would, in future, be compelled to "comply with applicable legislation". Hence there are now legal barriers to join a union. The NUM has been unsuccessful in being involved in all mine decision-making about sub-contracting. The union has also issued a set of guidelines on sub-contracting work. The union wants each mine to provide reasons for contracting and an explanation for why the work cannot be done by regular employees. It asks for details, on a mine-by-mine basis, of the numbers involved; the type of work; the extent of unionisation; and the level of compliance with collective agreements. The NUM also demands that wage rates and conditions of services should be no worse than those of ordinary employees and those sub-contractors be barred from hiring undocumented migrants.

Other sectors, such as agriculture and construction, are also supplied by foreign brokers. In the case of agriculture, recruiters in Mozambique and Lesotho and brokers from South Africa supply workers to farmers or groups of farms, primarily on short contracts for seasonal work. The main supplier in the case of Mozambique is Algos. However, the numbers recruited in Mozambique are very small. Algos has offices in South Africa, which are in a sense "internal recruiters", offering a legalisation service to Mozambicans already in South Africa. Algos also arranges the renewal of contracts for its recruits with the Mozambican labour delegate and local Department of Home Affairs (DHA) offices. In the case of Mozambique there is a subsidiary agreement to the main bilateral accord between the two countries that stipulates the conditions by which farmers in some South African districts can recruit and employ Mozambican farmworkers. A labour exchange was established on the South African-Mozambique border as a recruiting office for Mozambicans seeking entry to work on farms. The office performed a clearinghouse function for white South African farmers in possession of permission obtained from the DHA under Section 41 of the Aliens Act. The use of farmworkers from other countries –such as Lesotho, Swaziland, Zimbabwe and Botswana – does not fall under any bilateral accord. In this case, the provisions of the Aliens Control Act remained applicable. However, various special arrangements under the Act were put in place by the old DHA to regularise the status of undocumented migrant farmhands by allowing post-hoc registration and the issuing of temporary residence and work permits. The effectiveness of these "special arrangements" to protect workers was very much doubtful.

In the late 1980s and early 1990s, formal recruitment of non-South African farmworkers in their country of origin became increasingly unnecessary. The significance of temporary employment schemes regulated by the Mozambican bilateral accord was declining, given that temporary workers of non-South African origin have become increasingly accessible to employers within South Africa itself. This was due to a large-scale movement of refugees out of Mozambique in the 1980s and their resettlement in Bantustan areas close to some of the major farming districts, and to the growing movement of undocumented migrants from neighbouring states to South Africa, many of whom work initially on the farms before moving on to other employment. The refugee movement led to an increase in undocumented migration on a large-scale. Since the end of the war in Mozambique, farmers have had little need for formal recruiting under the contractual conditions of the bilateral agreement.

Most migrant farmworkers from Mozambique and countries such as Zimbabwe, Swaziland and Lesotho are individual temporary workers outside any formal management scheme. Farmers register the workers under "special agricultural permit". Then they register the workers with the Mozambican Labour Representative who organises identification papers and the local DHA office, which issues work permits. The system appears to be extremely lax, with large numbers of workers going unregistered. Even less is known about labour mobilisation and employment strategies in the construction industry, another major employer of non-South African labour.

The changing socio-economic context of South Africa in the mid-1990s and its impact on migration

Factors contributing to the change in shape, scale and scope of migration

Due to a number of factors, the shape, scale and scope of migration have altered significantly since 1994. The dismantlement of apartheid has opened up doors that were previously closed, or only partially open, for many potential migrants, particularly those from the rest of the continent, Asia and the Indian sub-continent. The newly established democracy turned out to become a pole of attraction to people who would normally not have considered South Africa as a receiving country, as well as to those seeking refuge from persecution and war.

The post-1994 restructuring of the economy has both closed and opened doors and opportunities for different groups of migrants. "Rationalisation" has led to massive job losses amongst unskilled and semi-skilled professions where many migrants from the region seek work. The numbers of mine jobs fell significantly due to retrenchments since 1987. Many more South Africans than non-South Africans were laid off during this period, but still contraction in the gold mining sector has reduced opportunities for foreign mineworkers as well. It has also led to significant changes in working practices and loss of income for those now subcontracted to the gold mines. In turn subcontracting has affected the time frequency when these mineworkers can return home.

The spiraling unemployment rate in the strongest economy of the Southern Africa region, soaring at 20 to 40 per cent, and the threat that the wages of illegal workers pose to the current low wage system and scarce social resources, causes unions to give tacit and sometimes overt support to stringent influx regulations. There is also a very strong opinion that the first preference for filling jobs should be given to South African citizens (S. Ryklief, 2003).

Despite the hurdles placed in the way of migrants trying to enter South Africa, with or without documents, it would seem that there has been a numerical increase in the number of migrants and immigrants. The size of these increases is unknown, but evidence suggests that they are not as great as in the imagination of the government and many citizens (Migration Policy Brief No. 10).

The reorganization of the South African economy within the context of globalization and the accompanying persistently high rates of emigration have led to increasing opportunities for skilled workers. Paradoxically, it is often difficult for skilled non-nationals to take advantage of these new openings, in spite of the fact that there is an insufficient supply of South Africans available to fill the new vacancies in the labour market.

Anxieties about documented and undocumented migration in the state and civil society have led to a shift in the way migration policy is implemented and administered. These changes have made it harder, although not impossible, or more inconvenient to be an undocumented migrant as well as to enter South Africa with documents.

Some new patterns of migration have emerged in today's South Africa. There has been a decline in the number of permanent residence and work permits issued to Europeans and North Americans but at the same time the number of tourists from Europe and North America has increased. People from Asia and the Indian sub-continent are working and opening businesses in South Africa, even creating a "Chinatown" in Johannesburg. Africans from the rest of the continent are working in corporate South Africa, running businesses and selling on the streets. Female migrants and immigrants entering as appendages to partners and as independent migrants and immigrants are increasing in numbers. The increasing feminization of agricultural labour has also led to increasing exploitation of these women who are employed in the most abusive areas of employment. Women are also working and migrating as independent entrepreneurs and skilled workers. These are the complex new forms of migration and immigration that are transforming traditional migration dynamics to South Africa.

The rise of xenophobia

Except for the small minority who are part of organized crime networks, research suggests that most migrants are in South Africa to work, to trade, to shop or to visit. In spite of that fact, xenophobic and anti-immigrant rhetoric clouds rational debate within South Africa. The most common charges are that "illegal aliens" cause crime, consume scarce resources, take jobs from South Africans, depress wages, consume social services and exacerbate unemployment (Migration Policy Brief No.10). The fact remains that the state of insecurity is very high in South Africa. A recent study shows that South Africans are more likely to be shot than suffer any other kind of unnatural death as gun crime pushes the country's violent death rate to up to eight times the global average. The survey showed 48 per cent of more than 22,000 unnatural deaths surveyed were caused by violence. Analysts estimate South Africa has between one million and four million illegal firearms in circulation (Zimbabwe Independent, March 24, 2005).

Reported incidents of human rights abuses and violence directed towards foreigners are now common. Bribery and corruption in the police force also abound. In much of South Africa, the term "foreigner" is regularly used to portray a coherent and uniform group of people with South African citizenship. The term "foreigner" is defined in the Immigration Act 13 of 2002, as *"an individual who is neither a citizen nor a resident, but is not an illegal foreigner"*. The term "illegal foreigner" is defined as *"a foreigner who is in the Republic in contravention of this Act"*. Although the difference between documented and undocumented migrants is relatively clearly defined in terms of legality, the two categories are not usually taken into account in practice by law enforcers. The various categories of documented non-nationals in South Africa, including refugees, asylum seekers and people with temporary and permanent residence who are legally in the country and who have applied for, and been granted, permission to reside in South Africa for a specific period, do bear the brunt of xenophobic and hostile attitudes adopted towards them. Non-Governmental organizations and the South African Human Rights Commission are active in their attempts to prevent unlawful arrest and to improve the conditions of detention. Documented migrants, especially black foreigners, are often incorrectly perceived a priori as being illegally in the country and treated as such. Direct human rights abuses and violations directed towards foreigners are often the combined result of xenophobia and other overlapping attitudes of hostility toward foreigners.

Insufficient communication between DHA and SAPS (South African Police Force) in handing over suspects resulted in a number of persons being detained in excess of the 30 days statutory limit on detention pending deportation without review. The Human Rights Commission launched a legal challenge against this DHA's practice. An alleged 1,674 people were detained for over 30 days between March 2001 and March 2002 (Migration Policy Brief No.14).

The turning point – Towards a new system of immigration control based on international norms and constitutional principles

The issues at stake

The exploitative and oppressive labour system that characterized the mines under apartheid and even post apartheid period, governed by the Aliens Act, needs radical changes, which the National Union of Miners (NUM) has been struggling for 15 years. The drive to eliminate the employment of undocumented migrants as temporary workers in mining is orchestrated by the NUM. In other sectors, unions are similarly involved but lack the power to force employers to stop the practice. Evidence concerning the working and living conditions of undocumented migrants in other sectors is anecdotal at best. It is impossible to estimate how widespread the reported abuse is until more research has been conducted.

Overall, if there is agreement that the contract labour system which brings foreigners to work in South Africa is in need of review and transformation, a number of questions can be raised: Can new policies be devised to further that process of transformation and to produce a labour system that is consistent with constitutional principles, democratic practices and human rights? Does transformation mean abolishing the system of contract migration altogether and, if so, how? Should foreign contract workers be treated instead as normal immigrants with the same rights, privileges and obligations? Or is there a case for the continuation of a humanized system of contract migration, which recognizes that not all migrants are or wish to be immigrants? In general, legalized, contract migration and undocumented, informal migration is considered to be linked at the household level. In other words, would the abolition or transformation of the contract system intensify or lessen the pressures for informal migration?

The issue of contract migration reveals that about half of the gold mine workforce is from outside South Africa. With unemployment rates of 20 to 40 per cent in South Africa, and many retrenched South African miners looking for work, should the mines be employing that many foreigners or, indeed, any at all? The regional labour market for contract migration has, over the years, been the object of various forms of political intervention designed to change the system. Any new policy on mine migration should recognize that the supplier states remain heavily dependent on mine employment and that any attempt to summarily eject foreign miners would have dire consequences for South Africa and the supplier states.

New initiatives to address the key migration problems

From the mid 1990's onward, a number of initiatives have been taken in order to address some of the key migration problems raised above. In 1995, following discussions with the NUM and the employers, the South African Cabinet offered permanent South African residence to mineworkers from outside the country who had been working on the mines since 1986 and who had voted in the 1994 election. Although through this miners' amnesty most sub-contracted labour will be unaffected, it does indicate the direction in which the South African government is moving at the executive level in its quest to normalise mine work and transform the migrant labour system to the mines. Of more pressing relevance is the decision, announced in February 1996, to offer a more general amnesty to non-miners. The general amnesty was approved by the Cabinet in February 1996 and handed to the DHA for implementation, in spite of reservation of some quarters in government in terms of consequences of such an amnesty for the country. Anyone is eligible to apply for permanent residence who: is a citizen or permanent resident of a SADC country; has lived continuously in South Africa for longer than five years; has no criminal record; and has been gainfully employed or self-employed since before 1991; or has a spouse or children born in South Africa. What are of interest are the potential implications of legalisation for the hidden temporary work regime in the country. By the end of November 1996, following an extension of the amnesty deadline by two months, about 200,000 people had applied (Migration Policy Series No.1).

Interestingly, in relation to the likely implications of the amnesty, a survey undertaken by the South African Migration Project indicates that over 93 percent of Basotho miners do not see a permanent move to South Africa as a desirable outcome while 68.3 percent of the miners who said they would move to South Africa also indicated that they would keep a home in Lesotho. These findings are highly significant for they contest the assumption commonly made in South Africa that most Lesotho citizens intend to move permanently to South Africa and give up their home country (J. Crush**)

The theoretical interpretation of the amnesty is that long-time undocumented migrants reliant on temporary work can now come out of hiding, regularise their status in the country and seek employment without fear of harassment, arrest and deportation, although this will not put an end to illegal temporary work. The decision does not affect migrants who came to the country in the last five years. This could mean that policing will now be more intensely targeted at the post-1991 immigrants to South Africa. The amnesty could, therefore, have positive consequences for some undocumented temporary workers, in as much as they will move outside the sanction of the Aliens Control Act. For others, it will make very little difference. There will still be employers who will continue to find post-1991 immigrants a better option because of their continued illegality and vulnerability.

The question is which of the various scenarios proposed in the 1990s should constitute the framework within which new policies of transformation are to be debated and developed. There are four basic policy positions currently being articulated in response to the influx of undocumented migrants and, by extension, undocumented temporary workers. The Fortress South Africa model, is the traditional "sealed borders" approach of the ancien regime – meaning blockading 7,000 km land border. The second model suggests that control must be exercised in the heartland not on the borders, making undocumented migrants' lives so insecure and unpleasant that incentives for coming to South Africa are reduced. The third model, which is the free movement model, is more of a vision of the future than a politically viable option, as exemplified by the SADC Draft Protocol on the Free Movement of Persons in Southern Africa. The Protocol would commit the SADC states to a policy of free movement along the European Union model, within ten years. The fourth model is the controlled access model. It is argued that it is better to regularise and monitor the movement of people, who in any case are

135

going to come to South Africa, by legalising it, directing it and managing it, thereby reducing the incentives for rampant corruption, exploitation and abuse (Migration Policy Series No.1).

The implications and impact of each would also vary considerably and these need to be carefully thought through. The normalization scenario is argued to provide the soundest foundation on which to construct a new policy for migrant miners. Prior to the formulation and implementation of a policy of normalization, it is recommended that the miners' amnesty be reopened and extended to miners who have worked continuously on the mines since 1991 (Migration Policy Series No.1).

As mentioned already, prior to 1994, control of migration was highly restrictive and security orientated. Influx controls were governed by the Aliens Control Act. The first migration reform policy was instituted in 1995, with the Aliens Control Amendment Act of 1995, and since then there have been successive reform measures. The South African Citizenship Act, 1995, was followed by the Green Paper, which was introduced in 1997. The Green Paper addressed the institutional and legislative deficiencies that are partly responsible for human rights abuses (Africa Policy E-Journal, 3 June 1998) and which was hoped would provide the blueprint for just, non-discriminatory international migration policy (Migration Policy Brief No.4). The Refugees Act was passed in 1998 and the White Paper came out in 1999. In spite of the fact that the White Paper was criticised on several counts, for example, for the fact that the composition of the Task Team responsible for drafting it was far from being representative and that public inputs appear to have been extremely limited in the drafting stages, with little attempt to draw on groups representing women's interests in the process, it remains the basis for policy reform (Migration Policy Brief, No.4). The Immigration Bill, which was tabled in Parliament in 2001, after four controversial years of formulation, was finally enacted in September 2002. Finally the Aliens Control Act has been repealed, and was replaced by the regulation of Refugees Act of 1998 and the Immigration Act of 2002.

Some key facets of the Immigration Act of 2002

The Immigration Act of 2002 favours strict regulation on immigration, including charging fees to employers for each foreigner employed and aims at setting in place a new system of immigration control which ensures that:

a) Temporary and permanent residence permits are issued as expeditiously as possible and on the basis of simplified procedures and objective, predictable and reasonable requirements and criteria, without consuming excessive administrative capacity;

b) Security considerations are fully satisfied and the State retains control on the immigration of foreigners to the Republic;

c) Interdepartmental coordination constantly enriches the functions of immigration control and that a constant flow of public input is present in further stages of policy formulation, including regulation making;

d) The needs and aspirations of the age of globalization are respected and the provisions and spirit of the General Agreement on Trade in Services is complied with;

e) Border monitoring is strengthened to ensure that borders of the Republic do not remain porous and illegal immigration through them may be effectively detected, reduced and deterred;

f) Ports of entry are efficiently administered and managed;

g) Immigration laws are efficiently and effectively enforced, deploying to this end significant administrative capacity of the Department of Home Affairs, thereby reducing the pull factors of illegal immigration;

h) The South African economy may have access at all times to the full measure of needed contributions by foreigners;

i) The contribution of foreigners in the South African labour market does not adversely impact on existing labour standards and the rights and expectations of South African workers;

j) A policy connection is maintained between foreigners working in the country and the training of South African nationals;

k) Push factors of illegal immigration may be addressed in cooperation with other Departments and the foreign States concerned;

l) Immigration control is performed within the highest applicable standards of human rights protection, and

m) Xenophobia is prevented and countered both within Government and civil society (Immigration Bill).

The objective and functions of immigration control under the new Act are many. Among some of the most pertinent ones, mention can be made of the following which demarcate clearly from the obsolete Aliens Act:

Section 2 (1)

a) Promoting a human-rights based culture in both government and civil society in respect of immigration control;

b) Facilitating and simplifying the issuance of permanent and temporary residence to those who are entitled to them, and concentrating resources and efforts in enforcing this Act at community level and discouraging illegal foreigners;

e) Preventing and deterring xenophobia within the Department, any sphere of government or organ of State and at community level;

h) Ensuring that, subject to this Act, migration to and from the Republic takes place only at ports of entry and illegal crossing of the borders is deterred, detected and punished;

j) Regulating the influx of foreigners and residents in the Republic to promote economic growth, inter alia, by –

(aa) Ensuring that businesses in the Republic may employ foreigners who are needed;

(bb) Facilitating foreign investments, tourism and industries in the Republic which are reliant on international exchanges of people and personnel;

(cc) Enabling exceptionally skilled or qualified people to sojourn in the Republic;

(dd) Increasing skilled human resources in the Republic;

(ee) Facilitating the movement of students and academic staff within the Southern African Development Community for study, teaching and research; and

(ff) Promoting tourism.

Section 2 (2) (f), in cooperation with the Department of Foreign Affairs –

(i) Promote programmes in foreign countries with the aim of deterring people from becoming illegal foreigners; and

(ii) Table the need for cooperation in preventing migration towards the Republic on the agenda of relations with foreign states, negotiating appropriate measures and agreements with such foreign states.

With regard to the question of human rights abuses mentioned above and in an attempt to remedy the problem of animosity against foreigners, the Department of Home Affairs introduced new guidelines for the police in relation to the arrest of illegal immigrants, which came into force in January 2002. Human rights organizations welcomed the policy. Unfortunately, these guidelines were apparently never put into action. Subsequently, unlawful arrests of foreign citizens, and long detention of refugees continued to be reported. If under the Aliens Control Act discriminatory patterns of detention and deportation were the order of the day, given its focus on discretionary action by immigration officers, the Immigration Act with its elaborate system of regulations promises better times. However, it can safely be said that little may change without true leadership and effective implementation.

In respect to regional development, the government favours a policy of regional integration. Already 14 countries involved in SADC agreed in 1996 to phase in a free trade area over the next ten years. The most radical and far-reaching vision for the transformation of Southern Africa's migration regime is embodied in the SADC Draft Protocol for the Free Movement of Persons within Southern Africa. The Protocol proposes progressively freer movement for all people, including job seekers, within the SADC region and the eventual elimination of all border controls within a period of ten years. If adopted, such a plan would mean open access to the South African job market for those from the SADC states seeking temporary work in South Africa. Second, it would discriminate the activities of undocumented temporary workers and bring temporary work above the ground. Third, it would obviate the need for bilateral accords and temporary employment schemes. In effect, there would be a single regional labour market open to all. However, the SADC member states are deeply divided on the Protocol. Within the next three years SADC should be a free trade zone. However, whether the policy of open borders will be instituted is questionable. The scarcity of both work and social resources such as food, water, education and housing in the region, including South Africa, makes this unlikely.

Concluding remarks

The Aliens Control Act was repressive and discriminatory and provided few answers and little vision for the governance of temporary migration for employment across national borders in Southern Africa.

After years of debate, the need to bring all immigration under a single Immigration Act was felt. Policy makers needed to make a clear distinction between migration and immigration and between temporary and permanent migration. In behaviour and intention, many temporary workers are migrants rather than immigrants. They come to South Africa for a specific purpose and intend to go back in due course. There was a policy gap that clearly required attention. What was also needed was a new multi-lateralism in the area of population movement, akin to those developing for trade, infrastructure and investment.

Many commentators have noted that the White Paper was unclear on numerous policy issues, sometimes making definitive recommendations and sometimes merely speculating on whether some measures might be desirable. Nonetheless, the Bill does contain many positive elements that are far superior to the Aliens Control Act which are enshrined in the Immigration Act (Migration Policy Brief No.2, 2001). In addition, the White Paper proposed a hierarchical approach to immigration policy in which the SADC countries would have "Preferred Status". It is important to note in this context that none of the SADC countries have ratified the ILO Convention on Migrant Workers adopted in 1975, which seeks to promote respect for migrant workers' human rights regardless of whether they are legally or illegally employed.

Moving from the White Paper, the South African government's effort for its ongoing commitment to developing a new immigration and migration policy framework, which finally led to the passage of the South African Immigration Act of 2002, is highly commendable, in spite of some potential gaps in the design and implementation.

Gender concerns have been markedly lacking in the development of a new national policy on international migration to South Africa, both in the policy-making process and in the content of the Green and White Papers. Yet according to ILO sources, women account for 49 percent of the world's migrants and are increasingly traveling on their own as their family's primary income earner (ILO, International Labour Conference, Report VI 2004). Given the lessons of international experience, as well as recent advance in the understanding of the relationship between gender, migration and development, this represents a major oversight. In the further development of policy, as well as in the drafting and implementation of subsequent legislation, gender considerations must be systematically included. This is important as the meaningful basis for a socially just, economically effective, and administratively workable policy framework in South Africa.

The South African labour market is highly stratified by gender, which provides very different incentives and opportunities for labour migration by males and females. Increasingly the only legal way for a SADC citizen to work in South Africa is in the mining industry. Yet 99 percent of mine employees are male. There is no equivalent employment sector for women in which there is comparable ease of entry.

The introduction of the new Immigration Act is unlikely to make a significant difference to most potential migrants, unless they are planning to work for a large corporation or institution. Similarly, it seems that the Act, despite its stated aims and objectives, is unlikely to dissipate the hostile environment that permeated the lives of many non-nationals, particularly those from the rest of Africa. Whatever legislation is in place, it is how it is administered that will shape future patterns of migration (Migration Policy Brief no.10).

Resources should be devoted to systematic and rigorous programme of sectoral and community-level research focused on the sectors in which temporary employment is prevalent – mining, agriculture, construction and the service industry. It is recommended that the government institute a formal enquiry into the labour practices and working conditions in the temporary employment sector.

References

Africa Policy E-Journal: Abuse of undocumented migrants, asylum-seekers, and refugees in South Africa, June 1998.

Bhorat Haroon, Lundall and Rospabe Sandrine: The South African labour market in a globalizing world: Economic and legislative considerations, Employment Paper 2002/32, Employment Sector, ILO, Geneva, 2002.

Crush Jonathan and Williams Vincent (edited by): NEPAD, the city and the migrant: Implications for urban governance, Southern Africa Migration Project, Migration Policy Brief No. 12, 2004.

Crush Jonathan and Williams Vincent (edited by): Gender concerns in South African migration policy, Southern Africa Migration Project, Migration Policy Brief No.4, 2001.

Crush Jonathan and Williams Vincent (edited by): The new South African Immigration Bill: A legal analysis, Southern Africa Migration Project, Migration Policy Brief No.2, 2001.

Crush Jonathan and Williams Vincent (edited by): The South African White Paper on International Migration: An analysis and critique, Southern Africa Migration Project, Migration Policy Brief No.1, 2001.

Crush Jonathan and Williams Vincent (edited by): The point of no return: Evaluating the Amnesty for Mozambican refugees in South Africa, Southern Africa Migration Project, Migration Policy Brief No. 6, 2001.

Crush Jonathan, Ulicki Theresa, Tseane Teke and Jansen van Vuuren Elizabeth: Undermining labour: Migrancy and sub-contracting in the South African gold mining industry, Southern Africa Migration Project, Migration Policy Series No. 15, 1999.

Crush Jonathan: A bad neighbour policy? Migrant labour and the new South Africa, Africa Policy E-Journal, March 1997.

Crush Jonathan: Covert operations: Clandestine migration, temporary work and immigration policy in South Africa, Southern Africa Migration Project, Migration Policy Brief No. 1, 1997.

**Crush Jonathan: Contract migration to South Africa: Past, present, and future (not dated, see http://www.polity.org.za/html/govdocs/green_papers/migration/crush.html).

Crush Jonathan and Williams Vincent (edited by): Thinking about the brain drain in Southern Africa, Southern Africa Migration Project, Migration Policy Brief No. 8 (not dated).

Crush Jonathan and Williams Vincent (edited by): Criminal tendencies: Immigrants and illegality in South Africa, Southern Africa Migration Project, Migration Policy Brief No. 10 (not dated).

Crush Jonathan and Williams Vincent (edited by): Policing migration: Immigration enforcement and human rights in South Africa, Southern Africa Migration Project, Migration Policy Brief No. 14 (not dated).

Crush Jonathan and James Wilmot (edited by): Crossing boundaries – Mine migrancy in a democratic South Africa, assisted by Moira Levy, Janet Levy & Gail Jennings IDASA/IDRC, Cape Town, 1995.

Dodson Belinda: Women on the move: Gender and cross-border migration to South Africa, Southern Africa Migration Project, Migration Policy Series No. 9, 1998.

Fultz Elaine and Pieris Bodhi: The social protection of migrant workers in South Africa, ILO/SAMAT Policy Paper No.3, Harare, 1997.

ILO: Summary Report and Conclusions of the Tripartite Forum on Labour Migration in Southern Africa, Pretoria, South Africa, 26-29 November 2002.

ILO: An overview of some issue and trends in migration, standards and policies for the Tripartite Forum on Labour Migration in Southern Africa, Pretoria, South Africa, 26-29 November 2002.

ILO: Towards a fair deal for migrant workers in the global economy, Report VI, International Labour Conference, 92nd Session 2004.

ILO: ILO Migration Survey 2003: Country summaries, Social Protection Sector, International Migration Programme, ILO, Geneva, 2004.

ILO: Reports on the knowledge network meetings, World Commission on the Social Dimension of Globalization, Policy Integration Department, ILO, Geneva, March 2004.

ILO: Labour migration to South Africa in the 1990s, ILO/SAMAT Policy Paper No.4, Harare, 1998

Haroon Bhorat, Jean- Baptiste Meyer, Cecil Milatsheni: Skilled labour migration from developing countries: Study on South and Southern Africa, ILO, International Migration Papers 52, 2002.

McDonald David A, Mashike Lephophotho and Golden Celia: The lives and times of African migrants & immigrants in post-apartheid South Africa, The Southern African Migration Project, Migration Policy Series No. 13, 1999.

Republic of South Africa: Immigration Bill, Ministry of Home Affairs, 2001.

Rogerson C. M: Building skills: Cross-border migrants and the South African construction industry, Southern Africa Migration Project, Migration Policy Series No. 16, 1999.

Rogerson C.M: International migration, immigrant entrepreneurs and South Africa's small enterprise economy, Southern Africa Migration Project, Migration Policy Series No. 3, 1997.

Sahra Ryklief: Migrant workers in South Africa: A brief overview, Paper to be presented to SASK Solidarity Seminar on Migrant Workers, 5-6 April 2003, Lahti, Finland, March 2003.

Southern African Migration Project: Migration News, November 2004.

Stalker Peter: Global nations – The impact of globalization on international migration, International Migration Papers 17, Employment and Training Department, ILO, Geneva, 1997.

Standing Guy, Sender John and Weeks John: Restructuring the labour market: The South African challenge, An ILO country review, ILO, Geneva, 1996.

Wickramasekara Piyasiri: Policy responses to skilled migration: Retention, return and circulation, Perspective on Labour Migration 5 E, Social Protection Sector, International Migration Programme, ILO, Geneva, 2003.

Zimbabwe Independent: March 24, 2005.

Part III: Recruitment and ILO standards

ILO standards concerning employment services

Eric Gravel[1]

Early ILO standards on employment services

The first ILO instruments which addressed the question of employment services date back to the origin of the Organization, in 1919. That year, the International Labour Conference adopted the Unemployment Convention (No. 2), which provided for the establishment of "a system of free public employment agencies under the control of a central authority", and, where both public and private employment agencies existed, "for the coordination of their operations on a national scale". The same year, the first paragraph of the first International Labour Recommendation, which also dealt with unemployment, recommended that every State should "take measures to prohibit the establishment of employment agencies which charge fees or which carry on their business for profit" and that, where such agencies already existed, "they be permitted to operate under government licenses, and that all practicable measures be taken to abolish such agencies as soon as possible".

Public employment services

Nearly thirty years later, in 1948, the International Labour Conference adopted Convention No. 88 on Employment Service and supplementary Recommendation No. 83, both instruments considering full employment to be the outcome of a rationally organized employment

---

[1] Team on Employment and Social Policies and Tripartite Consultations, International Labour Standards Department, ILO.

market. Convention No. 88, which has been ratified by 86 countries, provides that ratifying States "shall maintain or ensure the maintenance of a free public employment service", the essential duty of which "shall be to ensure the best possible organization of the employment market as an integral part of the national program for the achievement and maintenance of full employment and the development and use of productive resources". The Convention also stipulates that workers' and employers' representatives must be associated in the functioning of such services and in policy implementation.

Fee-charging employment agencies

The specific question of fee-charging employment agencies, which had a notoriously negative image in view of certain abuses, was addressed during the Great Depression and was the subject of a Convention adopted in 1933 (No. 34). This Convention provided for the abolition of fee-charging employment agencies, with certain exceptions contained in Article 3, in exceptional cases and only after consultation of the organizations of employers and workers concerned. It is interesting to note that in drafting this instrument, there was an indication that the International Labour Conference was concerned both with the prevention of abuse as well as the organization of the labour market.[2] Convention No. 34, which stipulated that fee-charging employment agencies were to be abolished within three years of the coming into force of the Convention for the Member State concerned, was only ratified by 11 countries and was revised by a new Convention (No. 96) in 1949 to introduce more flexibility in the treatment of this question. Once the new Convention came into force, Convention No. 34 was no longer open to ratification.[3] Convention No. 96 concerning fee-charging employment agencies leaves the ratifying States the choice either of prohibiting the existence of such agencies (Part II of the Convention), or of regulating their activities (Part III). For Member States that accept the first alternative, the Convention provides that fee-charging employment agencies conducted with a view to profit should be abolished within a limited period of time determined by the competent authority. However, Article 3(2) provides that this

---

[2] ILO: Record of Proceedings, International Labour Conference, 16th Session, Geneva, 1932, p.280.

[3] In fact, as of today, Convention No. 34 is still in force for only two Member States, Chili and Slovakia, both of which have expressed their intention to ratify the up to date standard on this question.

abolition should not take place until a public employment service is established. Of the 42 States that have ratified Convention No. 96, a great majority has accepted the first alternative offered by the Convention.

It is worth recalling that the application of Convention No. 96 gave rise to certain problems regarding the placement of performers and domestic servants, and later in the seventies and eighties with the widespread establishment of fee-charging employment agencies. Furthermore, with the development of temporary work agencies, the question had arisen as to whether these agencies were covered by the Convention. The question was put to the ILO in 1965 by the Government of Sweden and the reply from the Office was that these agencies were indeed covered by the definition of fee-charging employment agencies conducted with a view to profit given by the Convention. In view of these developments, it is interesting to note that as early as the beginning of the 1970's, Nicolas Valticos, then Chief of the ILO International Labour Standards Department, had already foreseen the necessity to revise Convention No. 96 and had wondered whether it would not be appropriate to move at the international level towards the adoption of new standards in this field. [4]

New standards on private employment agencies

But it was only at the 81st Session of the International Labour Conference in 1994 that the role of private employment agencies in the functioning of labour markets was included in the agenda for a general discussion. The Conference reached the conclusion that Convention No. 96 should be revised, since Part II of the Convention appeared to be removed from current practice in most labour markets, and Part III did not entirely reflect current realities, mainly because of its narrow scope and its inflexible type of supervision. This led to the adoption, three years later, of a new Convention (No. 181) and a supplementary Recommendation (No. 188) on private employment agencies, both instruments recognizing the contribution of private employment agencies in the functioning of the labour market and in the protection of temporary workers. The adoption of these new instruments marked an important change in

---

[4] See Nicolas Valticos, "Temporary Work Agencies and International Labour Standards," International Labour Review, January 1973, pp. 43-56.

the relations between public and private employment agencies as it moved away from the traditional ILO standards that had largely recognized a public sector monopoly in the provision of labour market services. This was clearly expressed in the preamble of Convention No. 181, which considers "the very different environment in which private employment agencies operate, when compared to the conditions prevailing when Convention No. 96 was adopted". The preamble also recognizes "the role which private employment agencies may play in a well-functioning labour market" and recalls "the need to protect workers against abuses". It also recalls the provisions of the Forced Labour Convention, 1930 (No. 29), the Freedom of Association and the Protection of the Right to Organize Convention, 1948 (No. 87), the Right to Organize and Collective Bargaining Convention, 1949 (No. 98), the Discrimination (Employment and Occupation) Convention, 1958 (No. 111), the Employment Policy Convention, 1964 (No. 122), the Minimum Age Convention, 1973 (No. 138), and the provisions relating to recruitment and placement in the Migration for Employment Convention (Revised) 1949 (No. 97), and the Migrant Workers (Supplementary Provisions) Convention, 1975 (No. 143). Convention No. 181 thus strikes a balance between the recognition of the productive role that can be played by private employment agencies in the delivery of specific labour market services, and the need to ensure that the basic rights of workers are protected.

Convention No. 181 defines the term "private employment agency" as "any natural or legal person, independent of the public authorities, which provides one or more of the following labour market services":

(a) Services for matching offers of and applications for employment, without the private employment agency becoming a party to the employment relationships which may arise;

(b) Services consisting of employing workers with a view to making them available to a third party, who may be a natural or legal person which assigns their tasks and supervises the execution of these tasks;

(c) Other services relating to job seeking, determined by the competent authority after consulting the most representative employers' and workers' organizations, such as the provision of information, that do not set out to match specific offers of and application for employment.

While Article 2 provides that the Convention applies to all categories of workers and all branches of economic activity, except seafarers, it is important to note that the new Maritime Consolidated Convention, which should be adopted in February 2006, will ensure that seafarers have access to an efficient and well-regulated seafarer recruitment and placement system.

Articles 4, 5, 9 and 11 of the Convention deal with the protection of the workers recruited by the agency. These guarantees concern fundamental rights at work such as freedom of association and the right to collective bargaining, equality of opportunity and treatment and banning of child labour. Special protection to migrant workers is laid down in Article 8, which provides that "Members should seek adequate protection for and prevent abuses of migrant workers recruited or placed in its territory by private employment agencies. These shall include laws or regulations which provide for penalties, including prohibition of those private employment agencies that engage in fraudulent practices and abuses."

While Article 13 of the Convention calls for the promotion of cooperation between public employment service and private employment agencies, the Convention stipulates that this cooperation is to be based on the principle that the public authorities retain final authority for formulating labour market policy and for utilizing or controlling the use of public funds earmarked for the implementation of that policy.[5]

Recommendation No. 188 calls, amongst other things, on States to combat unfair advertising practices and misleading advertisements, including advertisements for non-existent jobs, and requires that the agencies should not knowingly recruit workers for jobs involving unacceptable hazards or risks. It also recommends that the contract of employment be in writing. As for cooperation between public employment services and private agencies, the Recommendation includes the following:

(a)   "Pooling of information and use of common terminology so as to improve transparency of labour market functioning;

(b)   Exchanging vacancy notices;

(c)   Launching of joint projects, for example in training;

(d)   Concluding agreements between the public employment service and private employment agencies regarding the execution of certain activities, such as projects for the integration of the long-term unemployed;

---

[5] In this regard, see also Articles 1 to 3 of the Employment Policy Convention, 1964 (No. 122) and the General Survey on Employment Policies, Report III, (Part IB), International Labour Conference, 2004.

(e)   Training of staff;

(f)   Consulting regularly with a view to improving professional practices."

Ratification of Convention No. 181 and comments of the Committee of Experts

As of today, 18 countries have ratified Convention No. 181, the most recent one being Bulgaria in March 2005.[6] It came into force in May 2000. While the number of ratifications up until now could be perceived as relatively low, it has to be pointed out that Convention No. 181, unlike Convention No. 182 which was adopted two years later, has never been the object of a promotional campaign from the Office. Therefore, the pace of ratifications, which has been relatively consistent in the past few years, can appear reasonable. Furthermore, while two countries are still bound by Convention No. 34, and 28 countries are bound by Convention No. 96, most of these countries have expressed their intention to ratify Convention No. 181.

The Constitution of the ILO sets out the obligation for Member States to submit regular reports on their legislation and national practices for each of the Conventions that they have ratified.[7] In 1926, the International Labour Conference adopted a resolution providing for the establishment of a Committee responsible for examining the reports submitted thereof. The Committee of Experts on the Application of Conventions and Recommendations, composed of high-level jurists of independent standing, thus became the body responsible for the technical and legal supervision of the application of international labour standards.

In examining the reports of the Governments, the Committee of Experts draws up two types of comments: observations and direct requests. Observations are written comments relating to the application of a ratified ILO Convention. In general, observations are made in cases of serious and persistent failure to comply with obligations under a

---

[6] Albania (1999), Belgium (2004), Bulgaria (2005), Czech Republic (2000), Ethiopia (1999), Finland (1999), Georgia (2002), Hungary (2003), Italy (2000), Japan (1999), Lithuania (2004), Republic of Moldova (2001), Morocco (1999), Netherlands (1999), Panama (1999), Portugal (2002), Spain (1999), Uruguay (2004).

[7] See Articles 19, 22 and 35 of the ILO Constitution.

Convention and are published each year in the report of the Committee of Experts,[8] which is transmitted to the International Labour Conference. The observations provide the starting point for the examination of specific cases by the Conference Committee on the Application of Standards.

The Committee of Experts also addresses a number of comments directly to Governments instead of including them in its report. These direct requests usually deal with more technical issues, or are questions that are addressed for the first time following a first report from a Government on a recently ratified Convention. Copies of such direct requests, as it is the case for observations, are also addressed to the representative organizations of employers and workers in the country concerned.

While it is not the role of the Committee of Experts to promote the ratification of a particular Convention, it is worth mentioning that in its comments to Governments on the application of Convention No. 96, the Committee has systematically reminded the Governments concerned of the invitation addressed by the ILO Governing Body to the States parties to Convention No. 96 to contemplate ratifying, as appropriate, the Private Employment Agencies Convention (No. 181);[9] the ratification of which would, ipso jure, involve the immediate denunciation of Convention No. 96.[10]

In the specific case of Convention No. 181, the Office has received the first reports of ratifying States since 2002. The Committee of Experts has thus started examining these reports and has initiated a constructive dialogue with the Governments concerned by making a number of comments regarding the application of the Convention in law and in practice. In its direct requests, the Committee has, on several occasions, made reference to issues raised under ILO fundamental Conventions, such as violations of freedom of association or the use of child labour. In this regard, the Committee has reminded Governments that the professional qualifications required to obtain a license are not enough to guarantee in practice the absence of the use of child labour by private employment agencies and that the incorporation of a prohibition on child labour in

---

[8] See for instance 2005 Report of the Committee of Experts on the Application of Conventions and Recommendations, Report III (Part I A), International Labour Conference, 93rd Session, 2005.

[9] For example, see 2004 comments of the Committee of Experts under Convention No. 34 for Slovakia and Convention No. 96 for Luxemburg, Mauritania, Poland, Senegal, Sri Lanka and Turkey.

[10] See document G.B: 273/LILS/4 (Rev.1), 273rd Session, Geneva, November 1998.

the conditions for awarding a license to a private agency should be envisaged.

With regard to migrant workers, the Committee has consistently asked the various Governments to indicate the measures adopted to prevent fraudulent practices or abuses by private employment agencies in relation to such workers. [11] Furthermore, the Committee has persistently asked Governments to provide detailed information on any bilateral agreements that might have been concluded to prevent abuses and fraudulent practices in the recruitment, placement and employment covered by the Convention. [12] In its dialogue with ratifying States, the Committee of Experts has also suggested to Governments to refer to the Conclusions on a fair deal for migrant workers in a global economy, which were adopted by the International Labour Conference at its 92nd Session in June 2004. Finally, it has to be pointed out that the dialogue between the Committee of Experts and the various Governments on these issues is just at its initial stage, as several more reports from Governments on the application of Convention No. 181 are expected to be examined by the Committee this year and in the coming years.

Final remarks

If the early ILO standards concerning employment services considered that the public service would ensure the needs of workers and the business community as far as recruitment was concerned, a climate of economic liberalism and international competition led to the recognition that private employment agencies, with appropriate regulation, could contribute positively to the functioning of the labour market. Moreover, the fact that public employment services, with their resources being downsized in several countries, were unable to provide all job seekers with services, contributed to the debate and the realization for the need of new international standards in this field. This recognition, and the following tripartite discussion which took place within the Organization, paved the way for the adoption in 1997 of new international labour standards on private employment agencies, namely Convention No. 181 and Recommendation No. 188.

---

[11] See for example 2004 direct request of the Committee of Experts concerning Spain. Direct requests are available on line on the ILO website www.ilo.org, with a link to International Labour Standards.

[12] See 2002-2004 direct requests of the Committee of Experts under Convention 181 for Albania, the Czech Republic, Ethiopia, Italy, Japan and the Netherlands.

But as fee-charging recruitment agencies are increasingly involved in international migration, and as some recruiters have engaged in unfair and abusive practices, efforts should be increased both at the national and international levels to further regulate this market and ensure proper application of existing rules. In this regard, the licensing and supervision of recruitment and contracting agencies for migrant workers in accordance with ILO Convention No. 181 and Recommendation No. 188, with the provision of clear and enforceable contracts by those agencies, should be a key element in that process. But these efforts should also include promotion for wider ratification of Convention No. 181 and subsequent implementation by ILO Member States, in order to prevent abusive practices by certain recruiters and ensure greater respect of workers' rights.

ILO Convention 181: The employers' perspective

Christian Hess[1]

C. 181 on Private Employment Agencies (1997) – the employers' perspective

Convention 181 was elaborated and adopted with the support of the employers. The Convention has been considered by the ILO's Governing Body, namely the Working Party on Policy regarding the Revision of Standards of the Committee on Legal Issues and International Labour Standards (LILS), as an up-to-date instrument.

Yet Convention 181 has shortcomings, reflecting some mistrust in the functioning of labour markets. For instance, the Convention unduly restricts the charging of fees to workers by private employment agencies, see Art. 7. It also calls for minimum wages, which potentially discourages legal migration and encourages illegal migration, see Art. 11 paragraph (b).

Nevertheless it is major progress on Convention 96 on Employment Agencies (1949). While Convention 96 basically aimed at an abolition of private employment agencies, Convention 181 explicitly states as one of its purposes *to allow the operation of private employment agencies* (Art. 2). Moreover, the Preamble of Convention 181 recognizes:

- *the importance of flexibility in the functioning of labour markets; and*
- *the role which private employment agencies may play in a well-functioning labour market.*

---

1 Senior Adviser, Bureau for Employers' Activities, ILO.

In this way, Convention 181 reconciles two goals. Firstly, a better functioning labour market and full employment, and secondly, the protection of workers using the services of private employment agencies.

Unfortunately, Convention 181 has so far not been widely ratified. There have been 13 ratifications from European, in particular Eastern European countries, but only two ratifications from African countries, two ratifications from Latin American countries and one ratification from an Asian country. One reason for this relatively low ratification record may be insufficient visibility as there has never been a promotional campaign for this Convention. But there may be also other reasons.

Information about the implementation of Convention 181 – and possible difficulties and obstacles in this regard are only now becoming available: Convention 181 entered into force in May 2002 and the first reports due under Article 22 of the ILO Constitution have recently been received by the Office.

Possible ILO action to promote Convention 181

The ILO, in close cooperation and coordination with its constituents, could take the following action to promote Convention 181. Foremost, it could **collect information on implementation and difficulties in its application**, for instance, through a general survey under Article 19 of the ILO Constitution. Furthermore, the ILO may **facilitate the decision of ratification** for countries considering ratification, as well as **implementation** for countries having already ratified it. Action in this regard could include to collect, develop and update material on implementation (tool-box approach); to

- provide commentary on the interpretation of provisions;

- provide guidelines, e.g. the *Guidelines on special protective measures for migrant workers recruited by private agents* (1997); but also guidelines on improving the functioning of private employment agencies in helping better match demand and supply in the labour market; and

- keep a collection of good practices.

It would be vital that this material be made easily available, including on the Internet.

Furthermore, in close cooperation and coordination with its constituents, **the ILO could provide complementary technical cooperation to implement Convention No. 181.** It could, for instance, help **private** employment agencies better match demand and supply in the labour market and develop self-regulation. Also, the ILO could provide support to strengthen the capacities of **public** employment agencies (rules are also needed for them) and promote better cooperation between private and public employment agencies.

The ILO could also assist in the organization of awareness-raising campaigns, particularly in labour-sending countries and in the dissemination of good practices/lessons learnt by other countries as regards law and practice.

The ILO can facilitate bilateral agreements/cooperation between countries on extending legal migration and on better control of illegal migration.

Additionally it can help labour-sending countries in improving their labour market policies with a view to promoting investment, growth, proper education/training and full employment, thus reducing undue pressure on workers in labour-sending countries to migrate.

References

ILO Convention 181 on Private Employment Agencies (1997)
ILO Convention 96 on Employment Agencies (1949)

Private employment agencies: The challenges ahead from the workers' perspective

Luc Demaret[1]

The ILO Private Employment Agencies Convention (No. 181) offers better protection for temporary migrant workers and an opportunity for employers in the industry to combat unfair competition and clean its record, undermined by abuses. But will Convention 181 prevail over the liberalising spree in services? Much depends on the ILO staying on course with its decent work agenda and on ongoing campaign by trade unions.

Trade unions – inspired by the ILO Philadelphia Declaration according to which "Labour is not a commodity" – have always been suspicious of private employment agencies. Among key concerns has been the fate of migrant workers recruited by dubious private agencies in the developing world or exploited by Temporary Work Agencies on their arrival in the industrialised countries. Facts have proven these concerns to be right on too many occasions. In a report[2] tabled to the 85th session of the International Labour Conference in 1997, the ILO noted "many of the private employment agencies do not overstep their legal boundaries and contribute to national development. However, a disturbing number of them, often not widely known, exploit both workers and the countries involved, including the host countries." Later during the same year, Trade Union World,[3] the monthly paper published by the Inter-

---

[1] Focal Point for Migration, Bureau for Workers' Activities, ILO.

[2] ILO: *Revision of the Fee-Charging Employment Agencies Convention (Revised), 1949 (No. 96)*, Report IV (Part 1), 85th International Labour Conference, June 1997, page 11.

[3] ICFTU: "Modern-day slavery for temporary migrants", in *Trade Union World*, No. 3/97, November 1997, Brussels.

national Confederation of Free Trade Unions (ICFTU) said that "accusations against (these recruitment) agencies are beginning to accumulate throughout the world." Entitled "Modern-day slavery for temporary migrants," the article detailed abuses such as fictitious job offers, for a fee, the withholding of information, or false information on the nature of the job and the conditions of employment, the charging of fees above the legal maximum and even, in the worst of cases, mafia style-trafficking.

In one Gulf country quoted in the ICFTU article, 300 nationals were at the time suspected of dealing illegally in work permits. They were accused of recruiting Asian and Arab workers via agents abroad and in exchange for up to 3,000 dollars per head provide them with visas and promise them jobs. The promised jobs did not exist and the company that was supposed to employ them was fictitious. In an Asian country, some 60 local recruitment agencies were involved in smuggling workers abroad with the complicity of high-ranking officials from the police and the government. Cases like these have been regularly denounced by trade unions and non-governmental organizations. In fact, the trade union and ILO concerns for malpractices by unscrupulous employment agencies probably date back to the ILO's very inception. As recalled by Eric Gravel, the very first ILO Recommendation adopted in 1919 called on member States to "take measures to prohibit the establishment of employment agencies, which charge fees or which carry on their business for profit." Until very recently most trade unions would have supported that approach.

In 1980, the Swiss trade unions for instance, called for legislation prohibiting temporary work agencies, as "trade unions can not accept that workers are placed in employment by intermediaries seeking profits out of this operation." More recently, in April 2005, the Secretary-General of the Malaysian Trades Union Congress, Mr. G. Rajasekaran called for "all middlemen or recruiters to be eliminated."[4] He was speaking at a regional workshop on migrant workers jointly organised in Petaling Jaya by the MTUC and the ILO. According to reports from the meeting, Mr. Rajasekaran quoted many cases of foreign migrant workers being cheated of their savings by unscrupulous agents who demanded large sums of money to obtain the necessary papers, which were normally forged travel documents.

---

[4] Reported in *New Strait Times*, 20 April 2005.

Abuses were also recently revealed in Dubai where, according to newspapers, security guards who initially had signed a foreign service agreement with a basic salary of about 225 US dollars had seen their wage reduced to 185 dollars in the employment contract upon arrival in Dubai and again lowered to 150 in a revised contract later in the year.

It is in that context of abuses and calls for prohibition of private employment agencies that ILO Private Employment Agencies Convention (No.181) adopted in 1997 has to be considered. It was clear in 1997 that prohibition of private employment agencies was leading nowhere. At that time, it was said, for example, that fee-charging private agencies represented 80 per cent of all movements of labour from Asia to the Arab States. In Europe the growth of jobs provided by temporary work agencies was estimated at 10 per cent a year from 1991 to 1998.[5] The challenge for trade unions was how to ensure protection for the millions of workers who were calling for the services of recruitment or temporary work private agencies.

Employers also had an interest in promoting the recognition of private employment agencies. Convention 96, the Fee-Charging Employment Agencies Convention that dated from 1949 provided for the abolition of such agencies (art. 3). A new Convention would give an opportunity to adopt a more flexible approach that was actually more in line with reality. It would also provide an opportunity for the industry to revamp its image and put in place a number of regulations that would force black sheep out of business.

Indeed, abuses by unscrupulous private agencies either recruitment and employment agencies or temporary work agencies had cast opprobrium on the whole sector. Like trade unions, employers had also to adopt a new approach. For many years, they had resisted attempts by governments to regulate the profession. For example, in 1995, one month after the Migrant Workers and Overseas Filipinos Act was adopted in the Philippines, the Philippine Association of Service Exporters, Inc. (PASEI) filed a petition to nullify the law. The laws had been passed after abuses of Philippines maids in the foreign countries made headlines, including the Flor Contemplación case. A 42-year-old Filipino maid, Flor Contemplación was convicted by a Singaporean court of killing another

---

[5] ICFTU : "Modern-day slavery for temporary migrants", in *Trade Union World* No. 3/97 November 1997, Brussels. Reported in *New Strait Times*, 20 April 2005.

Filipino maid, Delia Maga and Nicholas Huang, the three-year-old Singaporean son of her employer on May 4th 1991. She had originally confessed to the murders. It was, however, later claimed that she made the confession under duress. She was hanged before dawn on Friday 17th March 1995.

PASEI had sought self-regulation in the overseas placement industry. According to a recent editorial published in the Manila Times "It wanted private initiatives to promote the welfare of migrant workers and to contribute to the country's socio-economic development."[6] When the Manila Regional Trial Court declared certain provisions of the Act unconstitutional in early 2005, PASEI saw this as a victory for free enterprise while the government announced it would appeal the decision. Much as prohibition of private employment agencies did not work, self-regulation of the industry did not prevent abuses that damage the entire sector. In 1999, in the General Survey on the ILO Migrant Workers Conventions (Nos. 97 and 143), the ILO Committee of Experts on the Applications on Conventions and Recommendations noted that not a single government nor an employer or a worker organisation had provided information that would enable it to determine whether self-regulation was indeed a widespread means of regulating the industry.

Convention 181 offered a solution both for trade unions seeking to protect workers employed through recruitment or temporary work agencies and for employers seeking to project an improved image and lay out a number of basic rules to be applied by all.

Not surprisingly, one of the key provisions of Convention 181 applies to migrant workers. Article 8 of the Convention says "Members should seek adequate protection for and prevent abuses of migrant workers recruited or placed in its territory by private employment agencies. These shall include laws or regulations which provide for penalties, including prohibition of those private employment agencies that engage in fraudulent practices and abuses."

Since the Convention recalls in its preamble the provisions of the Forced Labour Convention, 1930, the Freedom of Association and the Protection of the Right to Organise Convention, 1948, the Right to Organise and Collective Bargaining Convention, 1949, the Discrimination

---

[6] *Manila Times*, 18 January 2005.

(Employment and Occupation) Convention, 1958, the Employment Policy Convention, 1964, the Minimum Age Convention, 1973, the Employment Promotion and Protection against Unemployment Convention, 1988, and the provisions relating to recruitment and placement in the Migration for Employment Convention (Revised), 1949, and the Migrant Workers (Supplementary Provisions) Convention, 1975, it can be assumed that "protection for and prevent abuses of migrant workers" covers the human rights of all migrant workers, their equal treatment and opportunity (Convention 143) as well as the rights for *all* migrant workers to form trade unions and bargain collectively, including those contracted by agencies.

Beyond those basic rights for migrant workers, or actually any worker employed through a private agency, Convention 181 contains a number of important features. A number of provisions require consultation with the most representative organizations of employers and workers and/or conformity with national law and practice. It is assumed that the consultation process envisaged in the Convention refers to employers and workers organization in the country where the actual employment is taking place, not the recruitment country if the workers have been recruited abroad. Similarly reference to national legislation and practice is meant to suggest legislation and practice in the country of employment.

Hence after having considered the respective role of private and public employment agencies for decades (Convention No. 34 on fee-charging employment agencies dates back to 1933), the ILO tripartite partners have agreed to a Convention the purpose of which "is to allow the operation of private employment agencies as well as the protection of the workers using their services" (Convention 181 Art 2). Workers had to overcome their initial opposition to any kind of private employment agencies and employers had to accept that recognition of the contribution of private employment agencies could not be obtained without some regulations being put in place. This includes a system of licensing and certification, the prohibition of private agencies to charge any fees or cost to workers and the establishment of respective responsibilities of the employment agencies and of the user enterprise in a number of key areas such as collective bargaining, minimum wage, working time, etc.

The question for today and for tomorrow is to what extent the provisions of the Convention and the promotion of its ratification can be reconciled with efforts at regional and global levels to liberalise services.

The "Bolkestein Directive"

Today, 18 countries have ratified Convention 181. This includes countries in the European Union (Belgium, the Czech Republic, Finland, Hungary, Italy, Netherlands, Portugal and Spain). What would be their situation if the proposal for a European Directive on "services in the internal market," also known as the "Bolkestein Directive" were to be adopted?

On 13 January 2004, the then Internal Market Commissioner, Frits Bolkestein, submitted a draft Directive which is, according to the European Commission, aimed at creating a real internal market in services by requiring European Union members states to cut administrative burdens and 'excessive red tape' which are seen as preventing businesses from offering their services across borders or from opening premises in other member States. This might be seen as a positive step that can unleash energies and create wealth as well as jobs in the European Union.

However, trade unions and non-governmental organizations have sounded the alarm as to the contents of the draft directive. A number of governments, including Belgium and France, have followed suit. So what is wrong with Mr. Bolkestein's initial proposal?

First, the liberalisation proposal would apply to temporary employment agencies with, according to trade unions, a potential risk for social dumping. This is because of the "the country of origin principle", according to which once a service provider (such as for instance a temporary work agency) is operating legally in one Member State, it can market its services in others without having to comply with further rules in these 'host' member state. In other words, countries that would have put in place legislation to regulate employment agencies in line with the obligations of Convention 181 may have "to eliminate from their legislation a number of requirements listed in the Directive that hamper access to and the exercise of service activities," according to the authors of the draft Directive.

The system of certification, which is provided for in the Convention, does not fit with the Draft Bolkestein Directive. In fact once a temporary work agency complies with establishment requirements in one European Union member country (for instance one that has not ratified the ILO Convention) it would be free to move to another EU country without further obligations. That would clash with obligations under

Convention 181 if the country of destination has ratified this instrument. Only if EU member states would harmonize their legislation, in line with the provisions of Convention 181, would such a clash be avoided. But the Draft Directive does not contemplate harmonization.

The fears of trade unions are, therefore, that the country of origin principle comes down to a legal incentive for companies to move to countries with the least strict legislation on social, fiscal and environmental issues, and the creation of letter box companies offering services at low prices, which will be able to operate from their registered offices across the whole territory of the Union. Even if the temporary work agency has to pay the legal minimum wage in the country where it sends its workers, it could still chose for headquarters a country where taxes, social contributions and other cost are lower. The "anti-Bolkesteiners" have been accused of scare mongering. Yet some recent developments may give us a taste of what is in the can for the future should the draft Directive be adopted (which seems now unlikely because of growing opposition, including from a number of EU governments themselves).

In Belgium, for instance, an ice-cream company, Frisa, has told its work council that it will recruit Polish workers through a German temporary work agency to meet demand in the peak season.[7] The Poles are paid by piece. Another temporary work agency, Eurostar 25, based in the Netherlands, is also recruiting Polish workers for the Belgian market. In fact, it recruits Poles who have double nationality (German-Pole), which enables them to work in Belgium. The difference is their salary: they work for 6,40 euros an hours while salaries in Belgium should be closer to 8 euros. "Some people are using the liberalisation of the market to impose unacceptable working conditions in our country," said Greta D'hondt, a member of Parliament. The Labour Minister Freya Van den Bossche said an inquiry has been launched into the activities of the temporary work agencies concerned. She reminded that temporary work agencies should have an authorisation to provide services in Belgium and violation of this rule can be used to sanction them. What will happen if the draft Directive, which would eliminate such a requirement, were to be adopted?

On 19 April 2005, the rapporteur of the European Parliament, Evelyne Gebhardt, presented the first part of her report on the 'Bolkestein

---

[7] This was reported in Belgium's Flemish Weekly "Trends" dated 10 March 2005. Subsequently the question was raised in Parliament and Labour Minister Freya Van den Bossche confirmed that an investigation was underway.

Directive.' According to a press release from the European Trade Union Confederation, Ms. Gebhardt "tries to get it right and excludes, from the outset, labour relations and services of general interest from the scope of the directive." The ETUC said it was waiting for the second part of the report. It added: "It is important to make the directive watertight against social dumping, and totally to exclude labour and employment law from the scope of an internal market directive."[8]

It warned, however, that there were still some unconditional supporters of the initial Bolkestein draft who continued to stress the importance of the country of origin principle - which Ms. Gebhardt has deleted and replaced with mutual recognition.

GATS

The proposed Bolkestein Directive should not be looked at in isolation nor should it be considered accidental. The political will to liberalize services exists at global level. There is a concern among trade union organizations and NGOs for the existence and preservation of public services and social security, which may become victims of the prevailing trade agenda. In that context, a parallel can be drawn between the proposed EU Directive and the General Agreement on Trade in Services (GATS). The GATS agreement was negotiated during the Uruguay Round and entered into force in the beginning of 1995 when the World Trade Organisation replaced the GATT secretariat.

According to the GATS Agreement, "trades in services" is defined as the supply of a service:

1. From the territory of one member into the territory of any other member (selling goods or products by post or over the internet, e.g., insurance, e-products etc.)

2. In the territory of one member to the service consumer of any other member (tourism for instance)

3. By a service supplier of one member, through commercial presence in the territory of any other member (establishing a company or a subsidiary and investment)

---

[8] ETUC: "Ms Gebhardt's report on services is a step in the right direction", ETUC press release, Brussels, 20 April 2005.

4.   By a service supplier of one member, through presence of natural persons of a member in the territory of another member (labour migration).

These modes of supply are usually called modes 1, 2, 3 and 4.

For the purpose of this article our attention will be brought to the latter. GATS mode 4 indeed covers a very particular form of migration. It has three essential features:

a.   It is temporary

b.   The service supplier controls its purpose and prompts it.

c.   It neither defines nor protects the rights of the employees concerned.

Labour migration under GATS mode 4 is temporary migration at the initiative of the employer for the provision of a service. It has therefore nothing to do with freedom of movement for workers. Clearly there is a risk that mode 4 migration will lead to a situation where labour under WTO rules becomes a commodity. Although Mode 4 is about people, human rights, workers' rights and working conditions are not mentioned in the GATS Agreement. This may be corrected if requests, offers and commitments by members do include reference to those rights. However, this is far from certain.

To be fair, the WTO does not seem afraid of debating the issues. On its website it tries to explain the various aspects of these negotiations and their potential impact. It recognizes that "Recently, however, the negotiations and the GATS itself have become the subject of ill-informed and hostile criticism." Additionally, "Scare stories are invented and unquestioningly repeated, however implausible. It is claimed for example that the right to maintain public services and the power to enforce health and safety standards are under threat, though both are explicitly safeguarded under the GATS. How have serious people come to believe what is, on the face of it, out of the question? Why should any Government, let alone 140 Governments, agree to allow themselves to be forced, or force each other, to surrender or compromise powers which are important to them, and to all of us?"

This is all reassuring, but recall the Multinational Agreement on Investments, the famous MAI negotiations in the OECD, which collapsed in 1998. The aim of the agreement was to extend deregulation by giving multinational investors a guarantee that their foreign direct investment would not suffer from measures a national government may take to protect their national interests, its enterprises or its citizens. Designed to facilitate and expand international investment by preventing discrimination between national and foreign investors, the MAI was to be applied to emerging and developing economies. Trade unions had fought to include in the treaty an obligation to respect labour standards by means of a binding clause which would allow for steps to be taken against any government seeking to attract foreign investors by lowering its labour standards or violating internationally recognised workers' rights. Proponents of the MAI said it was inevitable. Yet the failure to enlist public support, despite very reassuring language, brought to MAI to a death.

This parenthesis brings us back to what will be the key challenges in ensuring that private employment agencies involved in migration contribute positively to the economic development of countries of origin and countries of destination by promoting decent work. A balance will have to be struck between the needs of labour markets and the human and employment rights of migrant workers, including equal treatment and respect for labour legislation in the countries of destination. This is what ILO Convention 181 is about. The question is: will it prevail over the present liberal trade agenda?

Implementation of Convention 181 through regulation—The ILO experience

Ellen Hansen[1]

Introduction

Growing international trade and other aspects of globalization, the accelerated development of information and communication technologies, the increase in temporary and part-time work, and growing unemployment have changed labour markets and given rise to the emergence of private employment agencies (PREAs) in those countries where they did not exist previously.

For much of the twentieth century the potential for abuse and exploitation of workers overshadowed the benefits of PREAs, and they were banned in a number of countries. However, the above changes in the structure and operation of labour markets have presented expanding opportunities for PREAs, and they are now increasing in many countries. The growing recognition of their positive contribution has led to a reconsideration of their role. This new attitude was codified in ILO Convention No. 181 on Private Employment Agencies, adopted in 1997. This Convention balances the recognition of the productive role that can be played by PREAs in the delivery of specific labour market services with the need to ensure that the basic rights of workers are upheld.

The Private Employment Agencies Convention also responded to the growing pressures faced by firms as a result of increasing international competition. The Convention balances firms' needs for flexibility to

[1] Senior Employment Services Specialist, InFocus Programme on Skills, Knowledge and Employability, ILO.

expand or reduce their workforce with workers' needs for employment stability, a safe work environment, decent conditions of work, and a safety net when they are unable to work. The Convention proposes criteria as a means of striking this balance.

However, there are two clarifications or delineations to be made at the beginning. First, Convention 181 does not resolve the issue of who is accountable for staff in the employment relationship—the issue of the scope of the employment relationship. The ILO has no standard in this area, although the topic will be under discussion again at the 2006 ILO Conference. In Convention 181, the government, in accordance with national law and practice, is vested with the responsibility to allocate the responsibilities between agencies and user enterprises.

This allocation of responsibilities covers the areas of:

(a) Collective bargaining;

(b) Minimum wages;

(c) Working time and other working conditions;

(d) Statutory social security benefits;

(e) Access to training;

(f) Protection in the field of occupational safety and health;

(g) Compensation in case of occupational accidents or diseases;

(h) Compensation in case of insolvency and protection of workers claims;

(i) Maternity protection and benefits, and parental protection and benefits.

(Article 12).

Second, there is often confusion in understanding the roles of government as they relate to public employment services as opposed to private employment services.

In the first case, the government is the financier and usually the direct provider of services, including job placement or labour exchange, labour market information and labour market programmes. Increasingly in some developed countries, however, this role is contracted out in part to private non-profit or for-profit employment agencies. But in all cases the government remains the source of funding. When the government provides the funding there are mechanisms within the contracting process to enforce adherence to rules.

However, in the case of private employment agencies as businesses that rely on customers paying privately, the government's role is to regulate them as businesses. In this role a government needs to determine whether or not private agencies can operate as businesses, and, if so, under what conditions. This regulatory role of government over the functioning of business exists over many sectors of private economic activity.

It should also be noted that this responsibility for regulating private employment agencies can be delegated to sub-national level, particularly in federal states.

ILO role in reviewing private employment agency operation

Since the adoption of Convention 181, the ILO has not launched a promotional campaign. Instead, the chief activity of the ILO has been to comment on draft national legislation regarding the operation of private employment agencies. In the last four years, sixteen draft bills on public employment services or private employment agencies have been commented upon, and the vast majority have been concerned with private employment agencies. Based upon this experience and discussions with constituents over the same period, some observations can be made about the regulation of private employment agencies. Four areas for attention are noted.

Definition of private employment agency

First of all, it is imperative that the definition of private employment agency be included in the legislation, because there are a number of different interpretations of the term. Convention 181 defines three types of agency(ies), but there are many possible specific definitions. It may also be that only certain types of private agencies are targeted for regulatory action. In addition, multiple laws can cover different categories of private employment agency(ies).

Private employment agencies in Japan, for instance, fall into three categories, each with specific license provisions: 1) job matching services, 2) temporary work, and 3) advertisement services of vacancies. There are two types of temporary work businesses; one is a general temporary work business and the other is a specific temporary work business. [2]

---

[2] Law for Proper Operations of Temporary Work Businesses and Improved Conditions of Work for Temporary Workers, Law no. 88 dated July 5, 1985 (Tokyo).

171

Prerequisites for operation of a PREA

Second, some basic prerequisites need to be established which form the basis upon which a private employment agency can operate legitimately. At a minimum, the following requirements for the operation of a private employment agency are suggested:

– Registration of the business (with possible payment of a registration fee);

– Registration with other government business regulation and tax authorities as appropriate;

– Agreement to comply with all the appropriate labour laws and equal opportunity laws;

– Agreement to report periodically on agency activities;

– Agreement not to collect fees from work seekers (unless specific exemptions are made in the law; and

– Agreement to maintain confidentiality of client and work seeker personal information.

In this way, the intent is to apply currently existing legislation and regulations to protect workers wherever feasible.

Additional prerequisites for operation

Additional prerequisites for the operation of private employment agencies are found in some countries. These additional prerequisites are often designed to prevent some commonplace abuses. These prerequisites could include:

– Demonstration of lawful behavior;

– Demonstration of sound managerial capability;

– Demonstration of financial resources; or

– Demonstration of professional competence.

The difficulties in these prerequisites lie in the standard of proof necessary to satisfy the requirement. Definition of what constitutes adequate financial resources can vary. Not supplying precise definitions leaves interpretation up to the discretion of individual government officials, which is not advisable.

In Germany, for example, a license for job placement is issued when four requirements are met:

1) The applicant possesses the required suitability for job placement. This is defined as at least three years of work which involved tasks in the field of personnel management, job placement, personnel consultation or the supply of temporary workers, as well as a recognised vocational qualification or a degree from a university or other higher education establishment;

2) The application must demonstrate that the applicant does not have a criminal record;

3) The applicant must demonstrate sound financial circumstances; and

4) The applicant must provide a business site which is used solely for business purposes. [3]

In Singapore, the requirements are defined somewhat differently:

1) The applicant must operate the agency on a full-time basis;

2) The applicant must have an appropriate agency premise;

3) The applicant must be the owner of the agency;

4) The applicant must be 25 years old and above;

5) The applicant must possess at least 5 GCE "O" Level of National Skills Qualification Evaluation;

6) The applicant must be a Singapore citizen or its permanent resident;

7) The applicant must attend and pass the Certificate for Employment Agency Course. [4]

In the case of overseas employment agencies additional requirements are suggested to address common abuses in this form of private employment agency:

– A non-national should have his or her credentials reviewed and authenticated;

– An applicant agency should document its financial capability to support international operations when required, to sustain possible claims for compensation by national workers or foreign employers or other business partners, to satisfy the legal requirements for cash-

---

[3] Walwei, Ulrich, "Job Placement in Germany: Developments Before and After Deregulation," IAB, Labour Market Research Topic no. 31, 1998, p. 12 (Berlin).

[4] http://www.gov.sg/mom/mandev/ea/ea2.htm 08.11.2001.

bond deposits, surety bonds or other financial guarantees that may be needed to carry out recruitment activities.[5]

Government regulatory responsibility

At the outset, any legislation or regulations should clearly state the government's authority to regulate in this area and should identify the responsible Ministry or agency.

Second, at a minimum the government's activities in relation to enforcement of the law and/or regulations should include:

1. Administration of registration procedure and (possible) collection of registration fees;

3. Monitoring of agency activities (desk audit of information provided and/or field audits);

4. Assessment of penalties for non-compliance with laws or regulations;

5. Administration of a complaint procedure for workers; and

6. Information reporting to responsible authorities.

Perhaps the most important point to be made is that the laws and regulations established should be within the capacity of the government to enforce thoroughly.

The UK, with over 8,200 private employment agencies, is a case in point. Just regarding the administration of a complaint procedure, approximately 10,000 telephone complaint calls were received in 1998 alone and 1,300 formal investigations were initiated.[6]

Conclusion

These comments are based upon approximately five years of experience in reviewing draft laws regarding the regulation of private employment agencies plus some preliminary research on the topic.[7] A great deal more research in this area could be useful to clarify the most important regulatory issues and provide more guidance on the development of legislative guidelines.

---

[5] ILO, SEAPAT W. Böning et al, Working Paper No. 3, "Protecting Indonesian migrant workers, with special reference to private agencies and complaints procedures," pp.14-15, 1998 (Manila).

[6] ILO, ATLAS database, 19.11.2003 (Geneva).

[7] This paper draws heavily on research conducted by former ILO labour economist Alexander Samorodov.

Combating criminal activities in the recruitment of migrant workers

Beate Andrees[1]

Introduction

In a recent investigation on human trafficking, a Ukrainian agent who advertised jobs in the local newspaper recruited a couple to work in the Czech Republic. The job turned out to be much different than advertised. Both the Ukrainian recruitment agent and the Czech employer threatened the workers and forced them to work without pay. A draft bill to regularize the business of private recruitment agencies is currently pending at the Ukrainian parliament. In the absence of clear standards, however, the recruitment industry has mushroomed under the disguise of travel agencies or other business. Workers have hardly any possibility to distinguish between trustworthy agents and those involved in criminal activities. As a consequence, they prefer to rely on personal networks such as friends, relatives or neighbours. One can assume that the case of Ukraine is symptomatic for many other countries in the world.

The following article will explore international standards that provide guidance on the eradication of informal or outright illegal recruitment practices. The challenge is to develop regulations and enforcement mechanisms in national law that address abusive recruitment under disguise as well as through illegal channels. These mechanisms should entail punitive measures as well as positive incentives – that is to stimulate informal recruiters to come forth and establish a legitimate business and to punish those who continue using illegal means to make quick profits.

---

[1] Anti-Trafficking Specialist, Special Action Programme to Combat Forced Labour, InFocus Programme on Promoting the Declaration, ILO.

175

The article evolves in three parts: the first section will give a brief overview of existing empirical evidence on the role of illegal and abusive recruitment in international trafficking chains drawing on recent ILO research carried out in Europe. The second section will highlight the relevance of international standards, in particular the ILO Private Employment Agency Convention, 1997 (No. 181), the ILO Forced Labour Convention, 1930 (No. 29) and the Palermo Protocol to Prevent, Suppress and Punish Trafficking in Persons, Especially Women and Children, supplementing the UN Convention against Transnational Organised Crime (henceforth the Palermo Protocol). Other international standards, such as ILO Conventions on migrant workers, have been discussed elsewhere and will therefore not be treated in this paper. In the final section, some proposals for enforcing these standards at the national level are presented.

Informal recruitment in migration: Empirical evidence from Europe

Many migrant workers experience violations of their fundamental rights. They may face discrimination foreign to local workers, and are often prevented from joining a trade union. One of the worst violations experienced by a significant number of migrant workers in today's world is the inability to change employment due to threats or coercion. Recruitment plays a key role in these modern forms of forced labour as, for example, when workers are held in a situation of debt bondage to pay off a recruitment fee. In 2003, the ILO Special Action Programme to Combat Forced Labour carried out a survey among 644 returned migrant workers in Albania, Moldova, Romania and Ukraine. [2] 300 of them experienced certain forms of coercion while working abroad, such as physical and sexual violence, restriction of the freedom of movement or retention of identity documents combined with threats.

The research identified several factors that make some migrant workers more vulnerable to coercion than others. One important factor was the channel of recruitment the respondents choose. The graph below shows that victims of forced labour rely more on intermediaries that are not part of their social network. Successful migrants, on the contrary,

---

[2] ILO survey on human trafficking and forced labour in Eastern Europe, unpublished document.

have better social and family connections or direct contacts with the employers. Victims of forced labour also depend on social connections but these connections are less reliable.

The most important result with regard to the questions raised in this article, is the fact that only about 12 per cent in both groups used formal employment agencies. This has important implications in terms of law and policy as will be discussed below.

Way of obtaining a job offer abroad

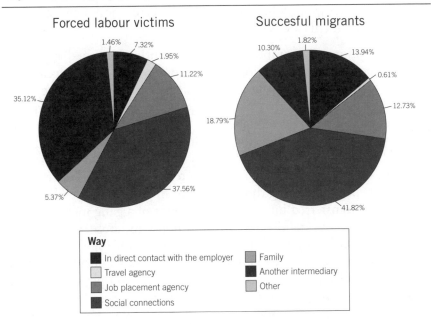

The data from these four Eastern European countries can be complemented by research results from major European destination countries. In the Russian Federation, for example, most migrant workers are recruited informally and scam operations are widespread. In a survey of 360 migrant workers, only 4 per cent indicated that they used official channels of recruitment.[3] Intermediaries approach incoming migrants at train or bus stations and transport them to construction sites or other places of employment. Sometimes, intermediaries travel to villages in the source countries to recruit workers. Below is an extract from an interview with a Russian recruiter:

---

[3] Tyuryukanova, Elena (2005): Forced Labour in the Russian Federation Today – Irregular Migration and Trafficking in Human Beings, ILO Geneva.

*"Organizing migration includes smuggling of migrants, job placement, settle-
ment and sometimes temporary registration. The trip from Uzbekistan to
Stavropol lasts approximately one week. We use either private or public buses.
The main problem is that the police collect "tributes" along the road. At some
places, if it is a big construction site (for example, an entertainment complex),
migrants live on the worksite."*

The respondent also admitted that migrants give him from a quarter to a third of their earnings. In addition, reductions are made for
expenditures that he had to make: bribes for the police, rent for the workplace, fees for temporary registration, food, accommodation, etc. Passports and documents are usually confiscated.[4]

The following example is from a recently published report on
forced labour in the United Kingdom: A group of Eastern Europeans was
brought to the UK by a gang to work illegally in a factory. They were
originally informed that they would be provided with regular work permits, but en route were given false British passports. When they realized
that they would be in the UK illegally they attempted to leave the gang's
control but with no success. They had to work seven days a week for one
year with no pay because they needed to repay their "debt" incurred for
various expenses, including those related to migrating to the UK. Their
salaries were transferred into the bank account of a gang member. They
were watched very carefully, moved from house to house, and kept isolated. If they broke any conditions, for example, if they spoke to anyone,
they were fined and this was all noted down in a book and added to their
"debt." Control was maintained through beatings and physical assault.[5]
Another report on "gangmasters" in the UK concludes: "we received a
wealth of evidence describing a range of abuses by some gangmasters.
Such abuses are often connected to the deductions made from wages to
pay for accommodation, travel to and from the workplace, and, in some
cases, the cost of coming to the United Kingdom."[6]

Abuses in the recruitment process are also gender-specific. Women
find it often more difficult to access formal recruitment channels, either
through private recruitment agencies or public employment services.
Female victims of trafficking indicated that they have been recruited

---

[4] Opus cit.

[5] Anderson, Bridget et al. (2005): Forced labour and migration to the UK, Trade Union Congress,
London.

[6] House of Commons (Environment, Food and Rural Affairs Committee): Gangmasters, Fourteenth
Report of Session 2002-2003, HC 691.

through friends or acquaintances, often, a woman already inside the trafficking chain. Married couples who offer assistance to impoverished families by recruiting the daughter and different types of cover agencies, such as modeling and entertainment agencies, tourist agencies, beauty contest, mail-order-bride or au pair agencies also serve as a means of recruitment. In most of the trafficking cases, women are deceived about the real nature of their work (i.e. prostitution) and sometimes also the destination country.[7]

These examples illustrate practices at the fringes of the labour market. They often escape the normal labour inspection routine as they operate in a grey zone between organised crime, illegal employment and sub-standard work. There is little research into the extent of these activities, partly due to the difficult nature of the subject. One can assume that there is a wide spectrum of illegal operations, ranging from sophisticated criminal networks at one end and semi-legal private agencies at the other end. Private recruitment is a dynamic business with fairly low entry barriers. Many recruiters are involved in other business activities or change their profile entirely when transaction costs increase – usually in the case of tighter controls. While "soft methods" of control, such as administrative sanctions, combined with positive incentives may be sufficient to clean up mainstream business, there have to be more efforts to prosecute those who are involved in criminal operations.

International standards on trafficking and recruitment

The ILO Private Employment Agencies Convention (No. 181) provides a definition of private employment agencies (PEAs) that is broad enough to cover a whole range of recruiters. In particular Art. 1 (c) refers to "other services relating to job seeking, determined by the competent authority after consulting the most representative employers' and workers' organizations, such as the provision of information, that do not set out to match specific offers of and application for employment." This definition could encompass some of the agencies that pose as travel, entertainment or professional career agencies through which people are

---

[7] ILO survey on Eastern Europe. See also: Nikolic-Ristanovic, Vesna et al. (2004): Trafficking in people in Serbia, Victimology Society in Serbia/OSCE, Belgrade.

trafficked. However, national legislation and regulations hardly ever specify these various types of agencies. Where a licensing system is in place, it usually targets easily identifiable PEAs, whereas, others are simply required to register with the state tourism authority (i.e. travel agencies) or like any other business (i.e. entertainment, fashion or model agencies).

C. 181 defines PEAs as "any natural or legal person". This may cover individual recruiters who have not set up a registered or licensed business. Further, in Art. 2 (2) it is stipulated that: "This Convention applies to all categories of workers and all branches of economic activity." The only exception is the recruitment and placement of seafarers. In practice, however, many informal economic activities as well as individual recruiters escape state regulations and are difficult to monitor. Even though the Convention and Recommendation No. 188 provide some guidance on the types of abuses that should be eliminated, they give little indication of how this can be done. Reference is made to "laws and regulations, which provide for penalties, including prohibition of those private employment agencies, which engage in fraudulent practices and abuses" (Art. 8.1). Penalties are not specified any further, and it remains unclear whether the drafters also considered criminal sanctions. Fines or revocation of a licence is not a sufficient deterrent for recruiters with a criminal energy as described in the first section.

Criminalizing recruiters who are involved in trafficking of human beings is a major feature of the Palermo Protocol. It defines trafficking as "the recruitment, transportation, transfer, harbouring or receipt of persons, by means of the threat or use of force or other forms of coercion, of abduction, of fraud, of deception, of the abuse of power or of a position of vulnerability [...] for the purpose of exploitation [...]" (Art. 3a). As such, the definition covers many forms of abusive recruitment as described above. State Parties are required to make these activities criminal offences when committed intentionally (Art. 5.1). The Protocol makes no reference to individual recruiters or PEAs specifically. It implies, however, that any legal or natural person engaged in one of the activities by using illegitimate means for the purpose of exploitation as specified in Art. 3 will be liable under criminal law.

The Palermo Protocol entered into force in December 2003 and as of July 2005, 87 States have ratified it. Ratification has been accompanied by changes in national legislation, often spearheaded by regional bodies such as the EU or ECOWAS. In Europe, major source countries of trafficking victims, such as Ukraine or Moldova, were among the first to introduce new legislation and prosecute traffickers. Prosecutors often target the recruiters since employers are at the other end of the trafficking chain and out of reach for national enforcement agencies in origin countries. Increasing cooperation among source and destination countries is likely to change this.

In addition, law enforcement activity has focused primarily on organised criminal networks most of which are involved in trafficking for sexual exploitation. While this is important, it has left the "petty crime" of smaller scam operations largely untouched. It has also prevented law enforcement agencies from focusing more holistically on forced labour, which can occur in a range of economic sectors. Advocacy on the ILO Forced Labour Convention, 1930 (No. 29) in relation to trafficking has helped to broaden this approach. In contrast to C. 181, C. 29 has a penal approach. It specifically requests State Parties to make the use of forced labour, and in particular the forms of coercion associated with it, a penal offence.[8] This may also apply to coercion occurring in the recruitment process, such as debt bondage.

A combined approach of ILO Conventions that generally favour administrative sanctions and the Palermo Protocol that puts emphasis on criminalization is therefore most likely to address all possible abuses in the recruitment industry. While criminal law should be the ultima ratio only, labour law offers a more gradual set of sanctions. The following section gives some ideas of how this can be done in practice.

Monitoring and enforcement

The first step in the development of an effective monitoring and enforcement mechanism is to improve the understanding of how the industry operates. In the United Kingdom, for example, several studies were conducted before a new licensing system for labour providers in agriculture was introduced.[9] The newly established Gangmaster Licensing Authority also made an assessment of the likely number of labour

---

[8] ILO (2005): Human Trafficking and Forced Labour Exploitation, Guidance for Legislation and Law Enforcement, Geneva.

[9] Temporary Labour Working Group (2004): A license to operate. New measures to tackle exploitation of temporary workers in the UK agriculture industry. (Editor's note: For more details on this see the contribution of Dan Rees in part IV of this volume.)

providers and their risk-profile. This will allow for a targeted monitoring approach where efforts are concentrated at the lower end of the spectrum.

Secondly, there has to be coordinated action between different law enforcement agencies in origin and destination countries. Recruiters who are involved in the recruitment and placement of migrant workers operate across borders. Experience has shown that they are very agile in changing locations and advertisement strategies. Labour inspectors usually alert police officers if there is an indicator that criminal activities are taking place under the cover of a PEA. However, if there is no coordinated action between these agencies, some cases may fall through the system. It is therefore important to develop an institutional framework that coordinates activities of various enforcement agencies. A mechanism of cooperation with trade unions and NGOs should also be in place as these organisations are often the first to receive complaints from duped or abused migrant workers.

Thirdly, law enforcement authorities can use a wide range of evidence to ensure convictions. This can also include intelligence, such as telephone or Internet surveillance. Victims of abusive recruitment practices are, however, the most important source of information. It is therefore imperative to empower migrant workers to come forth and report on the wrongs they have suffered. Migrants in an irregular status are especially in need of protection so that they are not deported before they can submit their claims. Legal and socio-economic assistance as well as the possibility of permanent residence should be granted to those who have been identified as victims of human trafficking.

Finally, sanctions will be more convincing when combined with positive incentives for law-abiding agencies. In countries with weak labour market institutions and law enforcement structures, PEAs find it very difficult to compete against criminal recruiters. Government authorities should therefore promote the activities of legally operating PEAs in the spirit of C. 181 and R. 188. Positive incentives have to be awarded according to the same criteria that stipulate sanctions. This can go hand in hand with measures of self-regulation, such as code of conducts or ratings. [10] Experience has shown that law-abiding PEAs have an interest in self-regulation if this helps to fight against unfair competition and if they can expect favourable government treatment.

---

[10] For more information see ILO (2005): Human Trafficking for Forced Labour: How to Monitor the Recruitment of Migrant Workers, Geneva.

Conclusion

This paper has argued for a combined approach of ILO and UN Conventions that stipulate administrative as well as criminal sanctions against abusive recruitment agents. New international standards that prohibit trafficking in human beings for the purpose of forced labour have helped to raise awareness on abusive recruitment practices in the migration process. Research into the nature of the trafficking cycle has shown that recruitment can play a key role in creating vulnerabilities in the final employment stage. Given existing restrictions on legal migration, many migrants fall prey to unscrupulous intermediaries who exploit their ignorance and their lack of financial resources. Excessive recruitment fees levied on prospective migrants are often the first step into the cycle of dependency and coercion.

While national regulations and enforcement strategies have to be reinforced to address these criminal practices, it is likewise important to develop positive incentives to reward law-abiding agencies and to encourage cover agencies to identify themselves. However, as long as legal possibilities of migration are highly restricted, PEAs will find it difficult to enter the market. Competition of informal smuggling and trafficking networks will remain a strong obstacle to the promotion of legal recruitment practices.

Part IV: Innovative policy and possible protection strategies

Strategies to combat forced labour in the context of migration

Mary Cunneen[1]

First, I would like to place the current discussions in a more structured policy framework, looking at forced labour within the context of migration, in particular in the informal sector. Then, I would like to look at the experiences of migrant workers themselves, and from these suggest that to protect migrant workers it is necessary that policy responses are set within a comprehensive human rights framework, protecting both migrant rights and core labour standards.

We are all well aware that the growing inequality of wealth within and between countries is increasing, leading more people to make the decision to migrate in order to seek a better life abroad. Equally, we are aware that the globalised nature of the economy is leading to increasing flexibility of the workforce, with deregularisation, movement, and informalisation. We are seeing this not only within traditionally informal sectors, but also sectors that are moving from formal to informal as well as those sectors that may not always be recognised as work.

Allow me to give you three practical examples from our own work at Anti-Slavery International.

First, in bonded labour in South Asia, we are seeing a change from the traditional, "feudal" relationships in agriculture, where often there was a long-term relationship between the bonded labourer and the landlord, that went beyond a purely economic relationship, to newer forms of bondage, both in agriculture and elsewhere in the economy. In these newer forms of bondage, labourers are often migrants, in short term

---

[1] Director, Anti-Slavery International, London, United Kingdom.

185

economic contracts with the employer. In some ways the relationship is harsher; there is no responsibility on the part of the employer for the bonded labourer in times outside the working contract, and as migrant workers, bonded labourers are in a weak position to negotiate favourable contractual terms.

In relation to previously formal sectors, such as construction, we are seeing increased infomalisation, through the use of migrant workers, short-term contracts, sub contractors and agents. An example of this is given in Bridget Anderson's recent research in the UK. The research showed that migrant nurses in the National Health Service, which is usually perceived as a highly formal, regulated sector, had been employed through the use of sub-contractors and agents. The nurses were paid, after unlawful deductions, £46 per week. When they tried to complain, they were informed that they would be viewed as untrustworthy, and so not registered as nurses in the UK.

Sectors such as domestic work are also highly informal, or not regarded as a work sector at all. We have recently been carrying out a programme of work looking at the conditions of migrant domestic workers in the Gulf States and Middle East. Work permits typically tie the worker to one employer, and contracts contain punitive clauses of up to three years wages if the employee fails to remain for the period of the contract. Workers have no access to any of the ILO core labour standards. Isolated in individual homes, they are particularly vulnerable to abuse.

In all these scenarios, organisation of workers and enforcement or claiming of labour standards is increasingly difficult. The sectors are highly informal, using a flexible, migrant workforce. Labour is cheap, expendable and exploitable, and thus vulnerable to forced labour. This vulnerability is increased by the status of workers as migrants, whether legal or illegal. The vulnerability of female migrant workers is more acute, with women more likely to migrate into unskilled, unregulated sectors.

In addressing vulnerabilities to trafficking and forced labour it is necessary to look at three factors: the vulnerability of the migrant worker, how to ensure core labour standards, particularly in informal or non work sectors and finally, how to provide protection and redress for those trafficked or in forced labour situations.

Formally, states have acknowledged issues of trafficking, forced labour and the demand for migrant workers in certain sectors. The European Union (EU), for example, is considering the debate on migrant workers and their conditions of entry with most recently their Green Paper on an EU approach to managing economic migration. However, instead of tackling xenophobic reactions to the issue of migration, many governments have sought political advantage by promoting more restrictive immigration policies. Such policies only reduce the opportunities for regular migration, thereby providing greater opportunities for traffickers and forced labour exploitation. Governments in developed countries are generally reluctant to publicly recognise their dependency on both skilled and unskilled migrant labour. However, the reality is that demand for migrant workers will be filled by irregular migration unless policy makers recognise that it is in their national interest to facilitate and manage this process.

Some countries have introduced schemes for work permits for migrant workers, for example, skilled workers or migrant domestic workers. However, legal migration schemes can also increase vulnerability to trafficking and forced labour, when restrictive conditions are attached, as can be seen with the abuses that occur in certain states in the Gulf and Middle East, or where migration is only available for certain, usually skilled workers.

Countries have also made steps to address the specific abuses faced by migrant workers. For example, Ethiopia has provided for training of embassy staff in Lebanon on support for migrant domestic workers and has made it mandatory that all work permits for migrant domestic workers should be supplied by one regulated agency.

These and other initiatives are significant in tackling specific aspects of abuses suffered by migrant workers. However, if they are not set within a more comprehensive policy framework, at best their effect can only be piecemeal, at worst they can simply divert abuses elsewhere.

Legal migration schemes need to be open and accessible to all, avoiding situations of dependency. Agencies facilitating migration should be regulated. Visas should not tie an employee to a particular employer or type of employment. Fees for providing work permits or visas should be clear and reasonable. Travel, visa and work permit documents should remain the property of the employee, and legislation should make retention of these documents by others illegal.

Safe migration needs to be promoted in origin countries. For many, migration is a survival strategy; for others, it is an opportunity to improve their lives; still, for others, it is part of traditional migratory routes (e.g.,

187

young people leaving home to seek jobs). In this context, awareness raising campaigns of the dangers of migration and trafficking have limited impact. Trafficking and exploitation are less likely to occur where established migration routes exist, with accompanying knowledge and contacts. States should therefore promote information about safe migration, for example, through clear processes to facilitate migration and regulated employment/travel agencies.

However, providing managed, accessible, open migration policies are only one aspect in combating forced labour, and by themselves, without the other elements mentioned above, cannot be effective. While addressing the issue of managed migration can reduce vulnerability, in particular to trafficking, exploitation and abusive labour practices also need to be addressed.

Although illegal migrants are more likely to be vulnerable to trafficking, and face more severe exploitation, all irregular migrant workers, even if they have initially willingly or legally crossed borders, are vulnerable to forced labour exploitation.

In protecting labour from trafficking and forced labour, it is necessary to enable safe, formalised migration. Accompanying this must be the enforcement of core labour standards, with accompanying rights, and supporting inspections and enforcement mechanisms. This is most important in the irregular, unorganised or informal sectors, such as domestic work, in which work, and abuses are often hidden.

Of course this is not easy, particularly in countries or sectors where labour rights are weak or non-existent. However, without access to core labour standards, all workers, be they regular migrants, irregular migrants, or indigenous workers, are vulnerable to exploitation. Policies that seek to manage migration, or to provide assistance to trafficked victims, will ultimately be ineffective without an underpinning of core labour rights that can be claimed by all workers.

Support for labour standards needs to occur on a multi-dimensional level. Organisation of workers should be encouraged. Migrant workers are often isolated, with limited access to either their own peer groups (e.g., in the case of domestic workers), or external groups (e.g., Chinese trafficked or smuggled migrants). Such isolation makes organisation difficult, and exploitation easier. Through organisation workers can become aware of rights they are entitled to, and seek to claim them. Both formal organisation (e.g., unionisation) and informal organisation (e.g., through church, community or outreach group) are important.

Enforcement of labour standards is increasingly difficult to ensure. Increasing movement of labour, and use of contractors and sub-contractors make the labour and supply chains harder to regulate. Policies to encourage companies to take responsibility for their supply chains throughout should be developed.

However, it remains the responsibility of states to ratify, ensure and enforce appropriate labour standards, including the ILO core standards. Additionally, states should develop a rights based approach to protecting the rights of migrant workers. A good starting place for this is ratification of the 1990 UN International Convention on the Protection of the Rights of All Migrant Workers and Members of Their Families.

It is perhaps tempting to concentrate on one specific aspect of labour policies, for example, the provision of legal migration channels, or regulation of migration agencies. While these are important, I hope what I have shown is that to tackle forced labour comprehensive rights based polices are needed to protect both migrant and non migrant workers alike.

Temporary migrant workers: Organizing and protection strategies by trade unions

Verena Schmidt[1]

Introduction

Work through temporary agencies is the most rapidly growing form of atypical work. According to the European Foundation for the Improvement of Living and Working Conditions, the use of temporary agency workers has increased five-fold in Denmark, Italy, Spain and Sweden and has at least doubled in most other countries (ETUC 2005: 1). Although figures for temporary agency workers outside of the EU are not available, it is likely that numbers there have also increased considerably. Even though temporary agency work can have advantages in that individuals can work flexibly or gain experience in a specific sector or country, work found by this method also has the worst record for working conditions, according to the European Trade Union Confederation (ETUC) (2005: 1). This type of work is reported to be more repetitive than in other forms of employment, less information is supplied to employees on workplace risks, there is generally little training and there is a higher rate of workplace accidents (ETUC 2005: 1-2).

This article will focus on recruitment agencies for migrant workers as one particular form of temporary agencies. Temporary recruitment agencies cover a large section of the labour market, which spans from unskilled seasonal agricultural workers to highly skilled computer experts. All temporarily recruited migrant workers and professionals have in common that they work abroad for a fixed term contract. Once the

---

[1] ILO Coordinator of the Global Union Research Network (GURN), Bureau for Workers' Activities, ILO.

contract expires, they usually have to leave the country since the visa is often linked to one particular employer or recruitment agency.[2] Research from the OECD suggests that the engagement of governmental authorities in the administration of the recruitment process guarantees a better protection of workers, a lower cost for the beneficiaries and a stronger control over the performance of employers. Even though this might make the programme less flexible, they can be more closely managed (ILO 2004, Booklet 3: 27).[3]

This article will deal with five different kinds of protection strategies: trade union campaigns to change the legal framework for temporary migrant workers, organizing temporary migrant workers, offering practical support to temporary migrant workers, information campaigns for temporary migrant workers and, finally other measures to include and integrate migrant workers within trade unions. The cases reported here were chosen by the workers delegates at the 92nd International Labour Conference as "good practice cases." Different national contexts, the migration history of a country and of trade unions as well as the subjectivity of the actors interviewed determine what is regarded as "good." It is up to the reader to draw conclusion of what s/he might regard as "good" or to see which of the various creative and innovative examples of trade union actions with migrants might be transposed to other countries.

Changing the legal framework for temporary migrant workers

In a number of countries trade unions are represented in tripartite commissions and can therefore considerably influence the governance of migration. One way in which trade unions are fighting against exploitation, especially of undocumented migrants, is by calling on the regulation of sub-contractors that hire migrant labour. In the UK some 70 percent of seasonal workers are supplied by so called 'gangmasters.' The gangmaster system originated in the 19th century. Farmers recruit workers

---

[2] Generally it would be important to distinguish between the different kinds of temporary migrant workers, however, this will not be possible in the space limits of this article. Undocumented workers will also briefly be dealt with since some temporary migrant workers overstay in the host country and then become undocumented.

[3] Reference to OECD (2003): Bilateral Labour Agreements: Evaluation and Prospects – Report for Seminar Jointly Organized by the OECD and the Swiss Federal Office of Immigration, Integration and Emigration (IMES), Montreux, 19-20 June, 2003: 5.

through gangmaster companies, yet the latter are the official employer. The enforcement of labour standards is much more difficult as often disputes arise over responsibilities for the workers between the gangmaster and the farmer. Between 1980 and 2000, gangmasters in the UK have developed into big business, with an estimated profit of £50 million per year. Many of these gangmasters have ties to smuggling and trafficking rings (ILO 2003: 13).

The British Transport and General Workers Unions (TGWU) has campaigned for a system of licences for these gangmasters. The slogan for the campaign, launched in 2004, is "Legislation not Exploitation." The TGWU reckons that in the UK's agriculture sector alone some 3,000 gangmasters employ about 60,000 people. The TGWU further estimates that about 100,000 workers, mostly undocumented migrants, are all dependent on a gangmaster for work. The union is calling for the introduction of a licensing system and a gangmaster register, which inspectors could then consult. These licences would be valid for a limited period of time and would be renewable as long as the gangmaster has not breached any obligations. [4]

A study on migrant workers in agriculture commissioned by the European Federation of Food, Agriculture and Tourism Trade Unions (EFFAT) also recommends that main contractors be made responsible to their subcontractors, and, to achieve this, cooperation should be organized between trade unions and consumer groups (ILO 2005: 7).

Organizing temporary migrant workers

From a trade union perspective, one of the most important protection strategies for temporary migrant workers is to organize in trade unions. [5] Trade unions' international networks in sending and receiving countries can share and exchange information on recruitment and placement of migrant workers. Trade unions can particularly use these international networks and their influence on drawing attention to abusive behaviour of recruitment agencies and to the victims of illegal recruit-

---

[4] Editor's note: As regards the UK Gangmaster (Licensing) Act 2004, see also the contribution by Dan Rees.

[5] In addition to organizing and the legal situation for migrants, the social capital of migrants (i.e. family and social networks of migrants) is seen as utmost important.

193

ment and trafficking, which are mostly women and children. Trade unions can also negotiate internationally recognized employment contracts that should be signed by employers, recruitment agencies and migrants in order to avoid undercutting and unfair competition with national workers (ILO 2004 Booklet 3: 48).

However, organizing temporary migrants is not always an easy task since there is a high turnover of workers given that the workers are only in their host country temporarily. By the time workers are organized and integrated, they might already have to leave the country. They often do not know the language in the country of their temporary residence and may live in isolated settings near their workplace rather than in towns or cities where the unions are usually more visible. As a number of workers depend on obtaining a temporary job abroad each season, they might be afraid that they will be sacked or not be selected the following year if their employer finds out that they are unionized or if they are seen to be active in unions. For example, the contract of the Canadian Seasonal Agricultural Programme stipulates that a farmer can decide to send a worker home before the expiration of their contract for 'non-compliance, refusal to work, or any other sufficient reason' (Human Resources of Canada 2004: 3). If the worker is sent home for any of these reasons, the cost of the flight has to be borne by the worker unless the employer specifically called that particular worker (Human Resources of Canada 2004: 3). The reasons for which the workers can be sent home are very broad and leave ample room for interpretation by the employer. According to the United Food and Commercial Workers Canada, the serious consequences of repatriation cannot be overestimated as the worker suddenly loses her/his income and in addition has to pay the cost for the accommodation at home (UFCW 2004: 14). Generally, an important prerequisite for organizing is, of course, that the ILO core Convention No. 87 on Freedom of Association and Protection of the Right to Organize as well as Convention No. 98 on the Right to Organize and Collective Bargaining are ratified and implemented in the country[6] and that there is a non-threatening environment for trade unionists.

Within trade unions, the organization of migrant workers is a complex and often ambivalent issue. The main goal of trade unions is to protect the individual and collective interests of workers. The aim of trade

---

[6] In June 2005, 144 out of 178 member states of the ILO had ratified Convention 87 while 154 had ratified Convention 98.

unions is to organize as many workers as possible in order to increase their bargaining power and to represent their members and workers at large to the best of their ability. Trade unions also try to build up solidarity amongst workers and to avoid a feeling of competitiveness. Thus they appear to be the obvious type of organization to protect the interests of temporary migrant workers. Lis, Lucassen and Soly (1994) have shown that the organized labour movement did not coincide with industrialization but rather with the development of the national state in the 19th century when the growing importance of the state fundamentally changed the relationship between employers and workers, and a triangle between employers, workers and the state emerged. With regard to migration and trade unions it is first of all important to stress the significance of the nation state: the concept of the nation state meant that an imagined community within a defined territory became the dominant framework for the organization of employers and workers. Citizenship and the deferral of those outside the boundaries as "aliens" indirectly evolved as a result (Penninx/Rosblad 2000: 2-3). Since trade unions as part of the triangle were partly responsible for the development of the modern welfare state, they also had to formulate positions toward migrant workers. To what extent trade unions are willing to include migrant workers in their ranks depends thus on the historic development of trade unions, the state and dominant migration regimes (Lis, Lucassen and Soly 1994).

In addition to this path dependency of trade unions relating to what extent unions are likely to integrate workers, Penninx and Roosblad show three dilemmas of trade unions with regard to migrants in a comparative research project on trade unions and migration in Europe (Penninx/ Roosblad 2000: 3-12).

The first relates to immigration itself: should trade unions in tripartite structures or commissions agree with employers and governments to the employment of migrant workers? Should they allow the licensing of employment agencies for migrants? On the one hand trade unions are afraid that the inclusion of temporary migrant workers will be to the disadvantage of local workers since migrant workers might be prepared to work for wages below the collective bargaining agreements negotiated by the unions. On the other hand, various European trade unions realize that there is at least temporary shortage of labour in some sectors and that domestic workers are not prepared to carry out tasks which have been described as '3D' i.e. dirty, dangerous and degrading jobs (Abella 2002: 1).

The second dilemma arises with the arrival of temporary migrant workers: Should trade unions include them fully in their ranks partly based on trade unions' tradition of international solidarity or should they exclude them? The exclusion of migrant workers might lead to a weakening of the bargaining position of trade unions towards employers and governments. The inclusion of migrant workers in trade unions can be seen as a threat of the national cohesion of the trade unions and of the labour markets. This of course depends very much on the national context. To give an example, the former Swiss union for construction and industry GBI (now amalgamated within Unia) had a percentage of foreign members of around 70, while the Japanese unions within Rengo have less than one per cent migrant workers. In case migrant workers form their own unions or NGOs, trade unions face the dilemma either to cooperate with these unions or NGOs or refuse cooperation because the NGOs might pose a threat to the hitherto monopoly of trade unions in disputes.

If trade unions decide to integrate temporary migrant workers, then the third dilemma is whether they should advocate equal treatment of all workers or special treatment of migrants?

The strategies on how trade unions deal with these dilemmas differ widely. Some unions exclude at least undocumented migrant workers from their ranks, while others proactively organize migrant workers regardless of their status. If trade unions include migrant workers in their midst they are likely to be confronted with cultural differences between domestic and migrant workers. The alternative between giving either special or equal treatment depends on how much special attention is given to migrant workers.

As Castles and Kosack point out, the two options on immigration and inclusion or exclusion are inextricably linked. Even though it may seem logical for national workers to oppose immigration for fear of wage dumping, once there are immigrant workers in the country, it is essential to organize them – not only in the interest of migrant workers, but in the interest of all workers. If the unions oppose immigration initially and continue to do so, they may find that the immigrants do not trust them and are unwilling to join trade unions. Where this happens, the unions have the worst of both worlds. Not strong enough to prevent immigration, their attempts to do so only serve to alienate the new workers from them. The result is a weakening of the unions and a deepening of the split in the working class (Castles/ Kosack 1973, cited in Penninx and Roosblad 2000: 9).

In the following sections, examples of attempts by unions to organize temporary migrant workers will be elaborated: Firstly on a bilateral level between German and Polish trade unions and the foundation of a European Migrants' Union, secondly by French and American unions by supporting workers centres for temporary migrants and thirdly on the international level by a Global Union Federation.[7]

Bilateral cooperation between trade unions leading to the foundation of a European Migrants Union

The German trade union IG BAU is the trade union for building, forestry, agriculture and the environment and an affiliate of the International Federation for Building and Wood Workers (IFBWW). Many Polish migrant workers come to Germany to work there temporarily. This is made possible through an agreement between Germany and Poland that enables seasonal workers to work in Germany for up to three months during a year within agriculture, and in the hotel and restaurant sector.[8] Despite this agreement, many workers are employed illegally, without any social protection and often far below the wages of the collective bargaining agreements. This was the case on the Potsdamer Platz in Berlin which was Europe's biggest building site during the 1990s. As a consequence, IG BAU opened an office and offered undocumented workers free legal advice and tried to organize migrant workers in general. However, they found out that the barriers for migrant workers to join a trade union once they are abroad are very high indeed. As a result, IG BAU opened an office in Warsaw in January 2004 where a German trade union officer cooperates with Polish unions and organizes workers who plan to work in Germany. In addition, in 2004 IG BAU founded a European Migrant Workers' Union. The aim is to organize migrant workers of all nationalities who work for a limited period of time in one or several Member States of the European Union (other than their own), especially in the

---

[7] These examples are mainly the result of an online conference on migration and expert interviews which were carried out in 2004. The online conference was organized in the framework of the Global Union Research Network (GURN) in preparation of the Migration Committee at the 92nd International Labour Conference which took place in June 2004. The expert interviews were carried out with delegates of the Workers Group in the Migration Committee during the above cited International Labour Conference.

[8] This agreement also covers the Czech Republic, Hungary, Slovakia and Slovenia. Poland and these countries all joined the European Union in 2004. A seven year transitional period is now in place during which the EU 15 member states can restrict the freedom of movement of workers from the new member countries. After this transitional phase, workers will enjoy freedom of movement within the entire European Union.

construction or agricultural sector. IG BAU supports the new organization and supports the costs of the start-up and consolidation period, which is planned to be completed by the end of 2006, when the new union aims to have organized at least 10,000 migrant workers (EIRO online 2004).

In the start-up period, the European Migrant Workers Union will concentrate its activities on migrant workers from Poland, who are the largest group amongst the 50,000 or so posted workers and estimated 200,000 seasonal workers from Eastern Europe who work with a legal permit for a limited time in Germany (EIRO online 2004). The new union provides:

- legal help and advice in various languages
- support in the event of sickness or accident
- support to ensure correct levels of pay
- collective bargaining in order to improve pay and conditions for migrant workers
- help to get in contact with German colleagues (language courses)
- help in finding better accommodation
- lobbying in favour of migrant workers
- support for undocumented workers (i.e. workers without an official work permit and residence status) so that they are able to organize themselves in the trade union's structure (see http://www.migrant-workers-union.org/ for more details).

It will be interesting to observe how the new union will be able to get access to the workers and what kind of organizing strategies are suitable and successful for migrant workers.

Trade union membership across borders

Another example on how to deal with the dilemmas trade unions face regarding temporary migrant workers is the Union Network International (UNI) Passport. The Global Union Federation UNI organizes crafts' and services' workers (postal, tourism, electricity, telecom, social security commerce, finance, media, cleaning and security) and launched a union passport scheme in 2000 to help mobile workers retain their union rights and obtain support as they travel and work in different countries. The passport allows a worker who is already a member of a union in his/her home country to be 'hosted' by a UNI affiliated union in the destination country. With the passport the worker has access to a list of local contacts, information on working conditions, the banking system, tax regulations, as well as on housing and healthcare. The migrant worker can also benefit from advice on labour issues and from legal support in the event of a dispute with the employer. The passport gives the holder the opportunity to participate in local union activities, including training courses.

Outside the service sector, several unions have also signed bilateral contracts that foresee the mutual recognition of trade union membership. This is the case between the following unions: All India TUC and Gefont (one of the trade union confederations of Nepal); CGTP-IN (Portuguese trade union confederation) with its counterparts in Switzerland, Luxembourg, Spain and the United Kingdom; UNISON (the British trade union for public sector workers) with its counterparts in Spain, Finland and Australia and the Philippines.

Offering practical support to temporary migrant workers

In 2003 the trade unions Confédération Française Démocratique du Travail (CFDT) and Force Ouvrière (FO) in France opened jointly with employers and local authorities a seasonal work centre near Béziers, which covers 19 communes. The aim of this project is to prevent the employment of clandestine workers hired through gangmasters under the guise of foreign temporary agencies. The centre informs seasonal workers of their rights, the options in terms of legal recourse as well as training opportunities. The centre is based on the versatility between the hotel and restaurant trade and the agriculture sector. It aims to offer workers whose contract has expired in one of the possible sectors job opportunities in the other. While the switch from one sector to another is not always easy, job rotation is common in the agriculture sector itself. For example, seasonal workers who have finished their job in a cooperative winery may continue working for the wine grower in the vineyards. This can help create lasting seasonal employment and even permanent employment contracts (ILO 2005: 16). In a similar way to France, migrant workers are also often organized in workers' centres in the USA.

This is particularly important for those who work in the informal economy as well as domestic workers, temporary and home workers. The workers' centres are usually staffed with lawyers who advise them on their rights and sometimes centres are supported by trade unions affiliated to the AFL-CIO.

Information campaign for temporary workers

This section will focus on a recent information campaign of the American confederation AFL-CIO for temporary workers. The AFL-CIO went through a remarkable evolution with regard to their attitude towards migrants. Before 1995 it was rather sceptical of migrants as they feared disadvantages for local workers. With John Sweeny's election in 1995 as President of the AFL-CIO a huge "changing to organize" campaign was launched which included the proactive organization of domestic and migrant workers, regardless of their status.

In 2002, the Building and Construction Trades Department of the AFL-CIO drafted model legislation for temporary workers which takes into account temporary migrant workers. NELP, the National Employment Law Project, which is an NGO with which the AFL-CIO cooperates, developed a guide for organizers and advocates on drafting day labour legislation that was however not adopted by Parliament. The resulting Day Labour Fairness and Protection Act (aimed at day labourers but all this applies to migrants employed through employment agencies) comprises the following:

– Ensuring a safe and healthy employment and work environment for all workers

– Protecting and expanding the wage and hour rights of day labourers

– Banning fees or wage deductions for

• Cashing a check issued by a day labour service agency or other day labour employer

• Health and safety equipment

• Transportation between the place of hire and work site

Furthermore:

• Establishing wage parity between temporary labourers with full time permanent employees performing similar tasks

- Mandating weekly and daily overtime rates
- Ensuring a minimum daily rate for workers
- Compensating workers for travelling time between the point of hire and worksite and for time spent waiting for employers
- Prohibiting employers from reneging on wage agreements
- Prohibiting retaliation by employment agencies against workers seeking to enforce their rights under the Day Labour Fairness and Protection Act
- Workers may not be dispatched to any worksite where a labour dispute exists

In case the Day Labour Fairness and Protection Act is violated, the Secretary of Labour would have the authority to suspend or revoke the registration of employment agencies.

Even though the draft legislation was not adopted, the AFL-CIO used it to bring the cause of temporary migrants into the public awareness and to make specific suggestions on what should be changed in the legislation on local, regional and state level.

In addition to organizing specific campaigns and information for temporary migrant workers, the latter will also benefit from other integrative measures trade unions have developed, and these will briefly be described in the following.

Integration of migrant workers into trade unions

Once trade unions decide to include workers in their ranks, there are a number of policies they can adopt to facilitate this. The most obvious practical measures include equal treatment and equality in opportunities as well as enabling communication with migrant workers by, for example, translating communications (bulletins, newsletters, legal advice etc.). More far-reaching elements are policies which take into account the special situation of migrants, for example, by including in collective agreements that employers must take care of housing of the migrants and enable special home leave (e.g. by allowing the migrants to save up holidays over a year or two year period to take long holidays). Other measures can consist of the following, which will be further elaborated on:

- Systematic integration of new migrant workers
- Provision of information material in different languages
- Offering language courses
- Agreements with banks on the opening of bank accounts for all workers
- Easy and cheap transfer of remittances
- Special provisions for undocumented workers
- Agreements on praying rooms at the work place
- Special structures for migrants within the union
- Campaigns against racism
- Intercultural activities including for and with domestic workers
- Information sharing of good practices on trade unions and migrant workers.

The Barbados Workers' Union (BWU) systematically gets in touch with all new documented migrant workers. When migrants enter the country legally, their names and countries of origin as well as the sector in which they work are listed in the newspaper. If a migrant worker is employed in a sector which is under the auspices of the BWU, s/he will be contacted and informed of the activities of the BWU.

The provision of trade union and legal material in the languages of the migrant workers is essential for the integration of migrant workers from the outset. The aforementioned Swiss GBI publishes information brochures in seven different languages. Three of these are the official languages of Switzerland, i.e. German, French and Italian. The other four languages are the ones most commonly spoken by migrants in Switzerland, i.e. Portuguese, Spanish, Turkish and Serbo-Croat/Albanian. Various contracts, especially in the hotel industry where in particular many migrants work, are also translated. In each members journal, the GBI translates a summary of two pages into different languages. In order to integrate migrants into the country and to the trade union in the medium term, the AFL-CIO organizes language courses for migrant workers. Sometimes these are combined with citizenship courses which are often required for immigration into the USA. The AFL-CIO has also negotiated special agreements with banks which will open bank accounts for all workers, as migrant workers often face difficulties opening accounts. Another important factor is that the AFL-CIO has made a number of deals with banks on remittances which facilitate better conditions for the workers. Both the AFL-CIO and the British Trades Union Congress (TUC) also realized that membership cards with pictures are very important especially for undocumented migrant workers as these are sometimes the only form of ID they have.

Furthermore, the aforementioned TGWU union in the UK accepts the postal address of a migrants' organization as home address since undocumented migrants need to protect their address details (TUC 2002:64). Undocumented migrants are also able to pay dues in cash as they often do not have bank accounts. AFL-CIO affiliated unions have also lobbied for special prayer rooms at the workplace for migrants. Some unions, such as the above mentioned GBI, offer special structures for migrant workers. Within the GBI, migrants have their own conferences and distinct representations, similar to that of women. Other unions, however, regard this as creating a form of ghettoization of migrant workers. Several unions such as LO Norway and the AFL-CIO organize anti-racist campaigns within their unions and for the population at large. The ICFTU launched a detailed action plan on how to combat racism and xenophobia (ICFTU 2001) and decided a Resolution on "Fighting Discrimination and Achieving Equality" during the 18th World Congress in Miyazaki in December 2004 (ICFTU 2004). The national training centre of the German trade union confederation (DGB Bildungswerk) has compiled an extensive selection on good practice cases with regard to anti-racism and equal opportunities at the workplace and they publish regular newsletters on migration. The good practice database and newsletter can be accessed via the internet on http://www.migration-online.de/.[9]

Conclusion

One important way to improve the situation of migrant workers in a sustainable way is to decrease the poverty gaps between countries. It is also important that unions fight for the ratification and implementation of the ILO's core Convention No. 87 on freedom of association and Convention No. 98 on collective bargaining, including that temporary migrant workers can organize and fight for their rights. For a number of reasons, temporary migrant workers pose a dilemma for trade unions.

---

[9] For a more detailed list of protection strategies for migrant workers for governments, employers' and workers' organization looking at recruitment, working abroad and reintegration see ILO 2004.

Migrant workers have been dealt with very differently in various national contexts, with experiences ranging from exclusion to active organizing.

Approaches to organizing temporary migrant workers by UNI, the Indian and Nepali unions and the IG BAU as well as the information campaign on temporary migrant workers by the AFL-CIO which circled around the draft legislation for temporary workers all provide good practice cases for protection strategies.

The above case studies have shown that there are a wide variety of approaches by trade unions towards migrants. Which policy option the trade union chooses depends on various factors, for example, the power position of the trade union in society, the internal organizational structure, the socio-economic conditions in society, the migration history of a country, the origin as well as the status of migrants in the host country and, last but not least, the commitment of migrant workers to organize.

However, migration expert Julie Watts shows that the policy choice of trade unions is by no means static. Watts argues that trade unions in several western European countries opt for more liberal immigration policies (Watts 2000:3). The same is true for the AFL-CIO in the USA. Watts sees four reasons for this change. First of all trade unions are normative organizations which have a tradition of international solidarity. However, when migrant workers appear to threaten the working conditions of domestic workers, ideological arguments in favour of liberal and open immigration policies create two dilemmas for trade unions, namely whether unions should protect the interests of all workers or only protect the interests of union members as well as whether unions should protect immigrants already present or protect also future immigrants (Watts 2000: 13-14).

The second reason for the support of more liberal migration policies is that the unions doubt the states' capacity to control migration. Even modern high-tech surveillance methods and border controls are not able to stop cross-border migration. Thirdly, migrants are seen as a new source of union strength. Fourthly, the organizing of migrant workers is seen as an important way to regulate the underground economy (Watts 2000: 11-36). According to Helen Schwenken, these variables could open a window of opportunity for migrant workers within trade unions (Schwenken 2005: 322).

References

Abella, Manolo (2002): Interview: Migrant Workers' Rights Are Not Negotiable. In: Labour Education 2002/4, Number 129. ILO 2002.

AFL-CIO (2002): Model Legislation. Temp Workers deserve a permanent Voice @ Work. Building and Construction Trades Department, AFL-CIO. Washington, USA.

EIRO online (2004): European Migrant Workers Union founded. 22 September 2004. Dublin. (http://www.eiro.eurofound.eu.int/2004/09/feature/de0409206f.html, accessed: 5 March 2005).

European Parliament and Council (2002): Proposal for a Directive of the European Parliament and the Council on working conditions for temporary workers Official Journal 203 E, 27/08/2002 P. 0001 – 0005 COM/2002/0149 final – COD 2002/0072. Brussels.

ETUC (2005): Temporary agency workers in the European Union. Fact Sheet of March 17, 2005. (http://www.etuc.org/a/501, accessed: 10 July 2005).

Human Resources Development Canada (2004): Agreement for the Employment in Canda of Seasonal Agricultural Workers from Mexico. Ottawa.

ICFTU (2001): Plan of Action for Trade Unions – NO to Racism and Xenophobia! Brussels.

ICFTU (2004): Final Resolution: Fighting Discrimination and Achieving Equality. Eighteenth World Congress. Miyazaki, 5-10 December 2004. 18 GA/E/6.9. Japan.

ILO (2003): Declaration on Fundamental Principles and Rights at Work: Forced Labour outcomes of irregular migration and human trafficking in Europe. Geneva 2003. Report of the Trade Union Consultation meeting 8 – 9 January 2003. A Series of Reports from the ILO's Special Action Programme to Combat Forced Labour.

ILO (2004): Preventing Discrimination, Exploitation and Abuse of Women Migrant Workers. An Information Guide. Gender Promotion Programme. Geneva.

ILO (2005): Bureau for Workers' Activities (ACTRAV): Trade Union Best Practice Initiatives for Migrant Workers. Geneva: 2005 (http://www.gurn.info/topic/migrant/index.html, accessed: 16 July 2005).

Lis, C., Lucassen, J. and H. Soly (1994): Before the Unions: Wage Earners and Collective Action in Europe, 1300—1850. Supplement 2 of the International Review of Social History, 1-11.

National Employment Law Project (2004): Drafting Day Labor Legislation: A Guide for Organizers and Advocates. February 2004. New York, USA.

National Employment Law Project (2003): The Day Labor Fairness and Protection Act. Fact Sheet for Workers. Advocating for the working poor and unemployed. July 2003, New York, USA.

Penninx, R. and J. Roosblad (eds.) (2000): Trade Unions, Immigration and Immigrants in Europe 1960-1993. A comparative Study of the Actions of Trade Unions in Seven West European Countries. New York/ Oxford: Berghahn Books.

Schwenken, Helen (2005): Auseinandersetzungen um die Grenzen Europas. Die politische Mobilisierung von MigrantInnen- und pro-migrant-Organisationen im Konfliktfeld irregulärer Migration in der Europäischen Union. Unpublished doctoral thesis. San Diego and Kassel.

UFCW (United Food and Commercial Workers) (2003): UFCW Canada National Report on the Status of Migrant Farm Workers in Canada, Toronto, Ontario 2004. Internet: http://www.ufcw.ca/cgi-bin/download.cgi/AgWorkersReport 2004ENG.pdf?id=1562&a=v&name=AgWorkersReport2004ENG.pdf (down loaded 15.2.2005).

Curbing malpractice – The role of information campaigns in international labour migration

Anna di Mattia[1]

Introduction

The 1997 Tripartite Meeting of Experts on Future ILO Activities in the Field of Migration recognised that a "well-informed citizenry is still the best protection against fraud and malpractice in recruitment" (1997:36). Furthermore, the meeting acknowledged that "Non-governmental organizations (NGOs) have played an important role in exposing fraud, graft and corruption in the responsible administrative bodies, and in assisting victims" (1997:36). The role of information in international labour recruitment is to comprehensively inform potential and actual labour migrants about choices, procedures and realities before, during and after migration to ensure that migrants are aware of the possible dangers involved. Potential migrants make their decision to leave the country only gradually. The type of information goes from very general in the early stages of the decision making process to very specific at the final stage (ILO, 2004:58). Detailed, timely and realistic information about the process of migrating, including using private or public recruitment agencies and the nature of work as well as the country of destination are crucial in deciding whether and where to migrate.

ILO Convention 181 does not refer to information campaigns, however, ILO Convention 97 and the International Convention on the Protection of the Rights of All Migrant Workers and Members of Their Families mention several times the importance of providing adequate

---

[1] Research Officer, International Institute for Labour Studies, ILO.

information to outgoing migrant workers[2]. As information distributors, these conventions suggest not only the state of origin, transit and destination, but also employers, trade unions or other appropriate bodies or institutions. Private or public recruitment agencies are not specifically mentioned in these conventions.

Ideally, all social actors would share the responsibilities of informing (potential) migrant workers. Information campaigns should be carried out by different providers, such as governments, NGOs, professional communication companies and, of course, international organizations such as the ILO, to ensure as impartial and balanced information provision as possible.

Many successful information campaigns have been carried out to inform people about the dangers of human trafficking but so far few have targeted labour migrants in particular. On the whole, the success of an information campaign lies in its objectives, design and implementation. In particular, a clear definition of the target group(s), a clearly stated goal of what the campaign should achieve, the careful preparation of clear and simple messages, the establishment of indicators and specific results and the capacity for the organizers to work with other social actors such as NGOs are crucial for the success of the campaign.

Information campaigns

Target groups

Possible target groups include:

- Labour migrants who should be informed about recruitment conditions, contracts and alternatives to using recruitment agencies;

- The general public which should be made aware of malpractices and what they can do, for example using their consumer power to boycott companies who employ migrants under atrocious conditions;

- Potential or actual employers, trade unionists, industry associations and concerned NGOs should learn about rules and regulations governing orderly labour recruitment.

---

[2] See Annex.

Ideally, the focus of any campaign for labour migrants is on those who are at the margins of information access. The specific target group is acted on three levels: first, to raise awareness of malpractices in migrant labour recruitment which is achievable in the shortest amount of time, second, to change attitudes and/or opinions and third to change behaviour. The latter takes the longest to achieve (IOM, 1999).

Mode of information dissemination

Potential and actual migrants can be informed through the internet, soap operas, radio programmes, theater, posters, newspaper and magazine advertisements, TV shows, distribution of leaflets/brochures/flyers/handbooks, public roundtable discussions and traveling exhibitions to name a few. It is perhaps better to use a mix of dissemination channels to ensure that the campaign reaches as large of a proportion of the target audience as possible. Since many different information campaigns are feasible, one can be very creative in designing an information campaign and even the illiterate can be successfully targeted.

Also, the International Migrant day on 18 December can be an opportunity to specifically address issues arising out of using private or public recruitment agencies to find work abroad.

Content of information campaigns

The information provided should include country-specific and labour market-specific information such as general conditions of work and life, unions and labour laws as well as practical conditions concerning jobs and finances and information on housing, schooling, etc. Information on procedures before departure should include visas, clearances, health certificates and, importantly, permissible fees or upper limits on fees paid to recruitment agencies or employers. Finally, job-specific information should include as detailed descriptions of the different jobs as possible (van der Linden, 2004:60-61)[3] and strategies to adopt in situations of exploitation and abuse. Nonetheless, the message(s) conveyed should be simply expressed and limited in number. Considering the increasing feminization of migration, it makes sense to include information more specifically directed toward women as has already been initiated in the Philippines (ILC, 1999:77).

---

[3] They may include means of reaching the work site, details about wages, benefits, health care, insurances and continuous learning provisions as well as information about the reputation and reliability of the employer.

Information providers

On the international level, international organizations such as the International Labour Organization (ILO), the United Nations High Commissioner for Refugees (UNHCR), the United Nations Children's Fund (UNICEF), the World Health Organization (WHO) and the International Organization for Migration (IOM) with their global expertise on different aspects of migration can and have provided national and international information campaigns. An example of a collaboration of an international agency and an intergovernmental agency took place in Albania 1992. The UNHCR in conjunction with the IOM launched an information campaign based on regular radio programmes with a question and answer format on emigration-related issues, and a call-in TV round-table featuring prominent personalities, including foreign ambassadors (UNHCR, 1998).

On the national level relevant ministries, trade unions, national institutions and NGOs and umbrella organizations, to name a few, can provide information to outgoing migrant workers. For example, the German AuPair umbrella organization Ring Deutscher AuPair Vermittler e.V. provides on their website relevant information and links for potential au pair girls and boys and their parents so that they can make an informed decision. Switzerland publishes brochures on working and living conditions in approximately 100 different countries for Swiss nationals intending to emigrate (ILC 1999: 75). Moreover, governments in receiving countries such as Hong Kong and Australia, provided information to prospective migrants in the languages of the most prominent migrant-sending countries (ILC 1999: 75). Furthermore, cooperation between providers' host and destination countries are desirable.

On the regional level, for example, social networks, community centres, local NGOs, the recruiting agencies/sponsor, schools or people who are thought to be multipliers, such as village elderly, mayors etc., can participate in workshops to receive more detailed information about recruitment agencies to increase the effectiveness of an information campaign.

Evaluations

The cost of conducting an evaluation should be included in the campaign budget for reasons of accountability, learning, strategizing and future planning (Karl, 1999). It is inherently difficult to measure the impact of information campaigns. Often, the assessments of the impact tends to be somewhat subjective and lacking in objective supporting data. Commonly, a "change in attitude" is expected, but there are difficulties in measuring this change of attitude. One has to be careful that the results are not merely methodological by-products. Whenever a quantitative analysis of the information campaign is not possible, a qualitative analysis based on the information collected should be conducted. It is advisable to use gender sensitive indicators. One proposition is to integrate monitoring and evaluation already in the planning process to make it more effective. Another proposal is to have integrated follow-up programmes or activities.

Case study Indonesia

Hugo and Böhning (2000) conducted a field study in Indonesia. The authors emphasise that not only the content and channels of dissemination are important but also to ensure that that workers fully understand what is involved and do not feel overwhelmed by the information presented. Providing information should in any case not replace tailored training for oversea contract workers (OCWs). In terms of the content of an information campaign they encourage that information on strategies to adopt by migrants in situations of exploitation and/or abuse. Suggested dissemination channels include directly addressing the individual potential migrant, the sponsor, the Department of Labour offices (DEPNAKER) and/or local leadership institutions and individuals.

Although it is generally agreed upon that social networks in destination countries can at least partly compensate for lack of pre-departure information, returning migrants may not give accurate information to potential migrants of their own community because they want to appear successful. Additionally, recruiting agencies/sponsors have a vested interest in persuading the worker to go overseas and paying them the highest fee possible, therefore, they would not necessarily paint an accurate picture of the realities OCWs face. Hugo and Böhning (2000: 26) propose a possible strategy, which in the case of Indonesia can be highly spatially focused because labour migrants tend to come from specific areas only. By modeling the information campaign on the successful Indonesian national family planning programme, that is, supplying information material and educating village leaders who will later act as multipliers about oversea worker programmes, they can spread the news and thus paint a more realistic picture of labour recruitment and conditions abroad.

Hugo and Böhning's survey on information needs of outgoing migrant workers also established that "[t]here are clearly significant differences between groups with the most pressing needs among women OCWs going to work as domestics (…)"(2000:7). It was suggested that this finding could become the initial focus for developing an information programme for potential female migrant workers who often face the worst forms of maltreatment during and after recruitment.

Case examples from other areas

Transnational advocacy networks

Transnational advocacy networks (TANs) are an additional, ever increasing force in world politics. TANs have been successfully utilised in environmental, human rights and gender issues. Transnational Networks for labour migration could be formed modelled on TANs such as the INGO Transparency International or the International Campaign to Ban Landmines, to improve protection measures for labour migration. Here the target audience would be the general public and governments, more than those who actually migrate. Keck and Sikkink (1988:4) remarked that scholars "have come late to the party," that is in paying attention to the rise of activist networks.

The political opportunity structure will, at least partly, determine the impact any TAN can have. Florini (2000:218) summarized that "If a significant, organized domestic constituency is lacking, external actors usually can accomplish little." The success of transnational advocacy depends to a great part on the strength of civil society in the particular country. Since many of the destination countries for labour migrants have only weak civil societies it will be challenging to mobilize the public in order to organize campaign work. This is also true for any attempt to inform consumers about malpractices concerning migrants and thereby pressuring companies into corporate social responsibility. Even in societies with active civil societies it depends whether the link between exploitation and the product is visible. Moreover, there are limits and time lags on visible outputs (if any) to TANs because they work indirectly.

There may also be problems arising out of cultural differences and misunderstandings. It may be hard to develop a truly transnational network involving members of culturally, socially and economically dissimilar countries in the decision making process as they each have their own conceptions and standards. However, it is vital for TANs to remain credible to all social actors, as this is the currency they work with and "It must be firmly connected to local reality"(Florini, 2000:217).

Ratcheting Labour Standards

Another, as of yet academic proposal, has been put forward by Fung, O' Rourke and Sabel (2001). They developed a strategy for strengthening labour standards named "Ratcheting Labour Standards" (RLS). Monitoring and public disclosure of working conditions are two measures to create incentives for companies to monitor and improve conditions in their own factories and those of their suppliers. Of course, it includes the employment and treatment of migrant workers in these factories. RLS is based on four principles: full transparency; competitive comparison; continuous improvement and sanctions; and it would be governed by a council made up of social certification organizations or collaboration between intergovernmental organizations. In the medium term detailed information about the social performance of firms will be collected which could be used to shame companies into improving labour conditions. The authors argue that these corrigible, nonetheless, imposable ratcheting labour standards would be the product and not the starting point of a process to provide and deploy information about actual labour practices.

Conclusion

Information campaigns can be utilized as a prevention tool to curb malpractice in international labour migration. The added advantage is not only that there are endless possibilities in designing and implementing those campaigns but also that numerous providers in addition to governments can carry out campaigns. Absolutely every effort should be made to repress misleading propaganda. However, simply proving information about possible alternatives, conditions and dangers involved can only be the starting point in any attempt to curtail unprofessional conduct and it should certainly not replace other protective measures. Therefore it makes sense to use information campaigns as an integrated element of broader labour recruitment, labour standards or labour migration programmes because it has up until now not been conclusively established what impact information campaigns have on changing migrant workers attitudes.

In addition, transnational advocacy networks or other forms of public monitoring can be utilised to curb malpractice in recruitment for international labour migrants.

The problem of who pays the costs of information campaigns is not easy to solve. It has to be ensured that the costs are not directly or indirectly paid by migrants. However, an accelerated development of cheap information and communication technologies as well as increased access to information for potential and actual labour migrants would make information campaigns more cost and time efficient in the future.

References

1999. "Migrant workers", in *International Labour Conference, Report III (Part 1B)*, 87th session (1999), pp. vii-xiv, 1.

Abella, M. I. and Abrera-Mangahas, M. A. 1996. *Sending workers abroad: a manual for low- and middle-income countries*, Geneva.

Douglass, Mike and Roberts, Glenda Susan. 2000. Japan and global migration, London, Routledge.

Florini, Ann. 2000. The third force, Tokyo, Japan Center for International Exchange ; Washington D.C.

Fung, A.; O' Rourke, D.; Sabel, C. 2001. «Realizing Labor Standards», in Boston Review, February/March 2001.

Hugo, Graeme and Böhning, W. R. 2000. Providing information to outgoing Indonesian migrant workers, SEAPAT working paper, 7, Manila, ILO/SEAPAT.

International Labour Organization. 1997. Protecting the most vulnerable of today's workers, Discussion paper, -MEIM/1997, Tripartite Meeting Of Experts On Future ILO Activities In The Field Of Migration. 1997

IOM Office of Programme Evaluations. 1999. Evaluations of IOM Information Programmes, Geneva, IOM.

—. 1999. Evaluation of the IOM Information Programme in the Philippines, Geneva, IOM.

IOM Migration Information Programme. 1995. Profiles and motives of potential migrants from Albania, Budapest, IOM International Organization for Migration Migration Information Programme.

Karl, Marilee. 1999. Measuring the immeasurable, New Delhi, Women's Feature Service.

Keck, Margaret E. and Sikkink, Kathryn. 1998. Activists beyond borders, Ithaca, NY, Cornell University Press.

Khagram, Sanjeev, Riker, James V., and Sikkink, Kathryn. 2002. Restructuring world politics, Social movements, protest, and contention, v.14, Minneapolis, University of Minnesota Press.

van der Linden, Mariska N. J. 2004. Trafficking for Forced Labour: How to Monitor the Recruitment of Migrant Workers Training Manual, Geneva, ILO.

UNHCR. 1998. Review of UNHCR Mass Information Activities, Geneva, UNHCR.

Available from: http://www.unhcr.ch/cgi-bin/texis/vtx/home/+TwwBmCe8Eudwwww
nwwwwwwwhFqo20I0E2gltFqoGn5nwGqrAFqo20I0E2glcFq2GnVoniadha1
DrqGaMw55aoDhdGMwBodDawVBoVoBon5Dzmxwwwwwww/opendoc.htm.

Annex

The ILO Convention 97 concerning Migration for Employment states:

Article 3

1. Each Member for which this Convention is in force undertakes that it will, so far as national laws and regulations permit, take all appropriate steps against misleading propaganda relating to emigration and immigration.

2. For this purpose, it will where appropriate act in co-operation with other Members concerned.

The International Convention on the Protection of the Rights of All Migrant Workers and Members of Their Families states:

Article 33:

1. Migrant workers and members of their families shall have the right to be informed by the State of origin, the State of employment or the State of transit as the case may be concerning:
(a) Their rights arising out of the present Convention;
(b) The conditions of their admission, their rights and obligations under the law and practice of the State concerned and such other matters as will enable them to comply with administrative or other formalities in that State.

2. States Parties shall take all measures they deem appropriate to disseminate the said information or to ensure that it is provided by employers, trade unions or other appropriate bodies or institutions. As appropriate, they shall co-operate with other States concerned.

3. Such adequate information shall be provided upon request to migrant workers and members of their families, free of charge, and, as far as possible, in a language they are able to understand.

Article 37:

Before their departure, or at the latest at the time of their admission to the State of employment, migrant workers and members of their families shall have the right to be fully informed by the State of origin or the State of employment, as appropriate, of all conditions applicable to their admission and particularly those concerning their stay and the remunerated activities in which they may engage as well as of the requirements they must satisfy in the State of employment and the authority to which they must address themselves for any modification of those conditions.

Article 65:

1. States Parties shall maintain appropriate services to deal with questions concerning international migration of workers and members of their families. Their functions shall include, inter alia:
(a) The formulation and implementation of policies regarding such migration;
(b) An exchange of information. consultation and co-operation with the competent authorities of other States Parties involved in such migration;
(c) The provision of appropriate information, particularly to employers, workers and their organizations on policies, laws and regulations relating to migration and employment, on agreements concluded with other States concerning migration and on other relevant matters;
(d) The provision of information and appropriate assistance to migrant workers and members of their families regarding requisite authorizations and formalities and arrangements for departure, travel, arrival, stay, remunerated activities, exit and return, as well as on conditions of work and life in the State of employment and on customs, currency, tax and other relevant laws and regulations.

2. States Parties shall facilitate as appropriate the provision of adequate consular and other services that are necessary to meet the social, cultural and other needs of migrant workers and members of their families.

New measures to tackle exploitation in the UK agricultural industry

Dan Rees[1]

Defining the issue

The recent deaths of 23 migrant cockle pickers in Morecambe Bay threw a public spotlight on an issue that has concerned the industry and government for over a decade. The exploitation of temporary workers in the UK agricultural and food processing sector is a feature of today's gangmaster system. The lack of effective controls on these labour providers has helped create an environment where it is easy for the unscrupulous to evade taxes and exploit the benefits system as well as the workers they employ. Labour users have no reliable way of distinguishing the good from the bad employers. Few of the workers involved are aware of their rights, many have limited English and all are vulnerable to exploitation.

There is worrying evidence that the exploitation of workers is worsening. Severe forms of abuse have been reported, including extreme forms of coercion and violence as well as health and safety malpractice leading to fatal accidents. Workers have been forced to work long hours for sub-minimum wages and subjected to poor living conditions. There is strong support in the industry for licensing and registration of labour providers in order to combat rising levels of exploitation and criminal activity.

---

[1] Director, Ethical Trading Initiative, United Kingdom.

The Temporary Labour Working Group and the Gangmasters (Licensing) Act

The Temporary Labour Working Group, a consortium of major retailers, growers, suppliers, labour providers and trade unions was set up in September 2002, convened by the Ethical Trading Initiative (ETI), with co-operation from government. Its aim was to establish a set of minimum standards for labour providers which could be enforced by new statutory controls. Partly as a result of the Group's lobbying activities a Private Member's Bill was enacted in July 2004 as the Gangmasters (Licensing) Act. This laid the foundations for a licensing and registration scheme which came into force in 2005.

What does the Act do?

The Act registers and licenses labour providers in agriculture, consumable produce including meat, fish and shellfish, food processing and packaging. The Act applies to the whole of the UK. It provides for new criminal offences making it illegal:

- For labour providers in these industries to operate without a valid licence;

- For labour users to employ the services of unlicensed labour providers (subject to a due diligence defence); and

- To obstruct enforcement officers exercising their duties under this legislation.

The Act is intended to create a 'paper trail' to make it easier to locate and prosecute labour providers. This should also reduce exchequer fraud and promote fair competition between labour providers. A register of licensed labour providers will provide labour users with an assurance that they are legitimate. Retailers will therefore be expected to insist that their suppliers and sub-contractors use only licensed operators and to ask their suppliers for evidence of this. The Act also covers labour provider and user contractual arrangements in order to prevent abuse of the licensing regime through sub-contracting arrangements.

The Act defines a gangmaster as anyone employing, supplying and/or supervising a worker to do work in these areas. It applies to gangmasters operating in the sectors outlined, whether based in the UK or offshore. It also covers all sub-contractors. In addition, any employment agencies/businesses (as defined by the Employment Agencies Act 1973) will come within the ambit of this Act if they are engaged in activities for which a license is required under its provisions. The Act extends the full protection of the law to any individual worker undertaking work to which its provisions apply.

The Act establishes the Gangmaster Licensing Authority and opens up 'gateways' between departments, the Authority and other enforcement agencies to facilitate the exchange of enforcement information connected with the legislation. The Gangmaster Licensing Authority is a Non-Departmental Public Body sponsored by the Department for Environment, Food and Rural Affairs (Defra) and consists of key industry stakeholders and representatives from government and enforcement agencies.

Enforcement

The success of this legislation will depend on the quality of the enforcement regime it inspires. The legislation gives the Secretary of State the power to appoint enforcement officers to enforce the criminal offences of operating without a licence and possessing false documents. In addition, the Licensing Authority is also able to appoint enforcement officers to carry out this function as well as compliance officers to enforce the licence conditions and take action for the purposes of the Act.

The Act gives enforcement and compliance officers rights to:

• Enter premises

• Search premises

• Take possession of any item from premises

• Require the production of relevant records

• Inspect and take away records (including computers)

• Order attendance of persons before them.

Enforcement officers will have the power of arrest for these offences. Offenders may be imprisoned for 12 months if convicted of operating without a licence or possessing a false licence/documents, while the deterrent value of the legislation has been strengthened by including sentences for repeat offences, up to two years imprisonment for a second offence; and up to ten years imprisonment for a third offence.

The Temporary Labour Working Group's code of practice and assessment procedures

The Temporary Labour Working Group took the view that a licensing and registration system had to be underpinned by a code of practice for labour providers and a robust method demonstrating compliance that probes workers' real conditions of employment. A code of practice was adopted in July 2004, with associated tools for labour providers establishing legal requirements and accepted best practice. These standards now provide an industry-agreed benchmark against which labour providers can be independently assessed.

The code and audit procedures developed to assess compliance with the code were trialled with six labour providers in Lincolnshire. Existing enforcement has prioritised tax evasion, benefit fraud and illegal working but field trials demonstrate that it is also possible to identify where workers are being exploited and how employers must improve working conditions. Trials undertaken by the Temporary Labour Working Group revealed serious and systematic abuses of workers' rights including payment of sub-minimum wages, excessive working hours and dangerous working conditions. A worker-focused inspection such as this is a necessary part of law enforcement and should be one component of a licensing regime.

Limitations and areas for development

The experiences of the enforcement agencies have shown that there are substantial training and awareness needs within the industry. Many employers are not sufficiently aware of the law or the advice and support that is currently available. In addition, many labour providers complain that when they try to seek advice about their legal obligations it is not always obvious where to go or that advice is difficult to access. If the industry is expected to comply with a code of practice in the near future, it must be recognised that businesses may require support in order to do so.

In the Group's experience, few labour providers are fully aware of the law and have all the necessary management controls in place to comply with the standards of the code. The Group recognised the constraints on small businesses that may not have an established culture of record keeping and were concerned to minimise any administrative burdens. Therefore, the Group developed a set of management tools to help labour providers implement the code and to facilitate the process of assessing compliance with it.

Local authorities, the Learning Skills Council, environmental health and Regional Development Agencies should be encouraged to facilitate the adoption of best practice among labour providers. This could be achieved by financing and delivering localised training courses and advice and guidance sessions on the code of practice. However at the moment this is a piecemeal approach and greater coordination is required. An analysis of the key skills that labour providers require in order to implement the code and meet the challenge of change within the industry may prove valuable.

Attempts to test the value of an awareness-raising leaflet and helpline for workers were met with mixed results. This experience suggested that the use of leafleting prior to assessment should be adopted as common practice. Workers must be made aware of their rights in their own language, and given a confidential means to complain with which they are very comfortable. However, some workers may not use this facility for months after they become aware of it. Leafleting via even the best employer and an impersonal helpline do not fully meet these requirements but are steps towards them. Trade unions and organisations that can advocate on behalf of workers can also have important roles to play. The group believes that an effective complaint mechanism would make licensing more credible and reduce its cost.

Making the legislation work

The new legislation has the potential to achieve benefits across the industry and society as a whole. A national register of licensed labour providers will help introduce fair competition between legitimate operators and place the responsibility on labour users and retailers to ensure that only their services are used. Government and tax payers will benefit through increased revenue from income tax and National Insurance and reduction in benefit fraud. Workers themselves will benefit as their conditions of work will be scrutinized routinely and the worst employers will be driven out of business.

The new Act, however, requires wide support and adequate resourcing if it is to deliver its potential benefits. Government, supermarkets,

221

growers, manufacturers, packers and labour providers all have a responsibility to stamp out exploitation of the workers who produce our food. All stakeholders must work effectively together to ensure the primary legislation is supported by the best possible mechanisms to license, register and assess labour providers. Crucially the Government must provide adequate resources to enable the newly-established Gangmasters Licensing Authority to implement, police and enforce the legislation. Industry stakeholders must also play their part to ensure that they promote a culture of compliance with the law.

Observations and lessons in brief

- A public interest case can be built to address responsible treatment of migrant workers.
- A broad based alliance is essential.
- Voluntary initiatives are most effective when employers are willing to change.
- Voluntary initiatives are not sufficient to protect the most vulnerable workers.
- There may be limits associated with the focus on a single industry.

References

"A Licence to Operate: New measures to tackle exploitation of temporary workers in the UK agricultural industry," Temporary Labour Working Group, November 2004.

The full Gangmasters (Licensing) Act 2004 may be seen online at www.legislation. hmso.gov.uk/acts/acts2004/20040011.htm

"Care trade": The international brokering of health care professionals

Susan Maybud[1] *and Christiane Wiskow*[2]

*T*he appealing, modern websites of the private agencies specializing in the recruitment of health care professionals for Western markets invite the loggers-on to explore a myriad of opportunities. Go ahead, they entice, just click on this website and you are one step closer to a better life. They advertise hundreds of fabulous hospital and health care nursing jobs in exciting places, and claim that they can make all the difference to health care careers. And it is so easy. Potential candidates just have to register, and they will be helped all along the way. Examination requirements will be demystified, job interviews will be arranged, and visas and permits will be handled. So fierce is the competition to secure scarce health care professionals that private recruitment agencies stage promotional events and aggressive recruitment campaigns in supplying countries, tripping over each other to attract suitable candidates.

How did the shortages of health care professionals become so acute, and how did international migration come to be viewed as one of the solutions to the problem? What is the role played by private recruitment agencies in the flows of international migration? How have they assumed their responsibilities towards individual migrant health care workers?

---

[1] Health Services Specialist, Sectoral Activities Department, ILO.

[2] Director and Research Consultant, Salumondi, Health Personnel and International Public Health, Geneva, Switzerland.

223

Introduction

Health care represents an important employment sector with an increasing demand for labour in most countries. An estimated 100 million people comprise the global health workforce. There are about 24 million registered doctors, nurses and midwives, and there are at least three times more uncounted informal, traditional, community and allied workers engaged in health care.[3] The majority of migrant health care workers are women, as women comprise 80% of the health work force. The feminization of the work force may seem advantageous to women, but often they may not achieve either economic security or personal empowerment. As migrant women continue to be motivated to repay debts and to cover the consumption needs of their families, it seems unlikely that there will be significant changes in gender power relations or more equality in social relations.[4]

The adequate supply of health care professionals has been a serious issue for developed countries in the last few decades. In general, developed countries have faced labour supply challenges due to ageing populations combined with insufficient planning and a lack of investment in attracting, educating and training domestic health care professionals. In the USA an estimated 20 percent deficit in the registered nurse workforce has been forecasted by 2020 if current trends are not reversed.[5] Yet strikingly, more than 26,000 qualified applicants were turned away from entry-level baccalaureate nursing programmes in 2004, in large part due to insufficient numbers of faculty.[6] In the UK 100,000 nurses are due to retire by 2010.[7] Across the EU, more than half of the physicians were aged over 45 in 2000; in Norway, the average age of dentists was 62.[8] EU

---

[3] Human resources for health: Overcoming the crisis, Joint Learning Initiative (Harvard, 2004).

[4] Kawar M "Towards gender sensitive labour migration management," Employment Strategy Department, ILO, 2004.

[5] Janiszewski G H (2003). The nursing shortage in the United States of America: an integrative review of the literature. Journal of Advanced Nursing, 43(4): 335–350.

[6] International Council of Nurses, "SEW News" No. 1, Jan-March 2005.

[7] Laporte C (2005). Diversity: Comment: The DTI must prevent private agencies recruiting nurses unethically overseas. Independent Newspapers, 27 January 2005. Available from www.factiva.com, accessed 20 April 2005.

[8] Hundley T (2005). Low pay leads Polish nurses, doctors to seek jobs abroad. Chicago Tribune, 2 January 2005. Available from www.factiva.com, accessed 20 April 2005.

Commissioner David Byrne warned that shortages would become critical and put health systems at risk, if these trends continued.[9]

Developing countries, on the other hand, struggle with harsh socio-economic situations to produce and retain a sufficiently qualified health care workforce. Around 36 African countries do not meet targets of one doctor per 5,000 people, according to the World Health Organisation. Even in non-conflict affected countries such as Zambia and Ghana, there is only one doctor for more than 10,000 people. Disparities between urban and rural areas are evident. In Nairobi, Kenya, there is one doctor for 500 people, but in the Turkana district the ratio is 1:160,000.[10]

The health care profession is not attracting enough new recruits in both developed and developing countries. In addition, it is also losing large numbers of trained personnel to areas outside the sector. Difficult working conditions and burnout are often quoted as root causes for this loss of talent. In the US, 500,000 trained nurses are not practising, 35,000 in South Africa, and 15,000 in Ireland.[11]

Nursing shortages specifically are not a new phenomenon. Concerned about insufficient supply, ineffective deployment and the worrying situation of nursing personnel,[12] the ILO Nursing Personnel Convention (C.149) and its accompanying Recommendation (R. 157) were adopted in 1977. Although nearly 30 years old, C.149 and R.157 were classified as up-to-date instruments by the ILO in 2002, reaffirming their relevance to today's socio-economic realities.

Once again, the effective management of human resources for health has recently re-entered the policy agenda after a long period of neglect. The challenge of implementing international development programmes such as the UN Millennium Development Goals, as well as the WHO/UNAIDS "3 by 5 Initiative" have highlighted the crisis in health personnel, especially in developing countries of the African continent. Worldwide, addressing the human resources for health crisis will constitute one of the prominent health policy issues for the next years to come.

---

[9] Reid L (2004). EU medical care chaos 'in decade' over staff shortfall. Independent Newpapers Ireland, 12 June 2004. Available from www.factiva.com, accessed 20 April 2005.

[10] Tripathi S "Africa's health sector needs more resources," Guardian Unlimited, Tuesday August 9, 2005.

[11] Health and Migration...The Facts, New Internationalist, no. 379, June 2005.

[12] ILO Nursing Personnel Convention, 1977; Preamble.

International migration in general also appeared on top of policy agendas in 2004, as witnessed by the outcomes of the International Labour Conference. [13]

Health worker migration – Brain drain, brain gain, or brain waste?

Where there is a gap, market forces will prevail, and the recruitment of workers from abroad represents a stop-gap solution for richer countries in addressing their shortages of health care personnel. The integration of migrants into the social and cultural fabric of receiving countries may be cause for concern, but it is also recognized that migrants bring "new experiences and talents that can widen and enrich the knowledge base of the economy…the self-selection of migrants means they are likely to bring valuable ideas, entrepreneurship, ambition and energy." [14] Already in 1977, the ILO R.157 made recommendations to facilitate the harmonization of education, training and practice regulations, as well as the mutual recognition of qualifications and nursing personnel exchange programmes on the basis of bilateral or multilateral agreements for migrating nursing personnel. Ethical aspects of migration were addressed, such as the protection of source countries, the equal treatment and opportunities of migrant nursing personnel, and the facilitation for return to countries of origin.

The international migration of health personnel became contentious in the 1990s when major recipient countries in the North were accused of "sucking in" health workers from the poor countries, regardless of the detrimental effects this had on the supplying countries' health systems. In the health sector, the 57th World Health Assembly adopted a resolution addressing migration as a major challenge for health systems in developing countries. [15]

The extent and flows of health worker mobility in general are difficult to establish due to the lack of consistent and reliable data. Inter-

[13] ILO (2004). Towards a fair deal for migrant workers in the global economy. International Labour Conference, 92nd Session, 2004. Geneva: International Labour Office.

[14] UK Home Office (2202) Secure Borders, Safe Haven: Integration with Diversity in Modern Britain, p. 11 (http:www.official-documents.co.uk/document/cm5387/cm5387.pdf.

[15] Fifty-seventh World Health Assembly (2004). International migration of health personnel: a challenge for health systems in developing countries. WHA 57.19. Geneva: WHO.

national migration most often occurs along post-colonial and linguistic lines, or within the same geographic region. Data from receiving countries show increasing trends of immigrating health professionals similar to general migration trends. [16] Compared with overall migration figures, the proportion of migrant skilled health workers may appear small. However, from the viewpoint of the health labour market the numbers involved are significant, and the effects on some of the sending countries health systems can be dramatic. For example, when a doctor from a small Pacific-island state migrates abroad, this may create a crisis if the professional is one of a handful of physicians serving the community. In 2003, nurses represented "only" 6 percent of the net foreign immigration in the UK; [17] nevertheless overseas nurses made up more than half of new registrants on the Nursing and Midwifery Council register in the previous year. [18] Foreign doctors constituted two thirds of all new full registrants according to the General Medical Council in UK. [19] In Queensland, Australia, 40% of the medical workforce was trained abroad. [20]

The richer countries can afford to resort to international recruitment as a "quick fix" [21] solution. The better payment and working conditions compared to low-income countries as well as professional development opportunities are attractive for skilled health workers from developing nations. The exodus of health professionals has jeopardized the provision of health services in some of the poorest source countries. Truly dedicated doctors leave the public sector in sheer frustration because of poor working conditions, unmanageable numbers of patients, lack of resources and lack of basic pharmaceuticals. [22] In 2002, the vacancy rates for doctors in Ghana was 47.3 percent and unfilled posts

[16] Stilwell B; Diallo K; Zurn P; Vujicic M; Adams O; Dal Poz M (2004). Migration of health-care workers from developing countries: strategic approaches to its management. Bulletin of the World Health Organization, 82 (8): 595-600.

[17] Migration Watch UK (2004). Immigration: the need for foreign nurses. Available from www.migrationwatchuk.com , accessed 24 April 2005.

[18] Buchan J; Dovlo D (2004). International Recruitment of Health Workers to the UK: A Report for DFID. London: DFID Health Systems Resource Centre. Available from www.dfidhealthrc.org , accessed 20 April 2005.

[19] Buchan J (2005). International recruitment of health professionals. BMJ 2005; 330:210. Available from www.bmj.com, accessed 20 April 2005.

[20] Mark L. Scott et al, *"Brain-drain or ethical recruitment?"* The Profession, MJA, 2004 vol.180, School of Public Health, University of NSW, www.mja.com.au.

[21] Buchan, 2005, *op.cit.*

[22] Correspondence posted by Bridget Farham on "Migration of health professionals," The Lancet.com website, 16 July 2005.

for registered nurses accounted for 57 percent. For the same year more Ghanaian doctors were registered abroad (about 1700) than working in the country (633). [23] Malawi reported a 52 percent vacancy rate for nurses. [24] A nurse in Uganda would typically earn US $38 per month and a nurse in the Philippines would earn US $380, but in the US the average monthly wage for nurses is about US $3,000. Health care professionals who leave most often do not return.

> "I have been working in a hospital in south west Ethiopia as a general surgeon for almost three years now. I work something like 16 hours a day for $200 a month. Beside the poor salary, how long can a person go on working 16 hours a day with no holidays throughout the year? I can understand it if doctors look for a place with better pay and reasonable working hours. But I feel very sad for the poor people who are left behind without quality health care." [25]

> "With the chaotic situation in the African health system, I can't condemn doctors who leave to look for pastures greener. Even if they remained, their knowledge would be of little help, as people would continue to die from lack of medicine. Our corrupt leaders are quick to travel abroad for quality health care and they don't care about us." [26]

Remittances generated by migrants are welcome national income sources for poorer countries and mitigate the impact of losing valuable professionals. "The economic impact of remittances in the areas that receive them are typically about 1-2, which means that $1 in remittances generates $2 in local economic activity as recipients buy goods or invest in housing, education, or health care." [27] Critics argue, however, that remittances flow directly to families, and do not compensate governments for their investment in the education and training of health care workers. Therefore the emigration of these professionals diminishes the capacities of many countries for general, sustainable development.

---

[23] Buchan and Dovlo, 2004, *op.cit.*

[24] Stilwell B; Diallo K; Zurn P; Dal Poz M; Adams O; Buchan J (2003). Developing evidence-based ethical policies on the migration of health workers: conceptual and practical challenges. Human Resources for Health 2003, I:8.

[25] BBC News World Africa website, Friday, 8 July, 2005, comment posted by Z. Baye, Ethiopia.

[26] BBC News World Africa website, Friday, 8 July, 2005, comment posted by K. Ntumba, Harare Zimbabwe.

[27] Martin P "Sustainable migration policies in a globalizing world," International Institute for Labour Studies, Geneva, 2003.

Migration does not only occur from the south to the north. South Africa, while losing health workers to other countries, also recruits from abroad to fill its own shortage. In 1999, 78 percent of rural doctors were non-South Africans, mainly from Kenya, Malawi and Zimbabwe.[28] In Namibia, half of the doctors in public services were reported being from abroad.[29] Some countries, such as the Philippines are deliberately supporting overseas recruitment of their nurses to other countries, partly because of an oversupply of nurses, and partly because of economic reasons with regard to the remittances of migrant workers as one of the biggest national income sources. The Philippines supplies 14,000 nurses abroad each year – twice as many as it trains – to work in the US, Saudi Arabia, Ireland and Britain, causing a shortfall at home.[30] More recently, countries like India, Sri Lanka and China have been looking at actively supporting the migration of their health care workers.

The complex issues surrounding health worker migration go beyond labour issues. Migration is embedded in the personal human right to freedom of movement, and the use of an individual's knowledge and skills to seek a better life. But it also affects human rights and social justice concerns where it contributes to worldwide growing health inequities. The loss of health personnel through migration usually results in a loss of capacity for the health systems of developing countries to deliver health care equitably.[31] The health of populations and thus the wellbeing of societies are at stake. The key is giving nationals valid incentives to stay in their countries as the primary solution.

International recruitment

Increased awareness of the detrimental effects of haphazard health worker recruitment from poor countries has galvanized key players into

---

[28] Martineau T; Decker K; Bundred P (2002). Briefing note on international migration of health professionals: levelling the playing field fro developing country health systems. Liverpool: Liverpool School of Tropical Medicine.

[29] Commonwealth Secretariat (2005). Report of a Consultation on the Recruitment and Migration of the Highly Skilled (Nurses and Teachers). Marlborough House, Pall Mall, London, 25 January 2005. London: Commonwealth Secretariat, Social Transformation Programmes Division, March 2005. Available from www.thecommonwealth.org, accessed 20 April 2005.

[30] Howell M "Doctors leaving Philippines to become nurses," 2003 www.sfgate.com.

[31] WHO (2004). Recruitment of health workers from the developing world. Report by the Secretariat. Executive Board 114th Session EB 114/5. Geneva: World Health Organization.

active discussion of the ethical issues involved in international recruitment. Several international organizations, professional associations and trade unions[32] have addressed the topic by issuing guidelines and policy statements. Ethical international recruitment has been endorsed, taking into account the potential effects of recruitment activities on the health system of source countries while at the same time protecting the rights of individuals to freedom of movement. In essence these efforts aim at balancing the needs of communities and societies, i.e. equitable health care, with the rights of individual health workers to move and select their employment.

At the international level, the 2003 Commonwealth Code of Practice for the International Recruitment of Health Workers is the only instrument officially adopted.[33] It addresses the principle of mutuality of benefits for source and receiving countries and recommends compensation for the loss of investment in education in source countries. This code has not been signed by Australia, Canada and the UK, indicating the conflicting interests of recruiting and sending countries.

At the national level, the UK is the first country to implement a code of practice on ethical international recruitment of health personnel. Recently the code has been revised according to lessons learnt and is now intended to include the independent sector and recruitment of temporary staff in its provisions.[34] All NHS employers are strongly commended to adhere to the code, which restricts recruitment from over 150 developing countries, including South Africa, Ghana, Uganda, Malawi and some Asian countries.

Guidelines and codes are generally considered as positive initiatives, serving as references for policy development. However, there is scepticism surrounding the limitations of such instruments due to their voluntary status. The instruments usually apply to active recruitment by employers or agencies. Yet applications by health care workers themselves are not restricted so as to avoid individual discrimination. The impact of guidelines and codes in terms of protecting poor countries from adverse effects of health worker migration still has to be evaluated. Initial experiences

[32] e.g. WHO, Commonwealth Secretariat, International Council of Nurses, World Medical Association, WONCA, Public Services International, UNISON- UK, Royal College of Nursing – UK.

[33] Commonwealth Code of Practice for the International Recruitment of Health Workers, Commonwealth Secretariat, London, 2003.

[34] Department of Health (2004). Code of Practice for the international recruitment of healthcare professionals. London: DH Publications. Available from www.dh.gov.uk , accessed December 2004.

with the code of practice in the UK have shown that the impact may only be short-term. For example, there was an initial decline in recruitment of nurses from South Africa, which subsequently increased again in the registration period 2001-2002.[35] In 2003-2004 more than a quarter (3,795) of new registrants on the Nursing and Midwifery Council's (NMC) register came from countries from which recruitment had officially been proscribed.[36] It has been argued that the UK government could not monitor the effectiveness of its code because it would not record the number of international health workers it employed.[37]

The role of recruitment agencies

Recruitment intermediaries fulfill various functions in facilitating the labour needs of international capital, the foreign exchange needs of labour-supplying nations and the employment and income generating needs of individuals. Furthermore, recruitment agencies promise to simplify the often thorny and confusing paperwork and migration processes that first-time migrants may face, thus demystifying what may seem complicated and insurmountable. Offering these services has shifted the nature of international migration from family or word-of-mouth initiatives to more commercial and internationally organized institutions. Recruitment intermediation has thus become a profitable and lucrative business[38] and has led to the "mushrooming" of recruitment agencies - some of them reputable and some not.[39] Much of their efforts to secure qualified migrants are active, through direct marketing and on site activities. However, since health care workers are educated and often have access to information technologies, there is a certain amount of "passive" effort through internet marketing and website management as well. Research is still needed in order to assess the roles of recruitment agencies

[35] Buchan J; Parkin T; Sochalski J (2003). International nurse mobility: Trends and policy implications. Geneva: World Health Organization.

[36] Williams S; Catton H (2005). Concern over nurses' code. The Guardian, 23 February 2005. Available from www.factiva.com, accessed 20 April 2005.

[37] Lincolnshire Echo (2004). Proposals to stop 'backdoor' recruitment don't go far enough. Lincolnshire Echo, 21 September 2004. Available from www.factiva.com, accessed 20 April 2005.

[38] Ball RE (1990). The Process of International Contract Labour Migration from the Philippines: the Case of Filipino Nurses. Sydney: University of Sydney, Department of Geography.

[39] Rajagopal S (2004). Big dreams, bigger pitfalls. The Hindu, 23 November 2004. Available from www.factiva.com, accessed 20 April 2005.

and to gauge their positive and negative impacts on migration flows and on the quality of service they offer individual migrants.

While in the beginning agencies charged individual nurses with the placement fees, these costs have shifted to the employer when the demand for nurses became acute. [40] In 1999, the rates to be paid per recruited nurse to agencies in the UK varied between 8-14 percent of their first year salary upon registration, not including the air fares between countries of origin and the UK. [41] According to media reports, UK hospitals have spent £28 million on hiring nurses from private agencies in 2002. [42] Many hospitals in developed countries have engaged in direct hiring processes, whereby their own staff will go abroad to recruit health care workers, thus economizing the middlemen fees paid to the recruitment agencies.

The recruitment of health care professionals requires a higher level of capitalization than other workers. For example, nurse recruitment is an expensive process, highly bureaucratic and selective. A nurse recruitment agency in India claimed that it invested $10,000 per nurse candidate for placement in the US, including air ticket, relocation, visa and green card processing as well as the fees required for professional examinations. [43] In general, the recruitment process for nurses requires a high level of organization, appropriate facilities and competencies to screen, test and select, and a longer-term commitment to the individual compared to other occupational groups. The screening process is extensive, including the evaluation of formal qualifications and specializations, experience and personal skills and qualities. [44] In addition to the work permit processing, the professional registration procedures have to be organized; these often involve requirements for adaptation periods, known as supervised practice. These issues have to be considered by the agency to assure the successful placement of nurses or other health professionals, and the conditions need to be clarified to the applying candidates.

---

[40] Ball RE, 1990, *op cit.*

[41] Department of Health (1999). Guidance on International Nursing Recruitment. London: Department of Health. Available from www.dh.gov.uk, accessed July 2004.

[42] McGarvie L (2003). NHS Plunderers. Scottish Daily Record & Sunday Mail, 7 September 2003. Available from www.factiva.com, accessed 20 April 2005.

[43] Varghese N (2003). Nursing ambitions? The US beckons. The Hindu Business Line, 8 December 2003. Available from www.factiva.com, accessed 20 April 2005.

[44] Ball RE, 1990, *op cit.*

Recruitment agencies may act as intermediaries in the recruitment process or as employers themselves. In cases where recruitment agents act as employers, the recruited nurses sign contracts putting them at the disposal of the agents who assign the placements and pay the salaries. [45] These situations are not always easy on the migrant nurses, who may be exposed to additional resentment of being both a temporary worker and a migrant:

> *"I was working as an agency nurse – so every time I worked, I worked somewhere new and I found that really stressful – a new emergency department every time and that was tough. I always had to work with new people and they sort of had an attitude toward agency nurses because they were paid more but weren't part of the place. There's a sort of stigma attached to agency nurses."* [46]

Vulnerability of migrant health workers

While it has been suggested that the employment experiences of skilled workers are more favourable than that of unskilled labour, the vulnerability of migrant health professionals should not be underestimated. [47]

As reported in the media, professional associations are aware of the exploitation of health professionals in destination countries. The scope of abuse ranges from overpaid charges to agencies over contract and registration frauds to bullying and threatening by employers and even slavery-like living conditions. Some of these forms of exploitation experienced by health professionals, such as unacceptable or expensive accommodation, withholding of identity documents and permits or illegal deduction from salaries, are similar to experiences of other labour migrants, notably unskilled workers. Other abusive practices, as described below, are more specific to the health professions.

For example, numerous agencies in various countries aim to bypass checking systems for work permits and bring health professionals under

---

[45] Ball RE, 1990, *op cit.*

[46] Van Eyck K, editor "Who Cares? Women Health Workers in the Global Labour Market," Public Services International, UNISON UK, 2005, p. 38.

[47] Bach S, International migration of health workers: labour and social issues. Sectoral Activities Programme, working paper 209. Geneva: International Labour Office, 2003.

improper student visas. Nurses with this kind of visa are not permitted to take up employment on arrival. [48] However, they will often work over the maximum number of hours permitted under their visas and for lower rates. Reports on agencies in India have uncovered the opening of fake tuition centres for nurses which pretend to offer training for the professional entry examination in the US Commission on Graduates of Foreign Nursing Schools (CGFNS). The nurses paid significant fees yet ended up without the certified examination required for employment in US health establishments. [49] Such incidents have highlighted the need for the regulation of recruitment and training agencies.

A registration scam was uncovered in the UK, when the NMC identified 83 nurses on the register from India and Africa who had not undergone the required supervised practice. All the nurses had been placed on the register by an agency that had purported to having provided them with fulltime supervised courses. In reality these nurses had been exposed to only part-time orientation visits. The consequences for these innocent nurses were significant as they were removed from the register at short notice. [50]

The situation is aggravated by a critical shortage of adaptation placements, which leaves nurses vulnerable to exploitation by abusive employers, especially in the independent nursing home sector. In the UK, nurses are paid care assistants' salaries while they are fulfilling their probationary adaptation period over three to six months prior to registration with the NMC. However, many unscrupulous employers delay the registration in order to continue paying lower salaries to the nurses. The dependence on the employer's recommendation for the NMC registration and for securing the coveted work permits has resulted in reluctance by the nurses to complain.

Wage deductions may also be made by employers, agencies and third parties, and more often than not, a combination of all three. These broadly include: i) deductions to "repay" migration debt and accrued interest, including travel, visa and documentation costs, ii) deductions for the opportunity to work, iii) deductions for accommodation and iv) deductions for work related costs such as uniforms, transportation or

---

[48] Features (2004). Agencies exploit foreign nurses; Health. The Times, 6 July 2004. Available from http://global.factiva.com accessed 20 April 2005.

[49] Rajagopal S, 2004, *op cit.*

[50] Carvel J, 2004, *op cit.*

safety gear.[51] Many nurses "end up in poverty or as virtual prisoners of their employers."[52]

A specific case involving "Conrado", a highly qualified nurse from Asia, illustrates in detail the vulnerability to fleecing by deductions:

> Conrado was among many who were approached by a UK based company with offices in an Asian city. Applicants are interviewed by agency staff, and the videos shown to prospective employers/ agencies cost some £200 each. After passing the pre-selection test they were offered a further interview... over the internet that cost a further £200 a head. They were then told that they had to pay a further £300 for the work permit and placement fee. Having paid a total of £700 – for which no receipts were given, they were then informed that they needed to raise one month's deposit and one month's rent for their accommodation on arrival in the UK. The nurses were not told that the Trust had a policy of giving migrant nurses an advance payment of £500 on arrival. Nor were they told that their accommodation was in fact being provided to them by the agency.

> "We were all drained in terms of the finances and this was the exact timing a finance company offered a loan of £1,500 with a net loan of around £1100 with a monthly payment of £302. Desperate to grab the opportunity we took the loan though we knew that almost nothing would be left from our salary and besides we're not in the position to decline the offer."

> When the nurses arrived in the UK they were given tenancy agreements to sign for accommodation not yet seen. "Our employers were there and did nothing." After two months the nurses found that they were unable to pay for the accommodation and give themselves an adequate diet. They approached their nursing manager for advice, but were told that this was a matter that needed to be arranged directly with their accommodation agent and was not something in which their employer could intervene. Their manager informed them that if they did not pay the full house rental they would have proven themselves "not trustworthy" and that the NHS Trust therefore would not support their application to register to practice nursing in the UK. "We were caught between the fear of being sent home and the fear of not paying back the debt, when the interest was getting higher all the time."... So, while the nurses'

---

[51] Anderson B and Rogaly B, "Forced Labour and Migration to the UK," Centre on Migration, Policy and Society (COMPAS), Oxford University, and Trades Union Congress (TUC), 2005, pl.42.

[52] Cottel C (2005). Is this the way to treat nurses who want a job? The Guardian, 5 February 2005. Available from http://money.guardian.co.uk, accessed 20 April 2005.

average net salary was £805 exclusive of tax, the amount they received, after deductions of £305 for rent and £302 for loan repayment was £198, or £46 a week, from which of course they also had to pay the loans incurred for video interviewing and visas. Conrado described how he lived on £5 worth of food a week, having an apple for breakfast, a snack in the canteen for lunch, and rice for dinner. [53]

Regulation as a measure of protection

Reports on unscrupulous private agencies raised calls for better regulation mechanisms. Registration with government authorities provided for some control over recruitment practices, and in many countries recruitment agencies have to register with government authorities. Legally registered agencies may accept admission fees from nurses and charge them for services, but the amounts involved are prescribed. In India, only agencies with a licence from the Ministry of Labour can execute overseas recruitment. Unlicensed agencies were observed charging huge sums from the individual recruits although the employing clients were also being charged to cover the costs of the recruitment services. [54] Irish law requires that costs be borne by the employers and states clearly that deductions from wages by recruitment agencies was an illegal practice. [55]

The majority of guidelines and codes on international recruitment in the health sector address the cooperation of employers – both public and private - with private recruitment agencies. Orientation and guidance is provided on key principles, on stages of selecting an agency and indicators for assessing the company as well as legal requirements. The Companion Document to the Commonwealth Code of Practice recommends that governments enter "auditable" arrangements with recruitment agencies and set up monitoring mechanisms.

The UK National Health Service recommends that its employers only cooperate with agencies that apply the standards set out in the Code of Practice. For this purpose a list of approved agencies is made available to employers. For NHS approval, an agency has to obtain two references

[53] Anderson B. and Rogaly B., op.cit. pp 45-46.

[54] Rajagopal S, 2004, *op cit.*

[55] Congress Youth (n.d.). Developing a Mulitcultural/Intercultural Society. Available from www.ictu.ie, accessed 20 April 2005.

by NHS employers verifying that they adhere to the Code of Practice. This however may create difficulties for some agencies, as they come only on the list with two NHS references, but NHS trusts may not cooperate with them if they are not on the approved list.[56] Currently, the Code applies to 178 agencies with an intention to extend coverage to 200 more agencies in the private sector from 2005 onwards, to include agencies supplying domestic staff to NHS.[57]

Public Services International (PSI), the global federation of unions, has called on governments, health sector employers and trade unions to engage in a process of social dialogue in order to: monitor and regulate recruitment agencies at national and international levels; adopt ethical recruitment guidelines and even impose sanction on employers and recruitment agencies that do not respect workers' fundamental rights; and to secure the commitment by receiving governments to decrease their reliance on foreign health care workers.[58] UNISON, the Public Service International (PSI) affiliate in the UK, released "A Guide for Nurses from Overseas Working in the UK," which gives practical guidance to migrating nurses so as to empower the individuals to protect themselves from abusive practice.[59]

Initiatives for ensuring quality services are also taken by reputable agencies themselves. For example, the Recruitment & Employment Confederation (REC) in the UK, representing among others 250 nursing agencies, has developed its own Code of Recruitment Practice, covering all member agencies. Two paragraphs of the code refer to overseas recruitment: member agencies are required to provide adequate information to the candidate on terms of recruitment and employment in order to enable the candidate to make an informed decision. Further, in the cooperation with overseas agents it should be assured that they would not charge recruits for services unless this was legal and normal custom. A standards team monitors the adherence to the code; quarterly reports on complaints and queries about agency conduct are issued.[60]

---

[56] Bach S (2003). International migration of health workers: labour and social issues. Sectoral Activities Programme, working paper 209. Geneva: International Labour Office.

[57] Parsons A (2005). New Code Of Practice Covering Recruitment Of Overseas Healthcare Staff. Mondaq Business Briefing, 1 March 2005. Available from www.factiva.com, accessed 20 April 2005.

[58] van Eyck, K., op.cit. p. 78.

[59] "A Guide for Nurses from Overseas Working in the UK" UNISON, London, revised 2004.

[60] Recruitment and Employment Confederation (2004). REC Quarterly Complaints Report: January-March 2004. Available from www.rec.uk.com, accessed 20 April 2005.

While these principles reflect major recommendations found in most instruments on ethical international recruitment, the REC has not signed up to the revised NHS Code of Practice, arguing that the government was not establishing a level playing field. The criticism refers to a provision in the revised code that precludes individuals from developing countries on the restricted list from seeking employment through agencies while allowing direct individual application to NHS. This highlights the difficulty in distinguishing between active recruitment in developing countries and "passive" recruitment of nurses who joined an agency after arrival in UK. [61]

Conclusion

The adverse effects that the international recruitment of health care workers have on strained health systems of poor countries raises moral concerns. The migration flows from poor to better-off countries contributes to increasing worldwide inequities in health by jeopardizing the capacities of weak health systems to provide adequate health service in today's globalized labour markets. An ethical approach to international recruitment is needed, taking into account the potential effects on health systems in source countries, safeguard the individual migrant worker's rights while pursuing benefits for all in the international migration process.

The social partners have their particular responsibilities in the international recruitment of health workers:

Governments are responsible for ensuring adequate workforce planning and development in their health sector; they should take the lead in promoting ethical recruitment and assuring regulation and monitoring mechanisms accordingly. Employers, both public and private, as well as recruiters are critical for implementing international recruitment according to quality standards. Unions and professional associations have an important role in preventing migrant worker exploitation by disseminating information, fostering capacity building and developing support measures for victims of abuse. Finally the individual health care worker has the responsibility to obtain as much information as possible before committing to an overseas contract, and to learning about their rights once they have migrated.

---

[61] Carvel J (2004). Agencies defy nurse poaching code. The Guardian, 30 December 2004. Available from www.factiva.com, accessed 20 April 2005.

Merchants of medical care: Recruiting agencies in the global health care chain

John Connell[1] and Barbara Stilwell[2]

The migration of skilled health workers has, in the past decade, become more complex, more global and of growing concern to those countries who lose health workers from sometimes fragile health systems. The countries most affected by emigration are in sub-Saharan Africa alongside some small island states (though numbers have been greatest from such Asian countries as India and the Philippines). In both these groups of countries national economies are often performing poorly and economic inequalities are the key to migration. The migration of skilled health workers takes place within the broad context of the accelerated globalization of the service sector in the last two decades. Such professional services as health care are very much part of the new internationalization of labour, and in this context it has largely been demand led (or at least facilitated), with the growing global integration of health care markets.

The main destinations are the Gulf Countries, Europe and North America where demand is increasing, as national populations age, the recruitment of health workers has fallen (or has remained inadequate) and attrition increased. As demand in these countries has tended to increase so too has the active recruitment of overseas health workers. Recruitment agencies have become much more active in recent years and have stimulated migration, and, in some cases, increased resentment in labour supplying countries.

---

[1] Professor of Geography, School of Geosciences, University of Sydney, Australia. (Seconded by the Australian Government to WHO, Geneva, 2005, to work on migration issues).

[2] Coordinator, Department of Human Resources for Health, World Health Organization (WHO), Geneva.

While the broad structure of emigration and immigration has been in place for over thirty years, it has recently grown in volume and shows more obvious negative consequences in source countries. A quarter of a century ago it was mainly a movement from a few developing countries to a small number of developed countries, typified by the recruitment of nurses from the Philippines for the Middle East (Mejia et al 1979) but it has now extended, become more complex, increasingly involved governments and recruiting agencies (Bach 2004) and become more likely to be dominated by women. One of the more important changes of recent years is the entry of China into the market as a supplier of nurses. The size of China and its considerable interest in becoming a supplier of health workers has the potential to profoundly influence the system in the near future (Xu 2003, Stilwell et al 2005).

Where political circumstances change, as in the case of the expansion of the European Union that enabled migration from poorer eastern states to those in the west, then new structures of migration have followed. There has been, for example, substantial movement of doctors from the Czech Republic to the west creating gaps in the Czech health service (Mareckova 2004). This movement from the 'new' European states has been accentuated further during the present century, creating concerns over what has been described as 'social dumping', a euphemism for cheap labour, in some sectors of western economies. In this century patterns of migration continue to change: Japan is becoming a recipient nation for health workers and China and Central and Eastern European countries are becoming new sources.

The greater complexity of migration is evident in the interlocking chains of recruitment and supply, though some of these were in place thirty years ago (Mejia et al 1979, Stilwell et al 2005). Thus in the Caribbean, Guyanan nurses move to several countries, including St Lucia and Jamaica, and Jamaican nurses travel to several places, such as the Virgin Islands, but also to metropolitan countries. In 2004 Bermuda was concerned about the loss of nurses to the United States; six months later Jamaica was worried about recruitment of nurses by Bermuda. There is therefore something of a hierarchy in global migration – the global care chain – from the poorest African and Asian states and the relatively small and poor island states of the Caribbean and the Pacific, to the developed world, culminating in the United States. Moreover, as demand in developed countries has increased, the structure of recruitment has grown and extended.

Most migration follows broad former colonial, geographical and linguistic ties. In many countries it is not unique to the health sector but is part of a wider pattern of the global movement of professionals. Thirty years ago doctors were the main migrant group, but migrant nurses have now become much more numerous, hence international migration has taken on a new gendered structure. At the same time as international migration, and partly as a response to it, rural-urban migration of skilled health workers has become more common alongside a movement from the public sector to the private sector, with negative consequences for the public sector and a reduction in equity.

Migration is a response to uneven development and its local repercussions including poor wages, poor working conditions (overtime, shift work, limited access to technology), poor ongoing training or research facilities, and limited and biased promotion prospects. Demand for health workers has increased in developed countries with the aging of their populations, while jobs in the health sector are seen in many developed countries as too demanding, poorly paid and lowly regarded (in line with reduced public sector funding, and disregard for the public sector) and occurring within a context of poor working conditions. The demands of working with patients with HIV/AIDS has been a further factor in some countries, as have crime and political factors. Migrants often choose to migrate to benefit their children and their extended families. Economic restructuring has imposed restrictive conditions in some countries that have made developing and retaining a health sector workforce more difficult, mainly because of constraints on hiring workers in the public sector. The same reasons that have stimulated migration have also reduced recruitment into, and increased attrition rates from, the national health workforce. Migrant health workers tend to be those with a high level of skill and experience but are usually younger than those who remain (Stilwell et al 2005).

It has become increasingly evident that, in a very crucial sense, the intention to migrate actually occurs even before entry into the health system. In the Philippines, for more than twenty years, some people have sought to become nurses at least in part, and sometimes primarily, because that provides a means of international migration (e.g. Ball 1996). By the end of the 1980s a medical degree at the Fiji School of Medicine was being widely seen as a 'passport to prosperity' (WPRO 2004). More recently this kind of situation has become more widespread. In India one Dean of a medical college has expressed his concern over 'the growing danger of a large number of new doctors who have no commitment to this country or to ethical standards of practice. At least if they go abroad we are rid of them' (quoted in Mullan 2004: 29). In such contexts developing a valuable national workforce is increasingly more difficult.

The issues

The migration of health personnel from relatively poor to relatively rich countries has been a source of growing international and national concern, especially over the past decade. It has been a critical influence on the ability of countries to plan for human resource management and therefore for health service delivery. Some categories of health workers – notably nurses – are in particular global demand because of shortages in richer countries. Many developing countries experience an absolute shortage of health personnel, which leaves gaps in the existing infrastructure and services, in both the public and private sectors.

The migration of nurses is particularly evident in terms of numbers but in some circumstances there are also significant migration streams of other skilled health workers, though these have usually been less well documented. So significant has the shortage of nurses become that, in the Philippines at least, doctors are retraining as nurses to become available for overseas employment.

There are substantial economic costs to sending countries who bear the brunt of the costs of producing the migrant health workers. This cost is greater than that for many other migrants because of high training costs, the lost care that they might have provided, and the repercussions of that throughout society and the economy, the cost of replacements (where this occurs) and the cost of referrals. Migration and loss of health workers has had negative consequences for many health care systems, where staff have increased workloads, facilities close and waiting times increase. Non-qualified workers may be introduced to undertake jobs that may be beyond their capabilities. These impacts are most severe in rural areas where migration has been greatest.

The challenges are greatest for the poorest countries, where wages and working conditions are usually least adequate. Moreover, the migration of health workers is of particular concern since in the health arena human resources are doubly significant because health workers directly improve the quality of life of others, who are then able to contribute more to wider society. This may constitute a basis for 'medical exceptionalism' – the need to formulate distinctive policies favouring health workers above other occupational groups.

The intensification of competition for skilled health practitioners has meant countries increasingly recruiting from each other, rather than addressing 'more difficult' causes of limited recruitment and greater attrition, that are linked to inadequate pay and poor working conditions. As demand for health workers has increased in recent years it has been paralleled by an increase in the active recruitment of health workers through trade fairs, visiting delegations and so on, that has increased pressure of health workers to become a part of the global health care chain. Recruitment agencies do not merely satisfy demand but, through their advertisements and promotions, actively *create a desire* for further migration.

In recent years the structure of migration has become increasingly privatised through the expansion of recruitment agencies, and the regular use of these by recipient countries and by particular hospitals. Irrespective of any existing intent to migrate, active recruitment has put growing pressure on, and impressive opportunities in front of, potential migrants. Moreover, recruitment agencies smooth the way in attending to bureaucratic issues, satisfying concerns over different countries and cultures, and providing induction training in destinations.

Recruitment agencies

There is remarkably little information available on the operations of recruitment agencies, despite their growing significance, as demand for workers exceeds supply. There is scant evidence on whether recruiters exaggerate the potential of overseas employment, but it is implausible that they do not increase its probability. Their advertisements alone stress the wide-ranging benefits of working overseas. They dominate the structure of migration in many places, especially in less developed states, their activities lie outside the domain of most codes of practice and there are concerns over their modes of operation.

For those who had emigrated from Cameroon the single most important reason was recruitment (Awases et al 2004), though obviously this would not have been successful unless other reasons were in place. Dozens of agencies have sprung up simply to market Polish doctors in the United Kingdom. In this century there has been active recruitment of Fijian nurses for the UAE, a country that few in Fiji would have had any knowledge of until then, and in the 1990s there was recruitment to work in several nearby countries, including the Marshall Islands, Nauru and New Zealand. In all of these cases recruitment agencies have expanded the scope of health worker migration.

A recent analysis of nearly 400 international migrant nurses in London has shown that as many as two thirds of all overseas nurses were recruited by agencies to work in Britain (Buchan et al 2005). Many nurses were also subsequently involved in 'back-door recruitment' by the NHS after an initial period of work in the private sector, and in most cases that initial employment was very brief, with nurses moving to the NHS as soon as they had completed adaptation. Most nurses paid for some of the services provided by the agencies, and some received no pay during early periods of work and adaptation, emphasizing the exploitation that can occur through unscrupulous recruiters. Many nurses also believed they were being underpaid in terms of their experience. This newly revealed extent of back door recruitment to the NHS emphasizes that codes of practice – designed to regulate unscrupulous recruiting and the exploitation of both workers and sending countries – are extremely difficult to implement, even in countries like the UK where there is a powerful rule of law, unless they is very strong commitment to them and they are very carefully monitored.

Where health workers are contracted by private recruitment agencies there are sometimes unforeseen costs, such as 'placement fees', that put migrants at an immediate financial disadvantage, and in some circumstances recruitment agencies simply exploit workers, even in countries like the United Kingdom, where there are trade unions and other forms of support. One recent example of this was a case where a recruitment agency recruited a Filippina nurse to work in Wales but, after migration, she was placed in a nursing home and told that she had to undergo a 'period of adaptation' before her credentials could be formally certified. She worked for some time at a wage of less than £5 an hour, barely above the minimum wage, performing unskilled work in the nursing home. Despite the low wages, monthly deductions were made for repayments of the 'loan' advanced to her for her recruitment fees that totalled almost £2000. After the probationary period was over she sought information from her employer on the status of her certification, and was threatened with deportation. In this case the trade union, UNISON, were able to support her and ensure that she was able to transfer to an appropriate job in the National Health Service. After this incident the recruitment agency returned to the Philippines to recruit more workers, offering even lower wages and stipulating a longer 'period of adaptation'. (Van Eyck 2005). Nurses have also been given orientation by a recruitment agency stressing that under no circumstances were they to join a union, and in particular, UNISON, stating that they would be deported if they did (Anderson and Rogaly 2004).

In other British cases nurses have been exploited by overwork, excessive accommodation costs and by undertaking periods of training and 'adaptation', which are supposed to last between three and six months, after which they are paid on a higher nursing pay scale. Many nursing homes have delayed such registration because of cost savings, reducing the ability of nurses to pay off loans which could be as much as £3,000 (Anderson and Rogaly 2004). While recruiting agencies may not be directly implicated they condone such practices. Indeed this is part of a widespread situation where the skills of migrant workers are deliberately undervalued or ignored in their destinations.

Even more recently, in April 2005, an agency recruited 55 nurses to the United Kingdom from a number of countries, promising to register their qualifications with the UK Nursing Council after facilitating a period of 'observation' in a British hospital. However, the agency did not request the hospital to host the nurses and simply left them there until the hospital eventually noticed their presence a few weeks later.

There is at least anecdotal information that circumstances may be both worse and more common in other destinations, where union protection and government support are absent. Many health workers move from countries where they are not members of, or familiar with, unions and lack the knowledge to gain union or other support in their destinations.

Consequently, in a number of places there has been concern over the activities of recruitment agencies. Thus in Mauritius it is argued by the President of the largest Mauritian nursing union that 'The British send recruitment agents who very discreetly make contact with nurses and directly negotiate the contracts. Last week, 26 nurses were lured away by a single recruiter' (quoted in *Afro News*, 28 May 2004). Ethical questions have also been raised about the use, operation and cost of recruitment agencies. It has been pointed out that a recruiter was hired by a US corporation to recruit nurses in the Caribbean for a fee of $1 million – a sum substantially greater than earned by the nurses or that might reach the region (*Stabroek News*, 18 July 2004).

Policy directions?

Migration is a basic human right and few countries have actively sought to prevent migration, while others have encouraged it as a source of capital. Moreover; in most cases individual health care workers and their families gain from migration, hence policies that directly oppose migration are very unlikely to be successful (Stilwell et al 2005). Indeed there is considerable evidence that women migrant health workers are often willing to put up with some degree of exploitation because of the economic gains to their families (Van Eyck 2005). Consequently a range of policies are required to address the growing imbalance of health workers between countries and regions, and the exploitation of those workers.

However, not all countries have sought to prevent migration, and some like India, Cuba, Egypt and the Philippines, purposefully export workers, including health workers, either to earn valuable foreign exchange, mainly through remittances, or to fulfil humanitarian goals. In several countries, such as the Philippines, there may even be tensions between government departments, where migration is perceived as a valuable economic policy but an inappropriate health policy. In many more countries migration may be perceived to be a right and intervening in that process is therefore unethical. Nonetheless, even in these countries there is concern about what may be perceived as excessive migration and exploitation and interest in developing programmes to mitigate or compensate for this.

All states have some opportunities to develop more comprehensive policies in support of skilled health workers, primarily in terms of working conditions, but in developing countries these are never likely to be as attractive as in developed countries. Improved wages alone in sending countries will not fundamentally change the structure of migration unless this is linked into a more comprehensive package of workplace reforms, that have been elaborated elsewhere (Stilwell et al 2005). Lack of numbers has partly followed underinvestment in the public health sector and in health worker education and training. All countries need to aim at self-sufficiency and produce adequate numbers of national health workers to meet their own needs rather than rely on migration, or experience its consequences.

Increased demands for ethical recruitment practices have resulted in some formal policy changes in receiving countries with the development of codes of practice, but these have not had binding powers and have often been circumvented. More dialogue is needed to establish policies and strategies that will maximize the benefits of health worker migration while recognizing its impact in the most vulnerable countries. Policies are needed that might reduce migration, or alternatively enable a more balanced and controlled structure of migration, and ensure that some countries and regions are not significantly disadvantaged by migration.

There is no agreed definition of ethical international recruitment and the purposes of ethical instruments vary, but a common understanding is found in most publications: ethical international recruitment (EIR) aims to prevent adverse effects on health systems of the source countries and to protect the rights of the individuals.

A more general definition of EIR, derived from the Commonwealth Code of Practice (Commonwealth Secretariat 2003), states that international recruitment of health workers should take "into account the potential impact of such recruitment on services in the source country", and the International Council for Nursing (ICN, 2004) has pointed out that "Ethical recruitment principles are the same in international and intra-national contexts." This broadens the view from international inter-country levels to recruitment practices in general and thus to employment conditions in the health sector. The ethical recruitment principles outlined by ICN provide a framework for retention strategies as well as international recruitment processes.

Ethical dimensions within international recruitment are explicitly described by some of the instruments as guiding principles: the World Medical Association statement refers to justice, co-operation and autonomy, in combining global social and individual needs and the co-operation as a way to problem-solving (WMA 2003). The Commonwealth Code of Practice applies the principles of transparency, fairness and mutuality of benefits, among Commonwealth countries, and between recruits and recruiter (Commonwealth Secretariat 2003).

However, information about the effects of and experiences with existing international recruitment (IR) instruments are scarce. This is partly because most of the instruments have only recently been developed and published. Some authors suggest a critical view on the instruments and their effects. Willetts and Martineau (2004: 13) point out that there may be a risk of codes of practice doing more harm than good: "The voluntary code is only a "quick and cheap" strategy to change employment behavior. At best the introduction of an instrument sends the message that something is being done to solve a problem; at worst the use of such instruments might be a cynical exploitation of the general sense of goodwill." Nevertheless, they appraise the introduction of IR instruments as a "good start which should be built upon by improving existing systems" (op cit: 14). Lessons learned from early experiences could help in shaping these improvements.

Whether the intended objective of protecting developing countries in decreasing the outflow of health workers has been achieved is difficult to say: a significant increase of nurse outflow from Sub-Saharan countries to the UK has been observed despite the introduction of the first ethical IR instrument in the UK in 1999. The impact of the instrument however cannot be evaluated as the data do not allow for differentiation between active recruitment and individual applications (Buchan 2003: 13). Another study suggests that there was a substantial fall in the number of nurses registered from South Africa and the West Indies in the UK in the year to April 2003. This may indicate that -given lags in the system – the guidelines are having some impact on employer behavior. All in all it will take several years before the impact of guidelines can be fully assessed (Bach 2003: 22).

The Department of Health Code of Practice in the UK first established guidelines in 1999 (Department of Health 1999), which required NHS employers not to target South Africa and the West Indies, where countries were seen as having particularly vulnerable health care systems. It then introduced a Code of Practice for international recruitment for NHS employers (Department of Health 2001). This Code was strengthened in 2004, and now covers recruitment agencies providing staff to the NHS, temporary staff working in the NHS, and private sector organizations providing services to the NHS as well as NHS employers (Department of Health 2003). The Code "promotes high standards of practice in the ethical international recruitment of healthcare professionals. All employers are strongly commended to adhere to this code of practice" (Department of Health 2004). The Code does not cover private sector employers (unless they are involved in providing services to the NHS) and does not prevent health professionals taking the initiative to apply for employment in the UK, or to come to the UK for training purposes.

This had two particular negative consequences. Firstly, one outcome was that Caribbean nurses, many of whom had hitherto gone to the UK, then went primarily to the United States. Secondly, there was nothing to prevent private hospitals and care homes recruiting in the banned countries and nothing to stop nurses moving from these institutions into the NHS at a later date. As one journalist argued: 'The NHS could say that its hands were clean' but still achieve more or less the same outcome (Carvel 2004). Since the code came into effect an estimated 7,000 nurses have registered to work in Britain (Volqvartz 2005). Thirdly, many workers in nursing homes and elsewhere are officially overseas students in Britain, working officially twenty hours per week but often much more, and are beyond regulation. The British government has observed that it has very little control over the activities of private recruiters in Africa or elsewhere. It did however ban the NHS from recruiting nurses from developing countries on renewable temporary contracts to evade the ban on hiring permanent staff, and later banned agencies from supplying the NHS by recruiting from the private sector.

It is difficult to protect nurses and others from the most unscrupulous dealings of recruitment agencies, given that there are so many of them (more than 800 in the Philippines alone) and they can appear and disappear almost at will. In countries like the UK the media have played a role in exposing fraud, and perhaps making it less likely in the future, while the Royal College of Nursing journal, the Nursing Standard, has been vigilant in exposing instances of discrimination and unfair treatment, alongside running a campaign to abolish racism. However, at times this is a lonely voice and in other countries there are no parallel voices.

It may be therefore that specific bilateral agreements, in a general context of managed migration, may be more effective in regulating excessive migration. Such agreements might be between countries or even between unions in different countries.

Bilateral agreements can be formulated in various ways. A memorandum of understanding (MOU) is a formal agreement between two governments. Sometimes, a less formal exchange of "letters of intent" is decided to be a sufficient procedure, as for example, in the case of Spain and the UK. The Indian Government was even content to agree verbally to the recruiting of doctors to the UK and decided not to enter into a formal agreement. The recruitment is authorized in states where there are no doctor shortages. Regular updating information for the Indian

Government about the recruitment activities is ensured by the UK Department of Health.[3]

An agreement between South Africa and the UK was signed in 2003 (Mafubelu 2004; Webster 2004) with the objectives of creating partnerships on health education, workforce issues and time-limited placements, and the exchange of information, advice and expertise. Within the frame of the MOU, opportunities have been provided for health professionals to spend time limited education and practice periods in the respective other country.

Collaboration is foreseen with the National Institute for Clinical Excellence in Quality issues and the Health Protection agency. The facilitation of mutual access for health professionals to universities and other training institutes for specific training or study visits is part of the MOU. It is planned that the professionals return home after the exchange period, for this purpose their posts will be kept open. They will use the new skills to support health system development in their own country. At the Commonwealth Ministers' meeting of May 2005, the South African Minister of Health reported on the success of the bilateral agreement in managing migration. Dissemination of this model of good practice is important if indeed it appears to be effective.

Conclusion

Shortages of skilled health workers occur in most countries in the world, and most significantly in countries where education levels are relatively high. Those shortages have been remedied mainly by migration rather than strategies for improved retention and recruitment, hence in the foreseeable future as shortages increase so migration will also increase. This is presently the case to the extent that countries such as the Philippines that previously exported an 'overspill' of workers are now feeling the adverse effects of their 'export policies' in the national health care system. Migration has tended to be at some cost to relatively poor countries where the costs of production are considerable and losses are not compensated. The costs of global mobility are thus unevenly borne by the poorer source countries and the benefits are concentrated in the recipient countries. These discrepancies are enhanced by the operation of recruiting agencies.

---

[3] Webster, DH-UK, Workforce Directorate ; personal communication.

There is a widespread assumption that the problem of health worker migration is worsening, as the care chain become global. Indeed there is now greater competition for workers between states, and intensified efforts at recruitment by both governments and specialized recruitment agencies. Migration is both more global and more complex than in earlier years. As demand for health workers has increased, the ability of both developed and less developed countries to meet this demand has worsened, and the costs of meeting this demand are now being increasingly borne in developing countries, as disparities in income and opportunity between countries are not reduced.

A range of potential, yet partial, solutions to excessive international (and regional) migration have been suggested – better wages, incentives, working conditions, management and supervision – to the extent that they have become as familiar and positive as 'apple pie and motherhood', yet they are not effectively implemented. While comparable wages may be out of reach of developing countries, what is at the core of the establishment of a an effective health care system is quite simply 'improved economic performance, a stable political situation and a peaceful working environment' (Awases et al 2004: 54) but all too often not only are these elusive targets but, in a climate where 'good governance' has become almost a global mantra, they are actually receding.

Were economic growth not to be substantially greater in the north than in the south then the context of uneven development in which international migration occurs would no longer exist. However, in the immediate future there is no prospect of significant change in global economic and social imbalances hence migration is likely to remain an attractive proposition. Indeed there is a greater probability that imbalances will worsen.

Recruitment, especially in developed countries has become more difficult, as fewer people are now attracted to health careers. Jobs in health are now more likely to be perceived as poorly paid and also dirty, difficult and sometimes dangerous compared with wider opportunities, especially for women, in the private sector. Consequently without substantial changes in global patterns of recruitment the global demand for health workers can only increase. Accelerated migration will be a further outcome.

High migration rates have contributed to low productivity, poor morale and frustration. Migration is usually not an overspill, but a definite loss, with negative social, economic and health outcomes. The lack

251

of skilled health workers has contributed to the less effective delivery of health services especially in poor and remote areas. This further emphasizes the challenge of meeting the Millennium Development Goals.

Since migration cannot be ended, and source countries have only limited scope for substantial policy change that will improve the number and status of health workers in the home countries, the onus has increasingly shifted towards the role of recipient countries in ensuring that, if migration is to continue, then it be more equitable and that there be adequate compensation for losses incurred in source countries. It is time for the notion of 'managed migration', that involves the regulation of recruitment agencies, to be given some practical basis.

References

Anderson, B and Rogaly, B (2005) *Forced Labour and Migration to the UK*, Centre for Migration Policy and Society, Oxford.

Awases, M, Gbary, A, Nyoni, J and Chatora, R (2004) *Migration of Health Professionals in Six Countries*, WHO Regional Office for Africa, Brazzaville.

Bach, S (2004) Migration patterns of physicians and nurses: Still the same story?, *Bulletin of the World Health Organization*, 82 (8), August, 624-5.

Ball, R (1996) Nation building: the globalisation of nursing – the case of the Philippines, *Pilipinas*, 27 (Fall), 67-92.

Buchan, J, Parkin, T and Sochalski, J (2003) *International Nurse Mobility: Trends and Policy Implications*, WHO, Geneva.

Buchan, J, Jobanputra, R and Gough P (2005) Should I stay or should I go? *Nursing Standard*, Vol. 19, No. 36 14-16.

Carvel, J (2004) Nil by Mouth. *The Guardian*, 27 August.

Commonwealth Secretariat (2003) Commonwealth Code of Practice for the International Recruitment of Health Workers and Companion Document.

Department of Health UK (1999): Guidance on International Nursing Recruitment.

Department of Health UK (2001): Code of Practice for NHS employers involved in the international recruitment of healthcare professionals (www.dh.gov.uk).

Department of Health UK (2003): New Agreement for Health Care Cooperation with South Africa, press release (www.dh.gov.uk).

Department of Health UK (2004): Code of practice for the international recruitment of healthcare professionals (www.dh.gov.uk).

International Council of Nurses (2004): The International Migration of Nurses; trends and policy implications. http://www.icn.ch/global/shortage.pdf

Mareckova, M (2004) Exodus of Czech Doctors Leaves Gap in Health Care, The Lancet 363 (9419), 1443-1446.

Mafubelu, D (2004) Using bilateral arrangements to manage migration of health care professionals: The case of South Africa and the United Kingdom. Presentation to IOM/WHO/CDC Seminar on Health and Migration, Geneva, June. www.iom.int//DOCUMENTS/OFFICALTXT/EN/PP_bilateral_SAFRICA.PDF

Mejia, A, Pizurki, H and Royston, E (1979) Physician Migration and Nurse Migration: Analysis and Policy Implications, WHO, Geneva.

Mullan, F (2004) A Legacy of Pushes and Pulls: An examination of Indian physician emigration. George Washington University, Bethesda.

Stilwell, B, Zurn, P, Connell, J and Awases, M (2005) *The Migration of Health Workers: An Overview*, WHO, Report to the World Health Assembly, Geneva

Volqvartz, J (2005) The brain drain, The Guardian, 11 March.

Webster, R (2004) Bilateral Agreements, presentation to IOM/WHO/CDC Seminar on Health and Migration, Geneva, June.

Willetts, A and Martineau, T (2004) Ethical international recruitment of health professionals: will codes of practice protect developing country heath systems?. Liverpool, Liverpool School of Tropical Medicine, Liverpool.

World Medical Association (2003) Statement on Ethical Guidelines for the International Recruitment of Physicians.

Western Pacific Regional Office of WHO (2004) *The Migration of Skilled Health Personnel in the Pacific Region*, WHO, Manila.

Van Eyck, K (2005) *Who cares? Women health workers in the global labour market*, Public Services International, Ferney-Voltaire.

Webster R (2004). *Bilateral Agreements.* Presentation at the IOM/WHO/CDC Seminar on Health and Migration, 9-11 June 2004 , Geneva; www.iom.int//DOCUMENTS/OFFICALTXT/EN/PP_bilateral_UK.PDF

Xu, Y (2003) Are Chinese Nurses a Viable Source to Relieve the US Nursing Shortage?, *Nursing Economics*, 21 (6), 269-274.

Annex I

International Institute for Labour Studies

Merchants of Labour
Policy Dialogue on the Agents of International Labour Migration
28 and 29 April 2005

ILO Headquarters, Geneva, Switzerland
Elimane Kane room (M3 South, room XII)

Agenda

Thursday, 28 April 2005

10:00 – 10:15	Opening

10:15 – 10:45	Session 1: Introduction and Overview
Chair	Jean-Claude Javillier (IILS)
Presenter(s)	Philip Martin (UC Davis)

11:00 – 13:00	Session 2 A: "Good Practice" examples from sending regions
Chair	Manolo Abella
Presenter(s)	Cesar A. Averia (EDI-Staffbuilders International, John Clements Consultants, Inc., Philippines), Elmar Hönekopp (Institut für Arbeitsmarkt und Berufsforschung – IAB) on Central and Eastern Europe
Panel	Ibrahim Awad (ILO Cairo) on North Africa, Nilim Baruah (IOM) on South and Southeast Asia, Asha D'Souza (DECLARATION) on Nigeria, L.K. Ruhunage (Sri Lanka Bureau of Foreign Employment, Sri Lanka Consulate Dubai)
General discussion	

14:30 – 16:30	Session 2 B: "Good Practice" examples from receiving regions
Chair	Patrick Taran (MIGRANT)
Presenter(s)	Alan Matheson (Australian Council of Trade Unions), Ng Cher Pong (Ministry of Manpower Singapore)

Panel	Mohammed Dito (Employment Services Bureau Bahrain), Rajendra Paratian (ILO Harare) on South Africa, Gerry Van Kessel (IGC Geneva) on Canada
General discussion	
17:00 – 18:00	**Session 3: Policies towards recruitment agencies: Lessons to be learnt from remittances' transfers?**
Chair	Philip Martin (UC Davis)
Presenter(s)	Dilip Ratha (World Bank)
Panel	Bernd Balkenhol (EMP/SFP)
General discussion	
18:00	Cocktail hosted by the Director of the IILS

Friday, 29 April 2005

9:30 – 11:00	**Session 4: Recruitment and ILO Standards**
Chair	Jean-Claude Javillier (IILS)
Presenter(s)	Eric Gravel (NORMES)
Panel	Ellen Hansen (IFP/SKILLS), Beate Andrees (DECLARA-TION), Luc Demaret (ACTRAV), Christian Hess (ACT/EMP), Sergio Ricca
General discussion	
11:30 – 13:00	**Session 5: Possible protection strategies such as**
	(i) self-regulation among employers
	(ii) media advocacy
	(iii) information campaigns
	(iv) bilateral agreements
	(v) public – private partnerships
Chair	Gloria Moreno-Fontes Chammartin (MIGRANT)
Presenter(s)	Mary Cunneen (Anti-Slavery International), Tasneem Siddiqui (University of Dhaka)
Panel	Anna di Mattia (IILS), Verena Schmidt (ACTRAV)
General discussion	
14:30 – 16:00	**Session 5: (continued)**
Chair	Christiane Kuptsch (IILS)
Presenter(s)	Bruce Goldstein (Farmworker Justice Fund), Dan Rees (Ethical Trading Initiative)
Panel	Susan Maybud (SECTOR), Barbara Stilwell (WHO)
General discussion	
16:30 – 17:15	**Session 6: Wrap up: Future options**
Chair	Christiane Kuptsch (IILS)
Synthesis	Jeff Crisp (GCIM)
General discussion	
17:15 – 17:30	Closure

Annex II

International Institute for Labour Studies

Merchants of Labour
Policy Dialogue on the Agents of International Labour Migration
28 and 29 April 2005
ILO Headquarters, Geneva, Switzerland
Elimane Kane room (M3 South, room XII)

List of participants

Mr. Manolo I. ABELLA
former Chief, International Migration Programme, ILO

Ms. Beate ANDREES
Anti-Trafficking Specialist, Special Action Programme to Combat Forced Labour,
InFocus Programme on Promoting the Declaration, ILO

Mr. Cesar A. AVERIA, Jr.
President, EDI Staffbuilders International Inc., Philippines

Mr. Ibrahim AWAD
Director, ILO Subregional Office for North Africa – Cairo

Mr. Bernd BALKENHOL
Head, Social Finance Programme, ILO

Mr. Nilim BARUAH
Head, Labour Migration Service, IOM

Mr. Roger BÖHNING
former Director, InFocus Programme on Promoting the Declaration, ILO

Mr. John CONNELL
Professor of Geography, School of Geosciences, University of Sydney, Australia
(seconded by Australian government to WHO)

Mr. Jeff CRISP
Director, Policy and Research, Global Commission on International Migration
(GCIM)

Ms. Mary CUNNEEN
  Director, Anti-Slavery International, United Kingdom

Mr. Luc DEMARET
  Focal Point for Migration, Bureau for Workers' Activities, ILO

Mr. Mohammed DITO
  Head of Employment Services Bureau, Ministry of Labour and Social Affairs
  Bahrain

Mr. Bruce GOLDSTEIN
  Co-Executive Director, Farmworker Justice Fund, Inc.
  United States

Mr. Eric GRAVEL
  International Labour Standards Department, Team on Employment and
  Social Policies and Tripartite Consultations, ILO

Ms. Ellen HANSEN
  Senior Employment Services Specialist, InFocus Programme on Skills,
  Knowledge and Employability, ILO

Mr. Christian HESS
  Senior Adviser, Bureau for Employers' Activities, ILO

Mr. Elmar HÖNEKOPP
  Head, Migration and Integration Study Group, Institut für Arbeitsmarkt-
  und Berufsforschung (IAB), Germany

Mr. Jean-Claude JAVILLIER
  Special Adviser, International Institute for Labour Studies, ILO

Ms. Christiane KUPTSCH
  Senior Research Officer, International Institute for Labour Studies, ILO

Ms. LAU Lee Jin
  Foreign Manpower Management Division, Ministry of Manpower,
  Singapore

Mr. Philip L. MARTIN
  Professor of Agricultural and Resource Economics, University of California-
  Davis, United States

Mr. Alan MATHESON
  Australian Council of Trade Unions

Ms. Anna di MATTIA
  Research Officer, International Institute for Labour Studies, ILO

Ms. Susan MAYBUD
  Health Services Specialist, Sectoral Activities Department, ILO

Ms. Gloria MORENO-FONTES CHAMMARTIN
  Migration Specialist, International Migration Programme, ILO

Mr. NG Cher Pong
  Divisional Director, Foreign Manpower Management Division
  Ministry of Manpower, Singapore

Mr. Rajendra G. PARATIAN
  Senior Labour Market Policy Specialist, ILO Sub-Regional Office
  for Southern Africa – Harare

Mr. Dilip RATHA
  Senior Economist, World Bank

Mr. Dan REES
  Director, Ethical Trade Initiative, United Kingdom

Mr. Sergio RICCA
  former Senior Employment Services Specialist, ILO

Mr. L.K. RUHUNAGE
  Employment and Welfare Counsellor
  Sri Lanka Consulate, Dubai, United Arab Emirates

Ms. Verena SCHMIDT
  ILO Coordinator of the Global Union Research Network (GURN)
  Bureau for Workers' Activities, ILO

Ms. Tasneem SIDDIQUI
  Professor of Political Science and Chair of the Refugee and Migratory Movements Research Unit (RMMRU), University of Dhaka, Bangladesh

Ms. Asha d'SOUZA
  Anti-Trafficking Specialist, Special Action Programme to Combat Forced Labour, InFocus Programme on Promoting the Declaration, ILO

Mr. Patrick TARAN
  Senior Migration Specialist, International Migration Programme, ILO

Mr. Gerry VAN KESSEL
  Co-ordinator, Intergovernmental Consultations on Asylum, Refugee and Migration Policies in Europe, North America and Australia, IGC, Geneva, Switzerland

Ms. Christiane WISKOW
  Director and Research Consultant, Salumondi, Health Personnel & International Public Health, Geneva, Switzerland